D1552759

JOHN WESLEY NORTH

AND THE REFORM FRONTIER

BY MERLIN STONEHOUSE

UNIVERSITY OF MINNESOTA PRESS, Minneapolis

Library of Congress Catalog Card Number: 65-15075

PUBLISHED IN GREAT BRITAIN, INDIA, AND PAKISTAN BY THE OXFORD
UNIVERSITY PRESS, LONDON, BOMBAY, AND KARACHI, AND IN CANADA
BY THE COPP CLARK PUBLISHING CO. LIMITED, TORONTO

To

JOHN W. CAUGHEY

INTRODUCTION

$\mathbb{A}$BOVE all, John Wesley North was a carpetbagger. His life offers a unique opportunity to examine the aims, character, and principles of a man typical of this group and to discover why the same man could succeed in three northern states and fail in the South — the more paradoxical since North went to Minnesota, Nevada, and California with an empty carpetbag. It contained a modest fortune when he arrived in Tennessee after the war.

Migration to the South after the Rebellion was no different from rushes to California, Pike's Peak, or Oregon, or movements to Iowa, Kansas, Wisconsin, and Minnesota before the war, unless it was that carpetbaggers to the South were somewhat more substantial, more experienced businessmen. We can never understand the reconstruction of the South until we examine it as part of a general expansion of the country, as a westward movement temporarily diverted southward.

No fallacy is more persistent in American history than that carpetbaggers were evil opportunists peculiar to one time and place. It would be the same fallacy in reverse to argue that North, a man of noble aims, high purpose, and unselfish ambition, was typical of all carpetbaggers — this would be a fallacy except for the fact that North's aims, ambitions, and ideas *were* common to many carpetbaggers, who took direction from a common inspiration, a common experience, and a common source.

The common inspiration was the evangelical humanism that flourished in the English-speaking world, save only in the slave-holding

South which had sealed itself off behind a cotton curtain. Major denominations split north and south. Local churches in the South were controlled by vestries, sessions, synods, conferences, or congregations which pro-slavery forces eventually dominated. The platform, press, pulpit, and post office were deprived of the opportunity to present the full range of evangelical humanism common to the rest of the English-speaking world.

The common experience of carpetbaggers was the westward movement. No political change achieved by the carpetbaggers in the South was so abrupt, complete, or long-lasting as the reformers' capture of Kansas, Minnesota, and California. The carpetbaggers, West or South, did not hesitate to use political means to achieve their ends. Though the clash of the carpetbaggers with southern conservatives is usually seen in a political light, southern hatred was directed against many who never engaged in politics, but represented an evangelical humanism southerners did not understand and which they regarded as self-righteous opposition to drink and duels, racial repression, and illiteracy.

The common source of carpetbaggers' ideas was the radical Republicanism which began in fact if not in name in the North and West before the war. John Wesley North's fight for negro suffrage in the South began in the constitutional conventions in Minnesota in 1857 and in Nevada in 1863. His efforts in behalf of free public schools in Tennessee were preceded by the founding of the University of Minnesota and plans for a mining college in Nevada. The positive program of evangelical humanism was free public education, equal opportunity for the races, female as well as negro suffrage, and condemnation of all violence, including mob action, duels, and war. An examination of the lives of North and his friends while they were in the West discloses that these were not ideals hastily adopted to bedevil the South with during reconstruction.

Everything that North did in Tennessee to his own destruction, he did in Minnesota, Nevada, and California to his greater wealth, fame, and honor.

The writing of biography places the author in debt to many persons whose cooperation is essential to its completion; this debt can scarcely be discharged by acknowledgment, but must forever remain as affection and gratitude. I am indebted inexpressibly to Professor John W. Caughey and Professor Brainerd Dyer of the University of California, Los Angeles.

I suppose every biographer labors with a constant sense of frustration at trying to make the past live again, watching for a twinkle of appreciation in the eyes of his first readers. For their encouragement I am particularly grateful to Professors Truesdell S. Brown and Clinton N. Howard and to the first lady of western history, LaRee Caughey. Professor Neal Brogdan of Scripps College supplied correctives to the Knoxville scene and Hugh M. Grauel gave me the benefit of his sound judgment as we traveled through scenes of North's adventures.

The Sunday mornings I spent with Chester L. North in his silversmith shop in Pasadena talking about his family will always be cherished. I rejoice in the friendship of North's granddaughter, retired teacher Anne C. Shepard of Santa Barbara, whose work in the desert at Palmdale was this year acknowledged by the legislature and a score of officials state and national.

North wrote to most important men of his day and his letters are preserved far and wide in manuscript collections and newspaper files. My search was aided in many places by the willing labors of many librarians. This biography could not have been written without the nearly daily access over four years to the North Papers in the Henry E. Huntington Library at San Marino, California. Researchers there become a family eating and working together, and to that paterfamilias of scholars, Dr. John E. Pomfret, and his staff, particularly Miss Mary Isabel Fry and Miss Anne Hyder, I am especially grateful. I should like to express my thanks to the staffs of Special Collections, UCLA Library; the Bancroft Library, University of California; the University of Tennessee Library and the McClung Collection of the Lawson-McGee Library in Knoxville; the State Library and Archives, Nashville, Tennessee; the Newberry Library and Chicago Historical Society; the Burton Collection, Detroit Public Library; the Massachusetts Historical Society; the Historical Society of Pennsylvania; the Manuscript Division of the New York Public Library and the New York Historical Society; the Nevada Historical Society; the Minnesota Railroad and Warehouse Commission and the Minnesota Historical Society; the Fresno County offices and Fresno Public Library; National Archives and the Manuscript Division of the Library of Congress; and particularly to the Onondaga County Historical Society, Syracuse, New York.

As a journalist who has spent a major part of a lifetime dealing with editors, I wish to express my thanks to Marcia Strout of the University of Minnesota Press from professional standards rather than as mere courtesy. Her able editing has saved me from embarrassments in both writing and scholarship, and I would trust any paragraph but this to her improving pencil.

MERLIN STONEHOUSE

University of California, Los Angeles

A CHRONOLOGY

1815   Born January 4 at Sand Lake, Rensselaer county, New York

1828   Converted at a summer Methodist camp meeting

1832   Moves with family to Cortland county, New York; teaches a district school near Albany

1833   Licensed as exhorter at Stockbridge; teaches in a select school in Madison county, New York

1835   Enters Cazenovia Seminary, Cazenovia, New York; engages in anti-slavery debates and attends the first state abolition convention, October 21, at Utica

*1838   Enters Wesleyan University, Middletown, Connecticut; in December *becomes agent for the Connecticut Anti-Slavery Society* (until 1843)

1841   Graduated from Wesleyan; surrenders preaching license

1843   Studies law in New York with William and John Jay and with Benedict and Boardman

1845   Marries Emma Bacon; with Forbes and Sheldon in Syracuse

1846   Forms partnership with Israel Spencer in Syracuse (to 1849)

1847   Emma Bacon North dies; North treated by Dr. George S. Loomis

1848   Marries Ann Hendrix Loomis of De Witt, Onondaga county, New York; visits Michigan colony settlements on honeymoon

*1849   *Visits Minnesota, summer; settles in St. Anthony November 6*

1850   Opens law office in St. Anthony and attracts immigration

*1851   *Member of the territorial legislature January 1; introduces bill*

NOTE: Important years in North's life are marked with an asterisk; important events in those years are in italics.

xi

founding the University of Minnesota February 13; sets stakes for first building August 4; opens academy November 26

1852   President of the temperance society, campaigns for the adoption of the Maine Law the following April

1853   Campaigns for railroads in Minnesota, now enlarged by new lands opened west of the Mississippi

1854   Invests in first bridge across the Mississippi and promotes immigration to new settlements

*1855   *Minnesota Republicans organized in North parlor;* first meeting in St. Anthony March 29; first territorial convention in St. Paul July 25; *proprietor of Faribault Townsite Company; founder of Northfield, Minnesota,* where he builds two mills on the Cannon River and develops townsite

1856   Builds two houses, ice house, American House at Northfield; organizes school and library and debating society; Minneapolis and Cedar Valley Railroad incorporated March 1

*1857   *President of the Minneapolis and Cedar Valley Railroad; leads Republican wing of the Minnesota constitutional convention,* contending for female and negro suffrage

1858   Begins construction of M. & C.V. Railroad with headquarters at Northfield; five-million-dollar loan voted in April

1859   Caught vastly overextended in converting mills to steam and promoting railroad, with failure certain

*1860   *Chairman of the Minnesota delegation to the Republican National Convention in Chicago;* campaigns for Lincoln in Illinois; M. & C.V. Railroad sold at foreclosure sale August 16

*1861   Accepts Lincoln's invitation to inaugural ceremonies; arrives in Washington February 22 with Hamlin; seeks office he fails to get; in surprise move, *Lincoln names him surveyor general of the new Territory of Nevada,* organized March 2; leaves New York May 21, arrives in Nevada June 22, first federal officer on scene; admitted to the Nevada bar, opens law office, and plans development of Washoe City, sawmill, and Minnesota Mill

*1862   Nevada bar and the Territorial legislature urge him as federal judge in territory; partnership with James F. Lewis; *Lincoln names him associate justice of the Supreme Court and judge of the District Court of Nevada Territory*

*1863   *President of the constitutional convention in Nevada*

1864   Defends himself against charges of corruption as judge

*1865   Cleared of charges of corruption before referee court; position

as federal judge ends with Nevada statehood; *goes South as carpetbagger in December*

1866   Buys foundry in Knoxville, Tennessee; saves negro from lynching July 4; promotes immigration and investment in Tennessee

1867   Organizes Knoxville Industrial Association, Knoxville and Jacksboro turnpike; named director of Knoxville and Kentucky Railroad; urges free public schools at Nashville Union Convention February 22; public attack upon him as carpetbagger begins September 23

1868   Promotes Northern and English migration to East Tennessee

1869   With enterprises boycotted, decides to take colony to California; sells foundry for less than is needed to cover debts

*1870   *Issues circular "A Colony for California" March 17;* prospective colonists meet in Chicago May 18; North reaches Los Angeles May 26; decides on Riverside location August 6; *takes up residence September 18 as president of the Southern California Colony Association*

1871   Completes irrigating canal and builds first school at Riverside

1875   Retires as president of Southern California Colony Association; practices law in Riverside and San Bernardino

1879   Opens law office with Nevada friends as North, Lewis, and Deal in San Francisco

*1880   *Becomes agent for the Washington Irrigated Colony at Fresno in June*

*1881   *Organizes colony at Oleander*

1882   Delegate to the California Republican Convention

1883   Opens lands at Malaga and Kings Canyon; returns east to visit Northfield and the University of Minnesota, and to make last speech at abolitionist reunion in New York, October 3

1889   Moves to daughter's home in Fresno and organizes Unity Club, a free-thought society in November

1890   Dies on Washington's birthday; buried at Riverside.

TABLE OF CONTENTS

Illustrations between pages 96 and 97

Loomis home, De Witt, New York; North's office and buildings, St. Anthony Falls, 1850; Ann and her "good husband" at the time of their marriage, 1849; two mills on the Cannon River at Northfield, 1860's; Washoe City, Nevada Territory, 1864, Riverside, California, 1870; North's house in Oleander, California, 1887

JOHN WESLEY NORTH

EVANGELICAL HUMANISM

$\mathbb{A}$MONG the oak groves below San Francisco, in 1888, an old man with a clear mind and firm hand sat down before a pile of foolscap to write "Random Sketches of a Crude Life," [1] recalling seventy-three years of personal history. The task would have been a major undertaking for a much younger man, for he would have had to write the story of founding a half-dozen cities and two states and the reconstruction of a third; he would have had to trace a score of careers, all his own. He would have had to sketch most of the national heroes of the most exciting period of American history, for he knew them all from Abraham Lincoln to Zachariah Chandler. He would have had to describe all the great movements in which he was prime mover, the rise of Abolition and the Republican party, westward expansion, railroad construction, development of the Comstock lode, Reconstruction, and land booms in California.

Above all, he would have had to explain himself, the most fascinating combination of idealism and practical good sense. The task was too great even for John Wesley North, and after a few hours of stroking his grey beard and bending his fine head over the manuscript, he put down his pen. Perhaps he had grown philosophic about misrepresentations in the press and in state history books, perhaps he knew that that was not the time to tell the true story of the Comstock lode or the reconstruction of Tennessee. Perhaps he had decided to let his great works bear testimony to his stature — the university and schools he founded, two state constitutions, and thriving cities sprung from the

3

wilderness and desert at his command. Or perhaps he knew that others in time to come would take up the pen.

John Wesley North was born at a sawmill owned by his father on Poestenkill Creek, a dark and rapid stream of considerable size rushing down a rocky bed to the Hudson. His first cries scarcely could be heard above the whir and whine of the great saws screaming through the green firs, freshly canted from the log booms of the millpond. His first playground was the galipot-fragrant sawdust of the lumberyard lighted on early winter nights by the great blaze of the towering incinerator that incensed the town of Sand Lake just to the west.

When he was two, his family moved to Oak Hill farm two miles south of the village in Rensselaer county. His grandfather had come to the New York frontier from Canaan, Connecticut, soon after the Revolution. The child born on January 4, 1815, was the third generation in the town. The people of the village were generally religious, but poorly educated. They were beyond good schools, but not good influences. No frontier was so remote as to escape the great evangelical movement then changing the course of history; when the baby was christened, it was with the name of the man who had wrought this wonder, John Wesley.

"Our house was always a home for preachers, and I grew up with a reverence and respect for them," wrote the aging North. "Their visits gave some variety to our otherwise monotonous life, and from some of them I borrowed books and learned to take an interest in intellectual themes." [2]

Five thousand itinerant ministers, at work on the frontier, shaped the lives and reshaped the thoughts of the American people. By the time he was forty, North would have become a rationalist with some distaste for emotional religion, but his whole life and the life of the nation would be marked by frontier Methodism. News of the world came to his home in the *Christian Intelligencer* (Presbyterian) until Boston Methodists began publishing *Zion's Herald* and New York Methodists the *Christian Advocate*. Here were the sermons read after family prayers, here were the topics discussed in the blacksmith shop by his elders as he played about his father's forge in the Glass House Village.

Once a year John and his five sisters were taken to Methodist camp meetings where they lived in tents under the hardwoods and twice a day went to the great tabernacle to hear the leading preachers hold forth a greater hope of happiness than was to be found on the frontier.— this "vale of tears." In a world where calloused hands soon grew hard and helpless, where women grew old before their time in giving life to numerous children too weak to survive this world for long, the only hope of a better life was to go at last to their reward. When he was thirteen, John North "experienced religion" at a camp meeting and was brought into the Methodist Episcopal church where he remained in good standing for thirteen years. In earnest determination to live a good life North thought the change supernatural; he was told it was so. He felt the call.

Once a boy felt this call, he became the cherished pride of his parents, the concern of the local church, and the object of special attention from the ministers. Indeed, if one wished to do good on the frontier, the ministry was one of the few fields of usefulness to be found. Not only did John North feel a call to the ministry, but his father also became a traveling preacher.

At seventeen, another field of usefulness opened to North when he taught in a district school for ten dollars a month. The "master" boarded around the district and was highly regarded by the unlearned people. The Dutch in his district brought North all their problems. A well-to-do farmer who had learned to read brought him a book he could not understand. The story did not make sense to him. It was Walker's *Dictionary*.

For pleasure, North walked to the eighteen-mile right-of-way of the Albany and Schenectady Railroad. The new steam engine made an impression on North, and he was never to lose his enthusiasm for railroading: he would build two railroads and take part in the frantic race of trains to the Republican Convention in Chicago in 1860 and in the first great excursion over the Union Pacific to California, but everything was anticlimax to his first ride on the Albany and Schenectady. North recalled:

The track was of strap iron laid on wooden rails. The cars were short with three apartments and two seats in each, facing each other and extending across the car. The conductor in passing from one apartment to another, had to walk on a narrow board outside, holding on to the iron rod extending along the top of the car. There was a steep incline at Schenectady where the cars were let down to the city by a long cable worked by a stationary engine on top of the hill. At Albany they did not venture into the city with the engine, but stopped two miles out, and took horses to draw the cars into the station which was on the hill near the capitol.[3]

While teaching in Madison county, North received his license as lay preacher at Stockbridge. The only service that lingered in his memory was one held on the reservation of the Oneida Indians. The road was through a bower of cherry blossoms, the Indian farms looked half-civilized like the Indians themselves. The neat colonial church had a high Episcopal pulpit with a clerk's desk below, where sat the interpreter who translated the sermon sentence by sentence. The church was full, women predominating; every squaw had a baby, all crying in unison.

When the Reverend Arnold Scholefield went to preach at Peterboro, he took young North with him, and Gerrit Smith, the Abolitionist, invited both to dinner. North came away with great admiration for Smith and with decided anti-slavery views.

Methodists at this time were trying to ignore slavery in order not to split the general conference north and south. Ministers, including the elder North, opposed discussion of a matter "settled" by the Constitution. When North entered Cazenovia seminary, he found the academy opposed to discussion; but under pressure from the students, class debates were allowed. An abolition convention at Cazenovia, New York, brought William Goodell and others into North's life. He called upon the principal (and later historian of Wyoming) George Peck, who allowed the formation of an abolitionist society among the students. Slavery became a favorite topic in the lyceum.[4] Since the students were mostly abolitionists, the debates became town-and-gown functions. Local preachers presented a resolution "That all ministers of the Gospel and others who profess to desire the abolition of slavery, and

GERRIT SMITH (1797–1874) Lifelong correspondent of North's. Heir to a fortune of nearly half a million in land, much of which he used for reform and philanthropy; settled whites and negroes in the Adirondacks, endowed colleges, supported John Brown and Eli Thayer's Emigrant Aid Company, temperance, vegetarianism, woman suffrage, prison reform, land reform, and anti-tobacco and anti-slavery movements. Vice president of American Peace Society, leader of Liberty party; served in Congress, 1853–54.

GEORGE PECK, D.D. (1797–1876) One of five brothers, all Methodist ministers, including Bishop J. T. Peck. Entered the ministry at 19; was member of every General Conference from 1824 to 1872. Editor of the *Christian Advocate*. Presiding elder of Lackawanna and Wyoming districts.

yet who oppose all action on the subject, give fearful evidence of un-blushing hypocrisy." [5] The opposing view was resolved "That all ministers of the Gospel and others who profess to love God, and yet labor to undermine the influence of his ministers and to destroy the Churches, give fearful evidence of unblushing hypocrisy." [6]

Under North's leadership, the student body tended to take the anti-slavery position, despite the fact they were all earnest Methodists (only one student in the school was not converted). Serious, if circumscribed, thinking was the result of a Spartan regimen. At five o'clock night and morning the students went to prayers and the rest of the day was spent in study, except when all ate together in forced silence. While North was there, discipline was relaxed in the evening hours to permit occasional parties where, at the cost of a shilling each, the men and women were allowed to mingle to refine their manners. Older students were given charge of mixed recitations and North became a teacher and was called "professor."

The elder North was so annoyed by the extreme anti-slavery views of his son that he gave no help with his education, so North reconciled himself to the cheerless prospect of leaving school. One Sunday evening he returned from a lonely walk through the snowdrifts and was attracted by the cheerful lights of a Presbyterian church. He entered, heard the minister declare there was nothing man could not do if he resolved to do it, and came away from the meeting determined to finish his education if it took ten years. He returned to Cazenovia for the summer term; in August 1838, he started for Middletown, Connecticut, to enter Wesleyan University. He had only money enough to pay his fare from Albany on the Hudson steamer. On board he met other students and learned for the first time of the availability of scholarships. He entered Wesleyan with his friend, John Curry, another "professor" from Cazenovia. Though they had been held in high respect as teachers, they now suffered all the indignities of freshmen. Curry withdrew in disgust to study law, later went to California with the Forty-Niners, and became chief justice of California. North stayed and was graduated in 1841, but not before he had shocked the university out of its complacency.

He was in the reading room one morning when the pro-slavery minister Francis Hodgson, censoring publications in the library, expressed astonishment at finding there the Methodist anti-slavery paper, *Zion's*

Watchman. He denounced the editor, La Roy Sunderland of New York, and seemed to direct his remarks to North. North came to the defense of Sunderland and the students present supported him. Growing angry, Hodgson called them young upstarts who thought they knew more than the Methodist Fathers.

"Now stop right there," said John Wesley North. "Our Father Wesley called slavery 'the sum of all villainies' and American slavery, 'the vilest that ever saw the sun.' Now do you agree with him, or do we?"

Hodgson, who was then as pro-slavery as anyone in the South, tried to dodge the question, but North demanded an answer. Backed into the darkest corner of his dim intellect, he said, "Wesley was wrong on that point."

North continued the attack. "Doctor Adam Clarke, the great Methodist commentator, was one of the Fathers, and he said that 'Slavery is an enormity and a sin for which perdition itself was hardly an adequate state of punishment.' Was he also wrong?"

"He was," insisted Hodgson.

Discussion continued for some time, and the students, many of them grown men, gathered round to hear the impromptu debate between the minister and North, forgetting their classes. They enjoyed North's victory as he continued to quote the Fathers Watson, Benson, and others in devastating numbers. Hodgson was mortified at the spirit of the attack and his obvious ignorance of the humanist base of Methodism. He retreated from Methodist doctrine and evangelical Christian doctrine of any variety. Officials of the school were highly indignant at what they thought a lack of courtesy to Hodgson, but they could take no disciplinary measures against North as long as he was so popularly supported by the students, nor could they risk a town-and-gown disagreement in Middletown on the slavery issue.

The news of North's victory became the pride of abolitionists all over Connecticut, and grew in the telling. In a few days the Connecticut Anti-Slavery Society invited North to lecture for them during the winter vacation. He did not feel equal to sharing pulpits with learned ministers

---

LA ROY SUNDERLAND (1804(2?)–85) Ordained at 22, but withdrew from his church in 1833 to lead the abolitionist cause among fellow ministers in New England, helping to organize first anti-slavery society of Methodists. Six times he was charged before successive conferences with such crimes as slander and immorality. In 1842 he split off to form the Wesleyan Connection of America, without slaves or bishops. He drifted from Mesmerism to Grahamism to his own pantheism, dying an unrepentant infidel.

of the state, but lecturing paid well, and his heart was in the cause. On a bleak day in December 1838, he began what he called his pilgrimage at South Manchester, Connecticut.

Connecticut had slaves for two hundred years. In 1774 when the importation of slaves stopped, there were 6,562 blacks in a white population of 191,448. By 1800, the slave population had dropped to 931. When North began his anti-slavery work, there were still 17. Abolition began in Connecticut in 1790 with the formation of the Connecticut Anti-Slavery Society of which Ezra Stiles of Yale was president, but the impulse went only to the state's borders and soon died. Growing trade with the South and accepting a states' rights theory of the Constitution made it unwise, even unpatriotic, to concern oneself with slavery beyond the borders of the state. It is sometimes claimed that Abolition developed from the stewardship tradition of the Calvinist past, making reformers believe they were their brothers' keepers. The good Calvinists of Connecticut did not interfere with slavery beyond their state's borders and did the job of abolition indifferently well even within the state. Abolition died out in Connecticut and almost everywhere in the North during the first generation of national life, a period when most Calvinists opposed abolition. A younger generation found inspiration not in the old Calvinist doctrine, but in the new worldwide evangelical humanism. Abolition was everywhere revived in the United States in the second quarter of the century: in 1833 the New Haven Anti-Slavery Society once more took up the struggle against the quintessence of all villainies. Under the inspiration of evangelical humanism, which had that year freed the slaves in the British Empire, this worldwide movement could no longer be stopped by state boundaries. Its objective was the regeneration of all mankind. Reformers with such an objective would not defer to a constitution that made immorality safe within southern states. Abolitionists everywhere cooperated heartily with each other, not only across state lines, but beyond national borders. Temperance, peace, education, domestic and foreign missions, and abolition became international aims.

North entered the Connecticut society when the "respectable" churches and "responsible" businessmen were opposed to an agitation disturbing to good order and trade and subversive of the Constitution. The work of the Connecticut Anti-Slavery Society was not well advanced. Only a few courageous souls tried to educate the negroes or to speak for freedom. No society functioned in South Manchester where North began his work. He called on a class leader of the Methodists and together they got up a meeting in a schoolhouse. At Bolton, a Congregational church was opened to him. At Rockville, three cotton-cloth manufacturers, the brothers Kellogg, sponsored his lecture.

All went well until the quarterly conference of the Methodist Episcopal church. Professor Augustus William Smith, acting president of Wesleyan, objected to the renewal of North's preaching license on the ground of his extreme position on slavery. The conference consisted largely of the faculty; its president was Dr. Nathan Bangs, who for years had been the terror of anti-slavery preachers in the New York Conference and had driven many of them from the ministry.

"This was the man," North recalled,[7] "who presided at the Conference and before whom I was somewhat suddenly arraigned by the most influential professor."

When his name was called for license renewal, Professor Smith objected, and North was forced to justify his position.

"This was my opportunity for delivering an anti-slavery lecture to Doctor Bangs that he had long needed and one that should make his ears tingle," said North. "I think I made them feel they were more on trial than I was. And when it came to a vote, the Conference was overwhelmingly on my side, and Professor Smith's solitary vote was the only vote against me."

In striking this blow for freedom, North struck off his own shackles. The Methodist Episcopal church would soon divide north and south on the question of slavery and the moneychangers would be driven from the temple, but North could not wait. Soon after the quarterly conference he went to Professor Joseph Holdich, the preacher in charge, and delivered up his preaching license and said he had decided against becoming a minister.

North remained at Wesleyan, organized a college Anti-Slavery So-

---

AUGUSTUS WILLIAM SMITH, LL.D. (1802–66) Professor at Wesleyan University from its founding until 1857, when he became its president. He resigned to teach at Annapolis, where he died March 26, 1866.

NATHAN BANGS, D.D. (1778–1862) Early missionary to Canada; returned to the United States in 1808, was elected book agent in 1820. Editor of *The Christian Advocate* and *Methodist Magazine*. Chief founder of the Missionary Society. President of Wesleyan University one year, 1841. Published *History of the Methodist Episcopal Church* in four volumes.

ciety, and invited Sunderland, whose paper had begun the dispute with Hodgson, to speak. After graduation in 1841, North worked full time until 1843 as lecturer for the Connecticut Anti-Slavery Society. He spoke in every city and town in Connecticut save one, "going to and fro as a flaming brand." [8] After all, he bore the name of the "brand plucked from the burning." He allied himself with Arthur and Lewis Tappan, Henry Brewster Stanton, William Goodell, William Lloyd Garrison, Gerrit Smith, Samuel J. May, and John Greenleaf Whittier. The way was not easy, for it was then estimated that even in liberal northern denominations ninety per cent of the clergy were pro-slavery.

The approval North did not find at Wesleyan he found in Middletown at the home of the lock manufacturer Nathaniel Bacon. North married the younger of the two daughters Bacon had living at home, Emma. Frail and delicate, a dream wife, in a year or so she was dead of tuberculosis. The shock of her death reduced North to a state of nervous prostration, a debility he would suffer time after time whenever great hopes failed of realization. After each breakdown, he would revive and go on to something bigger, but he never completely recovered from the loss of his dream wife. Her shadow lay even over love letters to his second wife.

To support a home, North had to leave the Connecticut Anti-Slavery Society and prepare for the law. The office of William and John Jay

---

ARTHUR TAPPAN (1786–1865) Importer at 21; credited with establishing one-price rule among New York merchants, but failed in panic of 1837. Chastened, he used his new wealth as "steward of the Lord" in reform causes: American Sunday School Union, American Bible Society, American Tract Society, American Education Society, American Home Missionary Society, New York Magdalen Society, American Colonization Society, American Anti-Slavery Society, New York City Anti-Slavery Society, British and Foreign Anti-Slavery Society. He helped found the New York *Journal of Commerce,* New York *Emancipator,* C. C. Burleigh's *Unionist,* Garrison's *Liberator, A. & F. Anti-Slavery Reporter,* Washington *National Era.*

LEWIS TAPPAN (1788–1873) Founded the first commercial-credit rating agency and was associated with his brother Arthur in reforms, supporting the Lane students in founding the abolitionist college, Oberlin, and backing such other causes as Prudence Crandall's school for negro girls, freedom for the *Amistad* captives, and Alexander M. Ross's work on the Underground Railroad.

WILLIAM JAY (1789–1858) Son of Chief Justice John Jay. Reformer. First contributor to *Emancipator* in 1833. Helped found New York City Anti-Slavery Society, called National Anti-Slavery Convention. President, American Peace Society; director, American Tract Society; a founder of American Bible Society. Sabbatarian, agricultural reformer, opposed dueling, supported temperance and Sunday School movements.

JOHN JAY (1817–94) Grandson of the chief justice, a third-generation abolitionist and reformer. Manager of Young Men's Anti-Slavery Society; secretary, Irish Relief Comin New York seemed to be a happy combination of law and reform,[9] and there he associated with Joshua Leavitt, Alvan Stewart, Beriah Green, William H. Burleigh, and many more abolitionists. All recognized the great work North had accomplished in Connecticut, but no praise remained in his memory like that of John Greenleaf Whittier, for whom he later named a son. He went to the cottage at Amesbury to introduce himself, quite unprepared for the warmth of his welcome, but his fame had reached the poet already. "I am glad to see thee," said Whittier. "I have heard of thee often — come in, come in."

mittee (1847); an organizer of the Republican Party in New York; a founder of the Union League Club; president, Huguenot Society of America; president, American Historical Association (1890).

WILLIAM HENRY BURLEIGH (1812–71) One of six reforming brothers, descended from William Bradford. Taught in Prudence Crandall's negro school and in 1833 printed, with brother Charles Calistus, the Brooklyn (Connecticut) *Unionist* to support the school. Lecturer for American Anti-Slavery Society (1836). Edited Schenectady *Literary Journal, Christian Witness*, and Pittsburgh *Temperance Banner*. While North was employed by the Connecticut Anti-Slavery Society, Burleigh edited the *Charter Oak*, formerly the *Christian Freedman*, for the society. North brought him to Syracuse to edit the *Prohibitionist* (1849–55). He published several editions of poems and propaganda poetry — *The Rum Fiend* (1871).

FREE SOIL AND LIBERTY

NORTH was thirty when he opened his law office in Syracuse with Israel Spencer. Never a great lawyer, he was too impatient of the past to linger over precedents and too active in the present to accept the routine and confinement of office chores. But law opened to him two avenues of great interest, politics and speculation. In lieu of fees, he too often shared his client's speculations, whether land or patent. Aside from some lots in Syracuse and an interest in a patent "regulator" for water control of the Erie Canal, he had little to show for his legal services; he developed, however, a wide acquaintance among Syracuse bankers and speculators which was to be important to him in his future careers.

Law was not a radical departure from the ministry. Disillusionment because of the pro-slavery bias of the ministry had made North reject the church as a means of righting social wrongs, and he regarded law as a secular means of accomplishing the social reforms the church neglected. It was abolition, temperance, and education — not religion — which brought him close to a great man, the Reverend Samuel J. May.

In 1843 May supplied the pulpit of J. P. B. Storer in Syracuse,

---

SAMUEL JOSEPH MAY (1797–1871) Unitarian reformer of Puritan descent, assisted William Ellery Channing in New England (1822–42), before going to Syracuse in 1845. Organized Windham County (Conn.) Peace Society, American Peace Society, New England Non-Resistance Society, a Cold Water army; served as general agent of Massachusetts Anti-Slavery Society; was active in reform movements in temperance, education, women's rights, and the Underground Railroad. His brother-in-law, Bronson Alcott, called him "the Lord's chore-boy."

13

and North revived their Connecticut acquaintance. They spent many hours walking along the Erie Canal towpath past the weighlock in the neighborhood of North's office. When Storer died the next year, May was called to the pulpit of the Unitarian church in Syracuse. The orthodox ministers had had a sample of May's preaching, and knew his power; they all combined with the pro-slavery men of the town to make him unwelcome. A meeting was called in the Presbyterian church to drive Samuel J. May out of town. North, who was on good terms with the trinitarians, now urged his friends to be reasonable and spoke in defense of the liberal preacher, helping to turn the tide of approval that would eventually carry May into the hearts of the people and make him Syracuse's first citizen. Thirty years later, North confessed to his daughter that no man had such influence upon him as May. "You can hardly know how much I am indebted to Samuel J. May. His genial influence, wise counsel and noble example have done more than you can think to shape my ideas of life and its duties." [1]

Another influence even more significant was that of Dr. George S. Loomis, who attended him during his illness after the death of Emma. Loomis, a remarkable man, an early and typical country doctor, lived on a dairy farm at De Witt, near Syracuse, and his gig was a familiar sight all over the region. What was not generally known at the time was that all his midnight trips were not to the sick. For twenty years he was a vital link in the Underground Railroad and carried many a poor negro along the road to freedom under the British Crown. North's daughter Emma recalled that food mysteriously disappeared from the Loomis kitchen and that woolly heads were poked out of the haymow when she played in the barn on summer visits.[2]

The Underground Railroad was not popular in Syracuse at that time. Davenport, a wealthy planter from Mississippi, on a visit to his wife's relatives in Syracuse, brought as her companion an octaroon slave, Harriet Powell. Negro servants at the Syracuse House helped plan Harriet's escape to Canada West. Mayor William A. Cook entertained the Davenports as the near-white companion walked calmly to a buggy on Onondaga street and departed for Canada. The reward handbill described her as fresh of complexion, so fair as to be taken for white. An attempt was later made to kidnap her in Ontario, for she was valued at twenty-five hundred dollars.

The most famous direct action against slavery was the Jerry Rescue,

14

an event later celebrated annually in Syracuse. At the celebration on October 1, 1857, Gerrit Smith declared, "Not a man can disapprove of that rescue, and yet be a Christian." [3] The issue was not that clear in the 1840's when North lived in Syracuse. Many Christians saw their duty not to the slave, but to the Constitution which provided that a person held to service in one state and escaping to another be returned.

The loss in runaway slaves was slight compared with the value of the whole institution of slavery which southern fanatics undermined by their insistence upon a strong fugitive-slave law. The fanaticism of public officials dependent upon political support from the South was worse than any excess of zeal in the North. The North never closed its press, pulpit, platform, or post office to debate. While North was working with the reformer Lewis Tappan, the abolitionist received a letter from Amos Kendall, who had barred abolitionist propaganda from southern mails:

You refuse to inform me where my [negro] boy is. Although you say he is beyond my reach, you will not permit me to ask him whether he prefers his present condition to that he has left. You will not permit him to *choose for himself*. This is no part of the liberty you give to the negro. . . . [You are] *man thieves* by land as well as by sea. Why do you not send abolition ships to Africa and *steal the slaves held by the petty chiefs and kings under the burning line*, to give them liberty among the snow drifts of Canada?

I trust you have a young and beautiful daughter. If so, teach her if you can to love this "noble young man" in whom you take so deep an interest. He is about twenty years old, well formed, has fine eyes, beautiful teeth, thick lips, a nose moderately flat, a mild temper, a skin as black as jet and does not smell worse than other negroes. *Take him as your son-in-law*, make your daughter proud of *kissing his black lips, nesting in his black arms, and raising up a family of woolly mulattoes to be dandled on the knee of their delighted grandfather*. . . . My Democracy has not been able to reconcile *black and white*. [4]

The Harriet Powells of fresh complexion and 411,613 mulattoes in the South in 1860 had, of course, been produced by spontaneous generation and not by any "reconciled Democracy."

Such indignation, fanaticism, and show of pistols made the calm and determined work of abolitionists like Dr. Loomis seem moderate. Yet southern fanaticism was legal and abolition illegal. None was more subversive of the Constitution than J. W. North, and his championship

15

of the negro made him romantic and appealing to Loomis's young and lovely daughter Ann.

At sixteen she was one of the belles of Onondaga county, trained in the academy graces of literature, voice, and piano. She worried about the length of her nose, always had her picture taken facing the camera, and could scarcely wait until the styles changed so she could wear a bonnet deep enough to hide the offending tip. For all this deformity, she was universally thought beautiful. Where she was concerned, and nowhere else, North took the popular view.

When Dr. Loomis brought his patient home after Emma North's death, Ann nursed him back to health. Although he was fifteen years her senior, she was determined he would become, as she always called him, "my good husband." She was far too intelligent not to know that she had caught North's affections on the rebound. She lived with the ghost of Emma Bacon North for forty years with rare complaints.

From Boston North wrote of the beauties of the Common on a summer evening, the magnificence of Theodore Parker's discourse on the Mexican War, and his fond hope that one day Ann and he might stand together above the clouds on the Bunker Hill monument. He attended a convention at Worcester, became "considerably acquainted" with Charles Francis Adams, and spent an hour with John Greenleaf Whittier as pleasantly as he could "with anyone but you." Still, the memory of Emma Bacon was in his love letters, for which he then apologized.

As to the sad strains of my first letter, I had almost forgotten them, and I am *very sorry* that it contained anything to make you shed tears. . . .

I assure you *Dearest Ann* that if you could read my heart you would not indulge in sadness for one moment. . . . It would be a greater luxury for me *just now*, to sit by the side of *My Dear Ann*, and enjoy the purity of her *sweet kiss*.[5]

He loved the balmy air and green hills of New England, loved to "pass like the flight of a bird from state to state," to be out of sight of land on the voyage to Portland, and to be recognized as an abolitionist of importance as he was at the Liberty meeting in Bangor city hall, where he was called on to speak from the floor. He met such old friends as Benjamin Edmund Messer, who would be one day the father-in-law of one of North's daughters. He met another abolitionist friend, Alvah Hovey, who had just come from Jamaica where he was agent for the Foreign Evangelical Society. There were new friends — John P. Hale of New Hampshire, with whom he would one day campaign in Illinois for Lincoln, and Hannibal Hamlin of Maine. But new friends could not distract him from his impatience to be with Ann. Travelling made his habits irregular and "unfavorable to the contemplation of moral and religious subjects. . . . It is very different with me now from what it was when I felt I had a *home*. When my Emma was living, we used *morning* and *evening* to unite in our devotions and ask the blessing of Heaven upon us." [6]

Pathos and religious sentiment were expected in love letters of the day, but "my Johnny" overdid them and caused tears as well as some girlish embarrassment at the academy when letters became too frequent. Ann had not yet given her answer to the proposal of marriage, but she seemed undeterred by the prospect of Methodist devotions. She hinted that she had come to a decision. North replied,

I am happy to know from your letter that it is a theme you will *love to talk about* when I get back. . . . The thought of *you* has done much to *hasten* my movements, and make *home* look desirable. . . . I have given up my trip to New Hampshire, and mostly on *your account*. . . . But my *sweet girl*, if you cannot bear such a separation as *this now*, how will you endure the separations of more than a year to come? [7]

This was the first indication that North expected to go alone to Minnesota for a year. He had expected to leave Maine before the Fourth of July 1848, but the Liberty party wanted him for an Independence Day rally at Exeter, and romance had to wait on duty. He spoke for two hours and then arose at four to catch the stage for Augusta. Even there he could not rest.

The stage was full of politicians, three Loco [Foco Democrat] members of the Legislature, one Whig Sea Captain who had been a member, and one War Whig from Providence. I was the only Liberty man in the Stage and had to talk against the whole of them. We kept it going for the whole distance, sixty-five miles, and when we got to Augusta I was so tired that I had to go to bed. I was nearly sick. But I had the satisfaction of *knowing* that I got the start of the whole of them, and that was "glory enough for one day." The next morning the Whig sea captain came and inquired *my name* and wished me to tell him what *Liberty Paper* he had better take. He said that he had not had the pleasure of listening to so interesting a conversation for ten years.[8]

During the early summer of 1848 romance and politics were inextricably confused in North's life. He was torn between his desire to be

17

with Ann and his devotion to his duty as an abolitionist. The Worcester Convention he attended on June 28, 1848, was the political antecedent of the Republican party. Five thousand Liberty party men were joined by the Barnburner Democrats and the Conscience Whigs who had now broken with the Cotton Whigs. These liberal reformers were now moving toward a combination in the Free Soil party, and eventually nearly all would combine in 1856 as the reform element of the Republican party. Charles Francis Adams, whom North had met at Worcester, had been freed from his allegiance to the old Whigs by the death of his father, John Quincy Adams, four months before. He could now help to divide the party, leading the Conscience wing against the Cotton wing, which in Massachusetts represented the large millowners who wanted to maintain business as usual with the South and not alienate Whig planters' support of the tariff. At Worcester, Adams reviewed years of Whig subservience to the South and quoted the words of his grandfather, John Adams, who, in signing the Declaration of Independence, said "Sink or Swim, Live or Die, Survive or Perish, to go with the liberties of my country, is my fixed determination." With the political parties splitting on sectional lines it would be only a question of time before the northern liberals of several parties would combine in a northern party stronger than any southern. This was the message North carried to New England meetings, and the desire to be part of this great moment in political history made him put his personal affairs, business and romantic, aside.

When he returned to Boston, he attended a meeting of the Conscience Whigs at Tremont Temple under the chairmanship of Richard Henry Dana, Jr., where Liberty sentiments were cheered with enthusiasm. A month later he was back in Syracuse ready to marry Ann, but the distractions of politics would continue to interfere both with his domestic and business responsibilities. The ceremony was performed by the Reverend A. Otis at De Witt on August 28, 1848.[9] North was thirty-three and Ann seventeen.

At that moment, North needed a less proud and pliant wife, one who would not encourage his concern, but would budget his hours and his overtaxed energies and keep his attention on law — on winning cases and winning bread. A reformer is not easy to live with, and a sick reformer is worst of all. Thoreau said that a reformer was sometimes

18

made by a stomachache. Whether the dyspepsia disposes the sufferer toward reform, or whether the frustrations of reform lead to dyspepsia may be debated, but it is certain that North had in him both the cause and effect. Whenever North was frustrated in business or politics, he took to his bed. A typical carpetbagger in that he did not always distinguish carefully between private business and the public good, he was frequently reduced by a combination of political and business failures to conducting his affairs from a sofa.

His purpose in going to Minnesota was given out as a search for health, but Ann — or possibly her father — believed that distance from political distractions rather than the salubrious climate of Minnesota would help North. The diagnosis was right: North improved. Yet he never gave up his concern for reform politics. Repeatedly he returned to New York for Abolition and Liberty conventions. He was at the Syracuse convention in 1855 when John Brown appealed for money to support his border war in Kansas. Here two evangelical reforms clashed head on. The pacifists led by Lewis Tappan refused the money, but the abolitionists were eager to subsidize direct action in Kansas. North rose with a compromise — a suggestion that they give John Brown the money and trust him to put it to some good use. This satisfied all consciences, and North's proposal carried.[10]

Just before he left for Minnesota, North, as a member of the executive committee, engaged his old friend William Henry Burleigh of Hartford to edit an abolitionist newspaper at a salary of twelve hundred dollars a year and expenses. To meet this expense, North was planning to organize conventions to raise collections in Rochester, Buffalo, Troy, Albany, or Poughkeepsie. Gerrit Smith had subscribed to fifty copies of the paper, but this did not prevent North from showing his Peterboro idol its feet of clay.

One of the Methodist customs that North held to long after he had ceased to be a member of the church was the practice of "plain talk." Rather than harbor any ill will, he would point out a friend's shortcomings in love and charity — but often with devastating frankness. On December 22, 1948, Gerrit Smith had taken Lewis Tappan to task for mixing abolition with politics and for "letting the world know which side he was on in politics." Smith wanted reformers to remain united and above politics. North, who now looked to politics as the machinery of reform, did not question Smith's motives, but inquired if his criticism

19

had not degenerated into faultfinding. "And is it not possible, too, that in watching so closely . . . to keep the wayward Abolitionists upon the track, you have sometimes failed to observe your own steps?"[11] North, no respecter of persons, pointed out that millionaire Smith had also supported Van Buren, calling him an anti-slavery candidate in the *Model Worker* and expressing a preference for Van Buren over John P. Hale at the time of the Buffalo convention. Moreover, North knew for a fact that Smith had given fifty dollars to Judge James Warren Nye to campaign for Van Buren.

"That fifty dollars," complained North, "secured more than fifty votes to Mr. Van Buren. And if Gerrit Smith, out of his abundance, can thus cast fifty votes for that gentleman, may not weaker men be excused for casting one?" He concluded in his best Methodist fashion, "I suggest these things to you, Brother Smith, in all plainness, and yet I trust with great deference and kindness of feeling."

Smith fumed over the rebuke for a few days and then denied that he had ever sent Judge Nye fifty dollars for any such purpose. North had been deceived either by his own law partner, Spencer, or by Judge Nye. North was to discover that neither of these men was the soul of honor nor the body of truth. In this case, however, it was Smith's abominable handwriting that was to blame. He had intended it for some other indecipherable cause, but the fifty dollars won votes for Van Buren.

The two men who were the cause of North's plain talk to Gerrit Smith would eventually receive the same treatment for the good of their souls. Judge Nye would have to wait until he was governor of Nevada Territory, but Israel S. Spencer's was already long overdue. North was perhaps the first to suspect that Spencer did not deserve the confidence of those for whom he drafted wills and acted as trustee of estates. The whole story did not come out until thirty years later, when Spencer died in his leather chair, a lawbook on his knees, in his old office in the Onondaga Savings Bank building, with a coachman and sleigh waiting for him beside the frozen Erie Canal. A long shelf of account books then disclosed that he was not worth a penny, and neither were his clients.[12]

It is unlikely that North knew of his partner's chicanery, which seems to have developed after Spencer had taken his son to Europe for his health, where the boy died. When North was associated with him, he was highly regarded as a pious man and reformer. As a judge, he

20

became known as a man whose decisions were seldom reversed.[13] It was apparent to North that Israel Spencer was careless as a lawyer and careless of truth, but this opinion may be inferred only in the slighting phrases that appear in his wife's letters to her parents. North's own letters contain no scandal, no gossip, and no harsh words except occasional "plain talk," but Ann North indulged her irritations and love of gossip in the privacy of family letters. North usually read her letters before mailing them, and then supplied the corrective by writing a more charitable explanation in his next letter. When he chided her gently for her lack of charity, Ann confessed that she could never be as good, noble, and kind as "my good husband" but said she would never give up trying to attain his patience and perfection.

The break with Israel Spencer was more than a clash of personalities, it was a break with the law. North never overcame a puritan distrust of lawyers, often pronounced "liars" on the frontier. That lawyers were sharp in practice and devious in speech was then part of American folklore. To talk like a Philadelphia lawyer was a common expression not meant to be complimentary either to the men who would argue either side of a question for a price or to a city then known for its vice. The attitude toward lawyers was expressed in Onondaga county folklore by a well-known recitation made in Syracuse streets:

Here's your nice India rubber suspenders; long enough for any man, short enough for any boy; give and stretch like a lawyer's conscience — pull a man out of debt, jerk a man out of jail, jerk a lazy man's breeches right over his head! All for a quarter of a dollar! [14]

No India rubber was in North's conscience. He could not be comfortable in the practice of law in a place where the profession was thus ridiculed. One of the Norths' close friends wrote,

Mr. and Mrs. North, have gone to Minnesota, to take up their abode, at the Falls of St. Anthony. We are very sorry to lose them, but were reconciled by the fact, that Mr. North could not enjoy any thing like health in Syracuse. He thinks very highly of the climate and resources of Minesota, and says it is rapidly filling up, with an eastern population, a great proportion of whom are from Maine and Massachusetts.[15]

Even in the year of Forty-Niners, Minnesota was attractive. Many would return from California disappointed, but North would return to Syracuse a railroad president, proprietor of new cities, and one of the founders of a new state and the Republican party.

Mᴵᴺᴺᴱˢᴼᵀᴬ was an idea without borders. In the minds of some it was the triangle bounded by the St. Croix River and the Mississippi, a remnant of the Old Northwest. The Ordinance had limited the Northwest Territory to the formation of five states. Wisconsin was the fifth state, oriented toward the more populous region bordering Lake Michigan, with little interest in the western boundary. When the line was drawn at the St. Croix, the triangular remnant of the Wisconsin Territory continued to exist under that name, but was more popularly called Minnesota. Some residents conceived of a greater Minnesota extending westward into the Dakotas; many with this ambition for the state proposed such borders in the Republican half of the Constitutional Convention of 1857. Still others hoped that Minnesota would be extended into Canada and embrace Winnipeg and everything south of Hudson's Bay Company lands. This expectation died hard on both sides of the border, for until coming of the railroad, the Manitoba trade found its outlet at St. Paul. As late as 1860 William H. Seward, visiting St. Paul, gave some encouragement to this idea, while an editor in Winnipeg supported the same proposal.

The Mississippi River was the broadest boundary that nature drew upon the continent. No immediate survey was needed to tell a settler when he crossed from Kentucky into Missouri or from Illinois into Iowa, but near St. Paul at Point Douglass (as Stephen A. Douglas originally spelled his name), the river turned abruptly west to Fort Snelling, and then turned again bearing northwest. From Point Douglass the north–south trend of the Mississippi was continued northward by the St. Croix River which in 1848 became the western boundary of the state of Wisconsin, leaving the "Minnesota" wedge between the two rivers with uncertain status.

Resistance to the remnant triangle's becoming part of Wisconsin came from special interests, notably from the fur traders. Routes in the fur trade ran from the Red River settlements in Manitoba down the Mississippi. It seemed unreasonable to put part of this trade route within a new state dominated by eastern or Lake Michigan settlements. The heart of Minnesota was a twenty-mile square running from Stillwater on the St. Croix west to the Falls of St. Anthony, thence south to Fort Snelling and east to St. Paul. Within this small square were the centers of population — Stillwater, St. Paul, Mendota, St. Anthony, Fort Snelling, and the Kaposia Mission. This square was dominated in 1849 by fur traders, lumbermen, military officers, Indian agents, missionaries, land commissioners, customs and Territorial officials.

Against this monopoly of local interests organized as Fur Democrats, North entered into a ten-year struggle, bringing in an Anti-Fur company and anti-Democrat population. But the newcomers agreed substantially with the old-timers on the extension of Minnesota in any direction — into Indian lands, into the Dakotas, or into Canada. On the Fourth of July 1849 this mood of manifest destiny was expressed in a "Desultory Ode." Of one thing, reader, be thou sure;/ The Yankee eagle *one* day/ Will stretch his wings from Bering Straits/ Beyond the Bay of Fundy/ And from Pole to Panama.[1]

When Seward mentioned in St. Paul for the first time the acquisition of Alaska (which he would achieve a decade later), he might astonish the nation, but he would be ten years behind the sentiment in St. Paul. By then, North would be a great man in Minnesota, but when he arrived in the summer of 1849, there were but four — Sibley, Steele, Rice, and Ramsey.

Henry Hastings Sibley was the most powerful man in the Territory.

HENRY HASTINGS SIBLEY (1811–91) Born in Michigan, of Puritan ancestry, sutler at Fort Brady until hired in 1829 by the American Fur Company. Organized an "outfit" with fur traders Hercules Dousman and Joseph Rolette to trade with Sioux. Built first mansion in Minnesota and the Dakotas. Delegate to Congress in 1848 from Wisconsin Territory and 1849 from Minnesota Territory. First governor of the state, 1858–59. Led the punitive expeditions against the Sioux after the War of 1862 and was commissioner in the peace-making, 1865–66. Businessman in St. Paul, and regent of the University, and on the board of the Historical Society. Not to be confused with H. H. Sibley, rebel officer in the Southwest.

He had come to Minnesota from Detroit as chief factor of the American Fur Company. When that company failed he became factor for P. Choteau, Jr., and Company of St. Louis. His mansion at Mendota on the south bank of the Mississippi opposite St. Paul, was the finest house in Minnesota. To this house came all important visitors. While North would oppose Sibley in politics and would from time to time give him a plain talk, they continued friends, closely allied as proprietors of the new town of Faribault and as directors of a railroad. Sarah Steele Sibley, wife of the fur trader, was the sister of the most important man in Minnesota, Franklin Steele.

Steele was two years older than North, the son of James Steele, Inspector General of Pennsylvania in the War of 1812. Franklin Steele became sutler at Fort Snelling, acquired military warrants, pre-empted lands, and in the end owned more of Minnesota than any other man in history. He held vast stretches of timber, built sawmills at St. Croix, St. Anthony, and elsewhere. He associated with the roughest sort of men in the forts and pineries, but always remained an Eastern gentleman. If he was ever tempted to swear, it was undoubtedly when North tried his patience. He gave the Norths a home in the wilderness and expected personal loyalty which extended into politics. As lumberman and trader, Steele's natural alignment was with his brother-in-law's Fur party. As one who received numerous favors and appointments from Washington, he supported pro-slavery Democrats most of his life. North differed with Steele politically almost from the start, but they were always in one business or another together. Periodic disagreements did not lessen their mutual respect and Franklin Steele the investor followed J. W. North the promoter as a sweet-toothed Indian follows a honey bear.

Henry M. Rice was one of the two or three hundred residents of St. Paul when North arrived in that village of birch-roofed cabins. Rice was also in the Indian trade. When he was not trading with them, he was in Washington divesting them of their lands. For several years he was North's best political friend in Minnesota — the one whipping up

HENRY MOWER RICE (1816–94) Born in Vermont. Emigrated to Michigan at 19, surveyed canal at Sault Ste Marie. Clerk at Fort Snelling (1839), traded with Winnebago Indians after 1842. In Washington was part of lobby for Minnesota Territorial bill and was elected delegate 1853 and 1855; senator (1858–63). Honored with statue in the Capitol's Statuary Hall. Regent of the University, president of Minnesota Historical Society.

support at home for roads, railroads, and land for settlement while the other got the proper bills through Congress. In politics, they were poles apart; Rice knew that politics was the art of the possible, whereas North always asked the impossible.

Governor Alexander Ramsey was the same age as North and arrived in Minnesota about the same time. North came as a penniless, unsuccessful politician, Ramsey full of honors as the first territorial governor. Back home in Pennsylvania, Ramsey had been a Whig; in Minnesota, nobody was ever sure what he was. North's attitude toward the governor was full of praise or censure, depending upon the current political shade of Ramsey's chameleon hide. He gave North his first public recognition, and they ended fast friends in the Republican campaign of 1860.

By the time of North's first visit, Steele had hired William Rainey Marshall to survey his lands about the Falls of St. Anthony, and Marshall, fifteen years younger than North, became his most intimate friend. Coming from Kentucky by way of Illinois and Missouri, William and Joseph Marshall opened, during the Norths' first winter in Minnesota, a general store in the new town that William had surveyed. Platting the village would have been easy if Franklin Steele had been able to acquire all the land in St. Anthony; but each of the other partners and proprietors planned to run streets of the future Minneapolis according to his whim or the most favorable disposal of his holdings. Each wanted the new city to crystallize about a public square centered upon his acres. Marshall discussed the problem with North and then appealed to Sibley — the one man who could influence all the proprietors.

Mr. Steele has adopted the plan of running the first street with the river and the others back, parallel to the first . . . Before anything permanent is done in regard to it [I would suggest] a general understanding and general agreement between the proprietors, for if each should adopt a plan of his own, it may make awkward work.[2]

WILLIAM RAINEY MARSHALL (1825–96) Born in Missouri of Scotch-Irish ancestry dating back to Pennsylvania in 1746. Reared in Quincy, Illinois, learned surveying in the lead mines. Staked a claim at St. Anthony, 1847. Elected to Wisconsin legislature, 1848 — but was disqualified by residence — and to the first Minnesota Territorial legislature. Chairman of the first Republican convention in Minnesota. Published the St. Paul *Daily Press*, combining it with the *Minnesotian*. Lieutenant colonel of Seventh Minnesota Infantry in Sioux war and Civil War: breveted a brigadier general. As war hero, elected governor of Minnesota in 1865 and 1867.

Sibley was not the best man in the world for Marshall to appeal to, for town planning was not one of his accomplishments. He had just laid out St. Paul with no alleys. The question in St. Anthony was whether to orient the streets to the river or to the road to St. Paul. Much depended on the expectation that riverboats would ascend that far, a hope that died only with the sending of local riverboats off to war in 1861. Before they could be returned in numbers the railroad had arrived to supplant them. Even Minneapolis across the river, platted in 1854 after New Orleans' plan, was laid out (with alleys) with reference to the river. Riverine orientation died hard; in seasons of high water when boats approached the Falls, St. Anthony and, later, All Saints (Minneapolis), would taunt St. Paul that it was no longer the head of navigation.

Steele took North to Nicollet Island at the Falls of St. Anthony and showed him a log frame which he promised to complete if North would move to Minnesota. This island had served Steele well. When, years before, squatters from the Selkirk settlements in Manitoba had settled there, they had been driven off by the War Department's declaring the site part of the military reservation. Steele, as sutler at the fort, had been on hand when the military reservation was declared excessive and reduced. Major Plympton filed the claim in 1836, built the original house on the island, and transferred the claim to Steele. To hold the claim, Steele put a *metis* from Pembina named Le Count (but called Le Gros) in the house. (Le Count was killed in 1840 when the explorer of Victoria Land, Thomas Simpson, shot his guides and then himself.) Steele made good his pre-emption and bought the land — nearly three hundred thirty-three acres of it — for $1.25 an acre when Steele paid for his St. Anthony claim at the Stillwater land sale in 1848. He had cultivated six or eight acres at the Falls as early as 1838, but his chief interest was in the water power. The mill begun in 1847 was still under construction when North visited the Falls in the summer of 1849. Steele alternately sold water rights and lands to complete his mill and then raised money on his mill to buy back his property.[3] (Among Steele's partners were Caleb Cushing, Robert Rantoul, Thomas E. Davis, John F. Sanford, Fred Gebhard, John S. Prince, Richard Chute (his resident manager), and Ard Godfrey (mill overseer). He sold property to A. W. Taylor for $20,000 which he bought back for $25,000. He had intricate financial relations with bankers in Boston, New York, St. Louis, Wisconsin, and Minnesota.)

Obviously, Steele needed a lawyer in residence at the very time North needed a residence. He urged North to return to De Witt for his bride, waiving any suggestion of rent — North could pay what it was worth a year hence. Very likely Steele also recognized North's talents and his enthusiasm for promotion of St. Anthony. North could be useful to a man whose financial entanglements could be relieved, as he hoped, by selling ten thousand dollars' worth of property by July 1849.[4] North would not fail him.

The only difficulty was that North had in mind peopling Minnesota with northerners who held strong convictions about temperance, education, peace, abolition, and free soil. Steele agreed with him about temperance, but the other reforms were not in harmony with the objectives of Steele's friends in Washington or the politics of the fur company, and thus every immigrant North brought in canceled one vote for the fur company in Minnesota. In fact, the immigration grew geometrically, for every person North attracted brought on others of his own kind, and each of them still others of like persuasions.

Because Steele would never accept political office, it has been assumed that he was no politician.[5] He was the most effective kind of politician: he controlled and delivered votes. When some of his hands at the mill and pineries were inclined to vote for Rice instead of Steele's brother-in-law Sibley, he threatened to fire the culprits.[6] That his threats were sometimes made good North himself would soon discover when he was proscribed.

Yet differ as they might in matters of public policy and private interest, these men of early Minnesota could never become permanently estranged. Each needed the other. Each recognized that the other was open of hand and heart in a way quite different from politicians and businessmen in more settled parts of the country. North was delighted that in the West every man's hand was stretched out to help his neighbor as a matter of self-interest — that none could prosper unless all prospered. Henry M. Rice noted the contrast with the East when he visited New York in 1848. He wrote to Sibley,

How great the difference between men who live to enjoy the comforts of this world and do what they can to make their neighbors happy and the man whose craven soul can see nothing but money. This city

27

presents an awful spectacle of human depravity. None seem to think that their graves are dug and hell is ready to receive them. No! all act as tho they had a liese to live to the end of time. After all the thoughtless unproviding savage is the only happy being.[7]

North did not doubt that he had found in Minnesota an ideal community, where alarming political issues were absent, where sound people might build homes, schools, churches, lyceums, and all the other institutions of civilization. He had met only generous men in Minnesota. North joined the nation moving west: returning for Ann, he was, by October, again on the road west, now with wife and impedimenta, the largest part of which was his enthusiasm. A choice had to be made between Ann's piano and his law books. Indulgence won over intelligence, and the law library was left in Syracuse; Minneapolis got its first piano.

On October 18 Ann wrote from the lake boat *Canada* which twice a week crossed Lake Erie to connect with the Michigan Central at Detroit and advertised "Through without Landing." The vibration of the engines turned Ann North's academy hand into a palsied scrawl. Scheduled to leave Buffalo at nine, the boat weighed anchor at midnight against strong headwinds, and tossed so furiously that many passengers missed breakfast. To avoid seasickness, the Norths read aloud from a package of books given them as a parting gift by William H. Burleigh, the abolitionist. Literature was no antidote. Bravely, Ann North tried to take minds off the rolling waves by playing and singing to the salon passengers with a quaver more fashionable in song than in penmanship.

The lake calmed in the afternoon, but the storm had caused them to miss connections with the cars at Detroit. The journey across Michigan took all day and they arrived upon the shore of Lake Michigan late in the evening. Its similar position on Lake Michigan to Buffalo's position on Lake Erie was responsible for the city's name, New Buffalo. There the Norths boarded the steamer *Sam Ward* for Chicago. On October 20 they settled themselves in the American Temperance House to await the arrival of their goods on board the slower *Superior*, which was delayed by fall gales in the Straits of Mackinac. They improved their time, according to the expression of that day, by seeing the elephant. Tourist attractions in pre-fire Chicago might more adequately have been described as a mouse. They found Chicago too flat and low, and their one pleasure was walking along the beautiful sand beach of Lake Michigan — scarcely a pleasure in late October to anyone not in love.

The Norths now had a choice of going down the Chicago River to St. Louis or crossing by land to Galena to connect with the riverboats to St. Paul. Every day's delay was worrisome, for they had been warned that so late in the season the riverboat might find the broad lagoon of the Mississippi called Lake Pepin frozen. Their nearly disastrous choice of the Galena route was decided by impatience and the assurance that Illinois roads were not so bad as usual. They boarded the cars at eight in the morning for the twenty-seven-mile ride to the railhead where they transferred at five o'clock to the Galena stage.

In Chicago, the Norths had had a preview of their new home in Lewis's *Mammoth Panorama of the Upper Mississippi*, but Ann was quite unprepared for the monotonous prairie broken only by oak thickets. For two days and two nights the twelve passengers crossed the prairie; in the early morning hours of the third day they neared Galena. About two miles outside Galena, the road descended precipitously to the valley of the Fever River, a drop that proved too much for the tired horses, and for the stage and driver — both loaded beyond capacity. Momentum carried the horses over the bank and dashed their brains out on the outcropping lead rocks below. The Norths and four other passengers were trapped inside the overturned stage. North disentangled himself, climbed through the upper side of the stage, and helped his bleeding wife out. An old woman from Kalamazoo refused to be extricated, declaring that she was already dead. North finally got her through the door, but she fainted and fell back inside. The rocks had ripped a hole in the carriage, and through this emergency exit the large woman was finally rescued.

Gathering their possessions in the dark, the injured passengers forded two small streams and walked on to Galena. After rousing the landlord of the Temperance House, the Norths had their lacerations cleansed and sewn. Although Ann North said she was bruised too painfully to spit, her greatest concern was for her broken comb and bonnet. The damaged headgear had probably saved her life; the strings and facings were in shreds, clotted with blood and ground-in dirt. In Galena she bought a new green satin bonnet lined with pink, more expensive than she would have bought without her husband's assurance that the stage company would pay for it. This was the lawyer in him talking, but when settlement was made the lawyer did not prevail. Stage agent Damon, from Northampton, Massachusetts, was a true diplomat. He refunded the sixteen-dollar fare and put himself and buggy at the Norths' disposal for seeing the lead mines and scenery until their baggage arrived by wagon freighter. It had cost twenty-nine or thirty dollars to get the goods to Chicago aboard the *Superior* and forty-three to get them from Chicago to Galena. The latter shipment was made in wagons which hauled grain to Chicago and usually returned empty. The cost from Galena to St. Paul was fifteen dollars by riverboat, and from St. Paul to St. Anthony, a dollar a mile, or ten dollars, making a total cost of nearly a hundred dollars. Such a sum would keep an average family all winter.

On November 1 the Norths boarded the steamer *Dr. Franklin* at noon. Fourteen others were going to St. Anthony Falls. The riverboat slipped down the seven miles of the Fever River and as it breasted the Mississippi one of the passengers, a lawyer named David Lambert, began to abuse everyone aboard in his alcoholic dementia. North calmed him down and the passengers retired believing the man rational again. But when they were in their berths they heard a scream. The *Dr. Franklin* backwatered and stopped. All ran on deck to discover that Lambert had jumped overboard and disappeared under the two barges the steamer had in tow. Ann North moralized to her young brothers about the evil of the "poisonous draught." Lambert had fallen into evil ways in Washington, not an uncommon experience. He had married there, but had not lived long with his wife. After the society of Washington, he could not face being wintered in at St. Paul again.

For three years St. Paul had been one of the regular stopping points for riverboats, but from December to May it had no communication with the outside world except by dogsled. It was said at the time that a thousand people lived in Minnesota exclusive of "French, Indians, Canadians and other fur-bearing animals." The figure was augmented by inclusion of such temporary residents as soldiers and *metis* when a show of population was needed on election day or to gain territorial status. The place had grown since North's visit a few weeks before. The Norths left their goods in storage at St. Paul and set out for St. Anthony Falls in a paper-and-book peddler's cart. Their island home was being converted from a log frame to a two-room house, sided, shingled, and com-

plete with cellar and garret. The house faced west, with gable ends
north and south and had a door in the west, with a window on either
side. Entering the house, a visitor found himself in the kitchen. The partition dividing the lower floor into two rooms was just to the left of the
door. Inside the outer door was a second, inner door to the parlor, which
North used as a law office. Both rooms were stowed full of furnishings.
The parlor contained not only the piano and mahogany livingroom furniture, but a bookcase and shelf upon which Ann displayed vases and the
forked candlesticks known as girandoles. Since the dividing partition
was a few feet south of the center of the house, the kitchen would have
been the larger room except for boxed-in stairs which went down to the
cellar and up to the garret.

Near the door, with its back to the partition, stood the Iron Witch
stove made in Albany, with a handy shelf above it. The stove was kept
red with hardwood fire as the mercury in the thermometer fell to ten,
then twenty below, and finally receded into the bulb. In the snug corner
with its foot to the fire was the bed; between the bed and the enclosed
stairs was a window in the east wall corresponding to the window in
the west wall by the door. This bedroom half of the kitchen was carpeted
and a bureau stood against the stairway enclosure. The culinary part
of the kitchen had a wood floor, but planed and therefore unlike other
floors in St. Anthony Falls, which were rough as they came from the
mill. Bragging of her new twenty-cent mopstick, Ann said, "I expect
to make a notable housewife."

On November 25, their first Sunday in the new house, Ann made a
cranberry pie (North had bought a barrel of cranberries for $4) but
forgot the sugar; it burned to "a dark handsome snuff color," but North
gallantly ate it soused with molasses (four gallons for $2.60). He im-
mediately invested $3.75 in thirty pounds of sugar as a conspicuous re-
minder, perhaps, and the next cranberry pie was superior to any cherry
pie. Cranberries, a newly discovered cash crop, carried all Minnesota
through the winter of 1849–50. Indians harvested them in the lakes and
swamps, Sibley and the other traders shipped hundreds of barrels downriver. It was the only fruit in Minnesota, and long before spring the
Norths were thinking fondly of New York apples. Ann said their style
of living was primitive compared with New York's, but far above the
usual style in Minnesota. They were so well off by St. Anthony standards that they could put up with having no knobs for their doors and

no feathers for their bed ticks. Chicken feathers sold for twenty cents a pound, goose feathers for fifty-five. Relatives were urged to cram at least one down tick into their luggage when they came west.

No sooner were the Norths settled in their island home than the Minnesota winter closed in. This is no figure of speech: when Minnesota's winter closes in, the experience is emotional as well as meteorological. The rustle of leaves is ended by a blast of north wind that denudes the trees. All living things depart or hibernate. Noise is smothered to silence by a heavy fall of snow, and as the pall deepens and drifts the sky lowers in snow clouds that stretch in thick pads to the horizon. Even breath congeals to puffs of cotton. The muffled landscape has no perspective: sky and earth blend in one diaphanous indefinitude.

On Nicollet Island, the thunder of the falls was quieted, the rippled millpond glazed. Curtains of snow descended, the difference between night and day was a faint luminosity far to the south. This twilight world gave way to a crackling cold universe with a sky as clear as ice that made the whole world crystalline. Trees snapped like rifle fire with frost. Snow glared in the sunlight and a field of diamonds sparkled in the shade. Spray from the falls covered the stark sugar maples with coats of crystal. Ice in the millpond was four inches thick and clear enough so the bottom was visible. A pavement of glass led to the village the Norths had been isolated from for a week. Ice packs drifted down from above and crashed in confusion over the precipice of the cataract. Winter alternated between gloom and glory. No mail arrived for three or four weeks at a time, letters went downstream in a canoe which could skirt the ice floes. Spirits shifted with the weather from depression to exhilaration.

One evening while waiting for North to drag himself through the drifts of the dead world beyond her door, Ann fought depression at the piano. She drummed out "The Switzer's Song of Home," but when she came to the lines

> "Give me those, I ask no other,
> Those that bless the humble home
> Where dwell my Father and my Mother . . ."

her voice broke, the keys would not obey her hands, and she sobbed against the rosewood. North came in, caught her up in his arms, the Iron Witch glowed to cherry magic, and, said Ann, "Of course, all was bright again."

PIONEERS AT THE FALLS

D URING Minnesota winters friends were tended as jealously as the fire. One of the four schoolteachers sent to the Minnesota frontier by former Vermont governor William Slade's Board of National Popular Education was Electa Backus. She planned a seminary for the projected city and promised Ann North that she might teach piano, understandable as long as Ann North had the only piano. Another friend was a young man with a good ear who tuned the piano in return for lessons. Still another friend was Abigail Marshall, the gay and overdressed mother of the local grocers. Her Kentucky charm was strange to the Norths, as strange as her endlessly amusing pronunciation. Southern manners and southern charm captivated them; but her discreet fondling of North, her efforts to appear young, and her uninhibited conversation shocked them to the rocky bottom of their puritan prejudices. But though Mrs. Marshall might not have done in Syracuse society, she became indispensable in Minnesota. Her warmhearted affection was returned measure for measure.

Rivals as well as friends appeared. The previous May, Ellis G. Whitall had come up from the South to compete with North for legal clients, rather successfully we might imagine, since North earned only fifteen dollars in fees in 1849. Whitall had the advantage of connections: he was the brother-in-law of Henry M. Rice. Ann thought Whitall irresponsibly young and rather "light," with a taste more for ladies than for law. In the face of this competition, North found it necessary to move his law office from his home to the post office. Neither Ard Godfrey, Steele's mill overseer and postmaster, nor North had a stove, and none could be had until navigation opened, so they did business bundled up in coats and mufflers. Despite his "downriver" sympathies — he was from Richmond, Virginia — Whitall was a welcome guest in the North home, but because of his sympathies, he did not remain popular after New Englanders began to arrive in St. Anthony; he eventually returned to the South to engage in the cotton trade and to fight in the rebel army.

Land, not law, filled North's thoughts. One night at eleven, when all decent folk had been abed for two hours, William Marshall pounded on the door to say he had overheard a conversation in the town which led him to believe a stranger planned to pre-empt a lot North wanted for himself. North shook off sleep and wandered through the bleak and black night for fifteen miles before he could find the lot, only a mile or two from town. He spent the night wrapped in a buffalo robe in the snow and in the morning staked his claim. The next Sunday, seated at the three-dollar walnut table, North wrote his father-in-law that he had paid a hundred and twenty-five dollars for the lot and could sell immediately for a hundred and fifty. The land boom had started; St. Anthony's size had doubled before navigation closed, and North predicted a great "filling-up" when it opened again.

His health had improved; Ann wrote that he looked fifty per cent better. He had worked hard cutting the winter's wood supply and scouting land, yet had gained weight. His improvement could not be laid to good food: They had had no milk since coming to the kineless territory; milk from downriver sold for ten cents a quart, an exorbitant price. Bread was made without milk. They lived on salt pork (seven-fifty a half barrel) until North's stomach rebelled and then they bought codfish for ten cents a pound. "Rather expensive living," worried Ann. Their accounts show that cod was followed by a salmon trout for fifteen cents and thirty-six pounds of beef at seven cents a pound.

It is typical of the Norths that even in financial straits they subscribed five dollars to the Library Association. Culture, such as it was, came before food. But more than culture, Minnesota needed cats. There was not a cat in the Territory and mice ruled the animal kingdom. North invented a mouse trap, but it was designed on such humane principles that the mice loved it. In desperation, Ann cut sleeves from her gowns to make bags for food which could be hung from the rafters. The most welcome settler to come on in the spring with Ann's Grandmother Lewis was a tomcat with a voracious appetite — three mice before breakfast.

Until relatives began to arrive in the spring, the Norths found Minnesota a lonely place, particularly at Christmas, when friends in St. Anthony went off to the gay attractions of St. Paul. North brought home Elder Chauncey Hobart and other ministers, but often the expected visitors could not get through the snow. Edward D. Neill — a later historian of Minnesota and secretary to Lincoln — was supposed to address the St. Anthony library association, but did not arrive. When the roads were clear, he did address it, and his talk became one of the first publications of the newly organized Minnesota Historical Society.

On February 10, 1850, North formed the first Sunday School with himself as superintendent, Ann as teacher, and William Marshall as librarian, but the teacher stayed home most Sundays on the plea that she could not climb the hill to the schoolhouse and the river bank was too steep for a sleigh. A sewing society of fifty members was formed, half men; from the sale of their sewing they made enough to buy a Bible and curtains for the schoolhouse. No church had been organized, but all united in weekly prayer meetings. Guests of the lyceum stayed overnight with the Norths. One speaker, Lieutenant Richard W. Johnson of Fort Snelling who became a general in the Civil War, spoke on the duties of a citizen. Morton S. Wilkinson from back home in Onondaga county, then living in Stillwater, defended the legal profession. He became a senator from Minnesota. Lawyer Bishop of St. Paul spoke of the progress of the human race, but invited a plain talk from North when he defended slavery. North held his tongue until his guest was ready to depart, and then "gave him some information on some points."

The Norths read Mrs. Lydia R. Bailey's *Friend of Youth,* and Ann sold nine subscriptions during afternoon walks. She gave piano lessons at the rate of twenty-four for ten dollars, but pupils were afraid to cross the millpond on the log boom. Abigail Marshall sent Rebecca regularly for lessons, accompanied by her son William, who wanted a wife "just like Ann North" and stood beside the piano in such frank admiration

---

MORTON S. WILKINSON (1819–94) Left Skaneateles, New York, as a youth to work on railroad in 1837 in Illinois, where he knew Lincoln; returned to Onondaga county to study law, was admitted to the bar in Syracuse (1842); moved to Minnesota in 1847. Elected to the Territorial legislature (1849); Republican senator in Washington (1859–65); representative in Forty-first Congress; state senator (1874–78).

that North was amused and Ann flattered. Mrs. Marshall praised Ann's industry and North's looks; the son praised North's industry and Ann's looks.

When pupils and guests were gone, the Norths spent evenings writing. North wrote to eastern papers touting Minnesota, and even placed a card in the *National Era* in Washington, D.C. For the next several years almost every mail brought three or four letters of inquiry which he answered in detail, describing the advantages of settling in the Territory. He had found a new concern, yet not unrelated to his old ones. He wrote only for papers dedicated to abolition, temperance, education, Free Soil, and liberal politics, and of course received inquiries only from the sort of people who read these papers. Like himself, they were carpetbaggers interested in speculative investment and settlement in a land where they might bring about the evangelical humanist reforms by founding a new political state. He was selective in replying, giving the greatest encouragement to the "right sort" of people. His acknowledged purpose was to build St. Anthony — the future Minneapolis — with citizens of such sterling worth that the community would become a political makeweight to what he believed was the dissolute, ignorant, drunken, Democratic, pro-slavery capital city down the river. He wanted as few wandering fur traders, lumberjacks, military men, Indian agents, immigrant Irish, and western roughs as possible. In a single year he was so successful that the control of the Territory seemed about to slip from the hands of Sibley and Steele. North helped bring in enough New Yorkers and New Englanders to carry Steele's own town by the two-thirds vote that eventually elected North to the second Territorial legislature. By ones and twos and families of twenty, the reformers converged upon St. Anthony, uniting politically some years before they would combine nationally in the Republican party.

A check on North's writing to the press and public was his lack of stamps. By late spring in 1850, only a timely contribution from his father-in-law saved him from an empty purse — his last shilling had been spent on stamps. Ann was his secretary, copying in her fine hand the long effusions of her husband and adding a feminine welcome to the female members of families who inquired. Like a true carpetbagger, North promoted his own interest at least as well as those of the prospective migrants; he would help select lands, take fees for arranging titles, and sell some of his own lots. So promising was the response that even before navigation opened those who owned property were expressing their appreciation for North's efforts by offering him special consideration in the purchase of lots.

On March 14, 1850, Ann wrote that total strangers had written North in response to his letters in the press. They promised to come, and come they did, as individuals, by families, and by congregations. Twelve arrived from Illinois in one family, and as time went on only families of thirty or forty (including in-laws) deserved comment. The sort of people North liked was the Christmas family with three schoolteaching daughters. Unfortunately, they married. They were undoubtedly feminists, for one, instead of saying "I will" at the altar, answered the "obey" question: "I don't want to lie about it — I'll do my very best."

Even letters to relatives were skilled promotional pieces and produced results. The first summer brought Uncle Gorton G. Loomis and Aunt Eliza Dean Loomis with other Deans, including James Dean, who soon defected to California. North's relatives came in numbers — the Reichards, the Finches, the Harrises. Sarah North came up from New Orleans where she had taught in a girls' school, Clarissa North from Albion Female Institute in Michigan. Friends came from Onondaga county: Sylvanus Jenkins of Jordan, G. B. Dutton, Bagg and Hall from Syracuse, Callender of Fayetteville, the Wheatons of Syracuse. Nathaniel Pitt Langford came on from Westmoreland. Other families sent their advance agents — McDougal, Bickford, Rexford, Sweetzer, a whole parade of old acquaintances that seemed never to end during the Norths' first summer (1850). A conservative estimate would place the number of newcomers lured to Minnesota by North's correspondence during the first year at a thousand. He had doubled the population of St. Anthony.

Of course, there were New Yorkers in Minnesota besides North who helped along the migration: Chief Justice Fuller was from Albany, Dr.

NATHANIEL PITT LANGFORD (1832–1911) Born in Westmoreland, New York. At 21 arrived in Minnesota with three sisters, one of whom married his banking partner, William R. Marshall. In 1862 he went with Captain James Fisk's Northern Overland Expedition to the goldfields. In Montana, Langford and fellow Masons organized vigilantes to deal with outlaws. He explored Yellowstone, advertised its attractions by his writings, and was its first superintendent. Returning to Minnesota, served as president of its Historical Society. Wrote a two-volume work, *Vigilante Days and Ways* (1890), *Diary of the Washburn Expedition to Yellowstone and Fire Hole Rivers* . . . (1905). He married first Emma and then Clara Wheaton, daughters of Charles Wheaton of Northfield.

E. G. Gear, the chaplain at Fort Snelling (and father of Governor John H. Gear of Iowa) was from "home," and Mrs. Stevens, the wife of a Steele partner and historian of Minnesota, was the former Helen Miller, daughter of "Jackass" Miller of Westmoreland (he sold the beasts). None of the New Yorkers wrote as assiduously as North, or as purposefully, but their modest accomplishments in Minnesota were his success stories to be related in letters home. On April 7, 1850, North received inquiries from New York, Vermont, Pennsylvania, and Ohio, a typical mail. One writer addressed North as "Northwestern Correspondent of the *National Era.*" Since he wrote only for the northern church papers and for the abolitionist and temperance press he would have been amazed to get a letter from south of the Mason-Dixon line, and none is on record as having been received.

On December 17, 1849, he wrote the editor of the *National Era*, his old abolitionist friend Dr. Gamaliel Bailey,

Having become settled in Minnesota, I am reminded of my promise to give you such information as I might gather . . . that may be of some service to those who contemplate making it their home . . . In extent, Minnesota reaches from Iowa on the South to the British possessions on the North; from Lake Superior and the St. Croix and Mississippi rivers on the east, to the Missouri and White Earth rivers on the West, containing as Governor Ramsey states in his message, "territory enough for four large States." That portion of the Territory lying West of the Mississippi is still owned by the Indians, except a small tract on the shore of Lake Pepin, that the United States commissioners purchased of the half-breeds in October last. The same commissioners [Governor Ramsey and ex-Governor Chambers] are authorized to treat with the Sioux for a large share of the remaining territory west of the river . . . and will no doubt result in a purchase, which will open for settlement a large share of the finest lands in the Territory.

At present, the only lands in market are those lying between the Mississippi and St. Croix rivers. . . . Most of the migration to this Territory has taken place from the Northern States. St. Paul, which is the temporary capital, stands on the East bank of the Mississippi . . . It has now about 1,200 inhabitants. This place had its origin in an order of the Government which forbade the sale of intoxicating drinks within five miles from Fort Snelling. Those who wished to pursue the traffic retired to the present site of St. Paul and dealt out the poison from there. . . . The Falls of St. Anthony are nine miles from St. Paul by land. . . . This village has been mostly built during the Summer [1849], and now contains between three and four hundred inhabitants.

Those who own the mill property here refuse to sell lots to any one who will sell liquor. . . . Indeed I never knew so young a village, where there was so little vice. It is said there is no man here who does not earn his own living, and I believe it is true. We have already two schools, a public library, and regular preaching by Presbyterian, Methodist, and Baptist denominations. A large and well-furnished school-house serves as a place of worship . . . The country round these Falls, on both sides of the river, is very beautiful, and when thickly settled and improved, will be one of the most delightful places in the West . . .

The water power here is unlimited. There is water enough to drive all the mills in Massachusetts . . . not a finer place for manufacturing in the Union.[1]

North's letter took up nearly two columns in the *National Era* and was typical of his letters to other papers. He described the farm land, Indian trade, the two forts, and other matters of interest to settlers. He appealed to the interests of the Northern, liberal Protestants who desired to live in a whiskey-free, vice-free, slave-free, care-free community. None others need apply.

The Norths opened their island home to as many as they could accommodate. Madison Sweetzer was one of the first from Onondaga county, but he smoked and was unwelcome, left without paying his board, and without as much as a "thank." He was followed by Jenkins of Jordan Junction, who did not smoke, shunned coffee, and worked off his weekly board bill of $3.50 by planting potatoes on North's property. On March 15, 1850, just before the opening of navigation, Ann North wrote, "One cannot help taking an interest in seeing our little village grow . . . It is thought by some, that one year from this time, there will be from five to ten times the present population." There were.

The first two boats, with a thousand on board, were held up by ice in Lake Pepin, and many walked the ice the rest of the way. The boarding house at St. Anthony had been crowded by the dozen who lived there along with the Norths while their house was being finished; now there were seventy. Some of the newcomers had failed to read North's warning about the character of St. Paul; they took one look at "Pig's Eye" and returned home by the next boat. "Quite a large number" came on to St. Anthony and by the end of May newcomers formed half the congregation on Sunday. North regretted that so few farmers had come, for potatoes were selling at a dollar and a half a bushel. No wonder Jenkins had planted potatoes on North's lot.

The potatoes led North to building a house of his own. Everything was so logical on the frontier. Potatoes were dear, so North planted potatoes. To keep the potatoes through the northern winter, a cellar was needed, but, said Ann, "We cannot have a cellar without a house, you know." This feminine logic did not appeal to Dr. George Loomis, who saw his son-in-law's speculations carrying him deeply into debt. North explained that he had acquired a block of city property at a special price from Steele and his partners with the proviso that he build upon it within the year. Pride, rather than potatoes, was the justification for North's new law office. Late in January he had purchased a lot from Steele on the main street with a view of the falls, in front of the now historic Pillsbury "A" mill. He wrote his father-in-law one Sunday, a business letter dated Monday by a Methodist conscience, that he had acquired the lot for a hundred and fifty dollars. Since Dr. Loomis knew that, what with postage, the Norths did not have enough money to live until spring, he was worried. When North said he had "bought" property, he spoke as a lawyer and not as a financier. He had merely contracted the obligation to pay for it. He quarried stone for the foundations of the office building from outcroppings on the island and drew the blocks across the frozen millpond. He had to have an office when newcomers, who imagined him a great man, arrived.

In February North had estimated that it would cost less to build an office than to rent, and he was nearly right. Lumber cost twelve dollars a thousand, but he got this from the mill on credit. The mason would charge fifty-nine dollars, the carpenter and joiner fifty. Starting with unlimited credit at the Marshall store and at Steele's mill, North made the following arrangements: on a lot that cost him nothing, an office was put up by a mason paid half in law services and half in trade at the store and lath from the mill, and by a carpenter and joiner who would be similarly reimbursed. The "best-looking office in the Territory" cost him in out-of-pocket cash only $19.50. Even this could be paid thanks to Alexander Ramsey who appointed North notary public, which meant a twenty-five cent fee for every acknowledgment of deed.

When North said his lot cost him nothing, he meant nothing *down*. But soon it appeared the lot would cost him nothing at all. Reverend B. F. Hoyt of St. Paul was setting up his son-in-law in medical practice. If Dr. J. H. Murphy could have part of the view lot of the Falls, Hoyt would pay North the entire amount promised to Steele for the whole lot. Marshall dampened North's enthusiasm by urging him to wait until the lot had increased in value, as it would do when navigation opened, but North could not wait. He justified his deal with Hoyt to Dr. Loomis by reminding him that Hoyt was a Methodist minister and the soul of honor — and that he would keep the deed in his own hands until every red cent was paid.

By May 20, 1850, North had moved into his office, his law books having arrived from Syracuse. The law books added greatly to his "dignity and consequence." With them housed in a case reaching across one side of his office, he could claim to have the finest office and the largest private library in the Territory: three hundred and fifty-six volumes.

He was ready to receive the immigrants he had invited. On a large map of Minnesota he could pinpoint the available lands, but he was disconcerted when so many visitors seemed to expect farms with views of the falls. He had overplayed the scenic attractions; the newcomers imagined themselves making hay beside the cataract.

He himself was buying land at a distance, and no man ever did so much on so little. When North had visited Minnesota in the summer of 1849, he had put ten dollars down on forty acres in St. Paul; that was the full extent of his investment during the many months he had proclaimed Minnesota far and wide. In January 1850 he had bought the view lot for his office and negotiated for the block on which he was growing potatoes and had promised to build a house. He had also preempted a farm. He agreed with Dr. Loomis that these speculations were "rather large" for one with no money, but he knew values were certain to rise greatly when the immigrants arrived. North had created a monster of inflation which might consume his hopes, however, for the very success of his promotion was pricing land out of his own reach. He wrote Dr. Loomis, "I told Major Godfrey and Steele that I was doing considerable in the way of writing letters, etc., to bring their Town into notice, and that they must give me a chance to make something . . . On this account I got lots on a little better terms."

After having given an additional ten dollars to the Library Association, he had no money for seed. Grandmother Lewis sent a land warrant for $150 to assist in speculation, but wanted the property put in Ann's name. Dr. Loomis sent a draft for $100 so that North could pay for the farm in St. Paul. North's buying of land raced well ahead of his in-laws' generosity, and a few weeks later Dr. Loomis had to send another draft for $250. North acquired two blocks, each divided into ten lots, or two and a half acres. This acquisition put him eight hundred dollars in debt, but he had arranged to pay it over five years at seven per cent interest. Though Steele and his partners waived the down payment because of North's promotional efforts, he was committed to build on one block in 1850 and on the second in 1851. He reasoned that the further he went into debt to the mill company, the more likely they would be to use his legal services; this was sheer rationalization, for he would have got their legal business anyhow.

Isaac Atwater, who had known North well in New York, became his partner in Minnesota, and later followed him to Nevada before returning to Minneapolis to write its history, said that North "largely lost the pecuniary benefit, which his foresight and energies merited, in founding the town, and which others have reaped . . . His perceptions of the natural advantages for town sites was unsurpassed, though he has not reaped the pecuniary advantages from the locations he made to which he was justly entitled." [2]

MINNESOTA, 1850

$\mathbb{P}$UBLICITY for Minnesota was aided considerably by the showing of five panoramas painted of the Mississippi in the 1840's — gigantic pictures unrolled before audiences all over the nation.[1] The landscape painter Henry Lewis showed his *Great National Work — Lewis' Mammoth Panorama of the Mississippi* (which the Norths had seen in Chicago on their way west) in Syracuse in 1850 while the North letters were appearing in Onondaga county papers. The high point of the program for many of the "capitalists" of Syracuse was the scene of St. Anthony Falls which was well-known locally as the "island home" of Mr. and Mrs. J. W. North.

When Ann North's parents wrote that they had seen Lewis's panorama, she replied that she hoped they would not be content with seeing only the picture, that there was more to Minnesota than could be represented on a slowly unrolling panorama. In his letters to the eastern papers, North described a dramatic Minnesota. He knew that the new territory was competing with California for immigrants, so he emphasized that finding gold was a gamble, but success in Minnesota could be achieved by industry. Migrants to Minnesota could bring all their possessions by riverboat and drive their stock overland. If California had its romantic pueblos and missions, Minnesota also had its exotics: North described the *metis* in their red sashes, beadwork, fringed jackets, and fur hats. Ann North recopied one of the articles for her young brothers:

Red River trains . . . have been down recently. One of these is composed of a thin, wide and long piece of wood, which is kept from splitting

43

by slats fastened across, and one end turned up for the front, and held in that position by cords passing from the end (which is bent up,) down to the main part of the board. This was drawn by dogs, of pretty good size, hitched in "tandem," which they were obliged to lead, being unable to guide them, in any other way.[2]

The dogs' harness consisted of a loop collar covered with buckskin and stuffed with hair; a strap connected the collar to the toboggan. After their nightly meal of fish, the dogs slept, their legs continuing to work as if they were still in harness. The halfbreeds with the train wore snowshoes. Mail was carried from Lake Superior to the falls of the St. Croix by such trains. After the snow melted, the Red River transports were two-wheeled ox-drawn carts of wood and sinew, built entirely without metal, and having greaseless axles. The ear-splitting squeal of the wooden wheels on their dry axles could be heard long before the carts came in sight.

The roads closed by the snowstorms of the winter of 1850 were blocked by the spring mud. Ice from the upper Mississippi cracked down, breaking into large cakes to form thunderous jams that tumbled over the rapids and the falls. The whole town came to the riverbank to see the sight. Ann walked the spillway when the water was an inch above the dam, but it rose a foot while she was in town; she could not return to the island and had to spend the night with the Godfreys. The next day the millpond had again frozen enough to bear her weight. The river was up ten feet at St. Paul and the Indians said it had not been so high in twenty-five years.

Thirty thousand dollars' worth of logs were tied in a boom in the millpond. In the freshet the boom broke, the logs went over the dam, and the frame gave way. Eight to ten acres of logs were reduced to one acre, a great loss to the hard-pressed Steele and to Ard Godfrey. These remaining logs, chaotic as jackstraws, were still the only bridge to the island in high water. Isaac Ives Lewis and his family were trapped on the lower island by water three feet higher than it had been in early spring. The continuing flood broke away large pieces of rock from St. Anthony Falls, changing the appearance of the cataract considerably. Over the years, the whole island would be endangered.

With the water so high, it was now or never for St. Anthony to make good its claim of being the head of navigation on the Mississippi. In May 1850 while North was off hunting land with his brother-in-law

44

Cyrenius Finch, Marshall escorted Ann to see the first riverboat approach the Falls, the *Lamartine*, Captain Marsh. She wrote:

They came up half way between St. Anthony City . . . and the Falls. On account of the strong headwind, they were unable to ascend the rapids to the Landing [as] desired by the people here. However, they came up to the *City* (about one mile from the Falls) without any difficulty, which, you know, is our great point gained.[3]

North was on hand as the central figure in the celebration of the next event. The *Anthony Wayne*, Captain Rogers, finally arrived at the foot of the Falls. At a meeting of citizens held aboard on May 7, 1850, North, as spokesman for the townsmen, presented the following testimonial with the two-hundred-dollar purse:

Resolved: . . . That Captain Rogers has earned immortality, which is justly due to those who lead the way in useful achievements . . . That we pledge [ourselves] to patronize boats which make trips to our landing, and particularly the *Anthony Wayne*. . . .[4]

The Sixth Infantry band mingled its roll of drums with the roar of the falls as North presented the money collected by grateful citizens. They could well afford the purse, for land values rose in St. Anthony and fell in St. Paul, which had temporarily lost the distinction of being the head of navigation. Even the St. Paul *Chronicle and Register* reluctantly admitted that the new town was forging ahead:

Within six months our neighboring town has done wonders. The only marks by which we can recognize the St. Anthony of last season are the falls themselves and the mill which has undergone great change — now running four saws instead of two. But the number of fine buildings that have sprung into existence, as if by magic, is truly astonishing. Stores, dwellings, and a large hotel — the largest and the handsomest in the Territory — are all there now where last September were fields and commons. There is a genuine Yankee enterprise at St. Anthony, more of it than is to be found in any other town in Minnesota, we are sorry to say . . .[5]

But St. Paul was only borrowing trouble: its place as head of navigation was not lost. When the flood declined in August, the riverboat *Nominee*, Captain Smith, could not make the upper landing, although it brought "considerable freight" to the town. While St. Anthony pointed with pride to southward navigation, they could also point with equal pride northward on the river. All spring there had been hammer-

45

ing and sawing on Nicollet Island as Captain John Rollins built a riverboat to navigate the Mississippi above the Falls. Early in June, the Norths, with Rebecca Marshall, boarded the new boat, the *Governor Ramsey*, Captain Todd, and started a hundred-mile trip to Sauk Rapids, tying up at nights because of uncharted islands and reefs.

On the return voyage, the ship was filled with naked, fierce-looking Chippewas on their way to a council with Governor Ramsey, who, as head of the Territory, was ex officio Indian commissioner. The most interesting passenger, Chief Hole-in-the-Day, spent his time on deck primping in a hand mirror. He already fully appreciated the charms that later in life, augmented by a million-dollar fortune, would make him attractive to white women. He was less than attractive to Ann North and Rebecca Marshall, although they went with the other women to the council at Fort Snelling.

The Indians took great offense at the presence of women at the council, but Hole-in-the-Day gallantly overruled all objections. The Norths saw the Bear Dance performed by Indians painted from head to foot and heard songs that sounded to Ann like a continual groan of changing pitch forced out by the exertions of the stamping dance. After the council, the Indians descended upon the wondrous new town and even invaded the precincts of Nicollet Island. They were not so nimble as popular fancy supposed, and had a hard time crossing the millpond on the logs. Ann wrote: "They were *so* timid . . . We watched them balance on two logs, try the end of one as it sank, jump back, set them all rolling, try again to balance on two, which . . . is impossible, and almost fall in the water."

Schoolteacher Backus was even less nimble than the Indians. On the way to the Norths she slipped off the logs into the water and since she was as heavy as North (a hundred and sixty-nine pounds) he had great trouble getting her to shore. It is little wonder that Miss Backus, so friendly with the Norths when ice covered the millpond, did not now visit them so frequently as she visited others in St. Anthony. Yet Ann grew peevish and jealous in her lonely hours on the island and complained of Miss Backus's neglect. While North read them a sermon one Sunday, calculated to improve Miss Backus, Ann wrote accusing Miss Backus of deceit, "notwithstanding her protestations of love." As usual, North followed up with a charitable correction, explaining that after Miss Backus had invited Ann to teach singing in her school, she had unaccountably changed her mind, but was still "a lady of much good sense and refinement." Furthermore, he said, he had had a plain talk with the schoolteacher and she seemed grateful to have her shortcomings brought lovingly to her attention — a remarkable woman. Before long Miss Backus called to announce her departure for Connecticut and the Norths had to make other friends.

Not all visitors were welcome. Those from downriver were taken to the Norths' house as a matter of course; it was a proud example of culture in the wilderness. Mrs. Stillman of Galena played and sang there, but offended Ann by her great surprise at finding a piano "out here in the woods." Even friends from home in Onondaga county became distant: Madison Sweetzer, once an unsatisfactory boarder because of his smoking, failed to call and even avoided North in town.

The reason was not long hidden. Sweetzer had bought a lot from Marshall on which to build an "eating place." Calling on him, North found the stock suspiciously liquid, whereupon he reminded Sweetzer of his mother back home and of the disgrace to her when word got back that her son was keeping a saloon. Marshall also objected, and in the end Sweetzer "cried copiously" — whether because of his sins or because he had now no way to pay for his lot, North did not say. Sweetzer moved downriver where, as the Norths put it, anything went. North would not tell Ann where Sweetzer was, perhaps to protect him from bill collectors.

The temperance spirit of the town was evident in the Fourth of July celebrations of 1850. The ceremonies took place in the triangular park of oak trees high on the bluff overlooking the river, and concluded with an Independence Ball in the newly completed St. Charles Hotel built by Anson Northrup. As Ann noted, the day was to be conducted entirely on temperance principles, in contrast to the goings-on down at St. Paul. North was toastmaster. A cannon wheeled from Fort Snelling saluted the flag and the military band played on a stage built under the scrub oaks. Abraham Edwards Welch of Kalamazoo (later the major in command of the Third Minnesota regiment and a local hero) talked for an hour and a half on "Our Country Right or Wrong." Welch would stay on in Minnesota and bring out his father, William H. Welch, who after a year's residence would be appointed chief justice of Minnesota by President Pierce. Young Welch's address on the Fourth did not augur well the later importance of the Welches. The reformers in St.

Anthony believed in a higher law (as their hero Seward would express it) and were not willing to accept the idea that patriotism bound them to all the evils of the Southern-dominated government in Washington. Ann's comment on the speech was perhaps typical: "What dough-facism!"

A procession formed after the address and North's reading of the Declaration of Independence to march to noon dinner at the St. Charles, where the toasts were drunk in water. Toastmaster North had long ago forsworn politics, but he was behaving very much like a candidate for the legislature on that Fourth of July as he discussed politics with the hundred or more townspeople who went for a ride after dinner on the *Governor Ramsey*. The townspeople were ready to take a political stand with North and the boat's owner, John Rollins, as their leaders. For North, this would mean a political break with his benefactor, Steele; Dr. Loomis wrote emphatically that North should not ungratefully antagonize Steele and the fur company party. Franklin Steele had hatched a serpent's egg; he would soon feel North's desertion and ingratitude sharper than a serpent's tooth.

Only personal problems kept North from greater participation in politics. By some delicate suggestion of indisposition not readily apparent to the reader of her letters today, Ann had conveyed to her parents that she was to have a baby. Her grandmother, Ann Hendrix Lewis, had arrived to take care of her in her "trial" and make a barrel of soap and flush the visiting Chippewas and Winnebagoes out of the bushes in the garden. This was no time for Ann to be frightened by Indians. "How would you feel," wrote Grandmother Lewis, "to have eighty of them mostly naked in your garden, some painted red and some an ash color." [6]

Dr. Murphy, with the help of his father-in-law Preacher Hoyt, had built his house and office on part of North's lot, and was ready to deliver Ann's baby. The baby turned blue and died — proof, perhaps, that Murphy's experience was not adequate to the needs of a frontier where cholera and smallpox raged. Another of his failures was with William Marshall, who was bleeding from the lungs. Soon Murphy would go off to Rush Medical College to learn how better to cope with the ills of St. Anthony. The Reverend Hoyt now moved into the back room of North's office next to the home of his daughter. The arrangement was pleasant to North who asked only four dollars a month rent which Ann supposed her husband would have "to take part in preaching."

North could afford the luxury of good company, for he was doing reasonably well. Steele had cooled toward him, but his new partner, Arnold Taylor from Boston, would trust no one else. He flatly made the condition that all the legal work of the mill company be done by North. He would not even use the deeds Steele had had printed at some expense, but insisted that they be copied anew by North, with the result that Ann worked all night with her husband copying deeds. The mill overseer, Ard Godfrey, would not sign the new deeds and Taylor would not sign the old ones; after some wrangling the Boston investor washed his hands of the whole affair and went off to St. Paul on his way home to Boston. This would have left North and his friends with insecure titles to their lots until Taylor could return another year, so North followed Taylor to St. Paul and after a plain talk and a plea for Guidance, persuaded him to sign the deeds. The profit to North, at seventy-five cents a deed, was three hundred dollars.

With land matters straightened out (for the time, at least) North was ready to step up his promotion of St. Anthony. An unexpected opportunity for worldwide publicity came in the late fall of 1850 when the novelist Fredrika Bremer visited the Norths. That same fall North got free postage as member of the Territorial legislature. He made the most of both opportunities.

As Miss Bremer came upriver with Captain Smith on the *Nominee* it was like a return to her own Sweden as she met the frosts edging down from Canada and spreading a royal pageant of colored woods to welcome the reigning queen of family literature. Beside her on deck was Henry Hastings Sibley, who was returning from Washington. He pointed out along the shore the curious Indian treatment of their dead: chests of bark were laid upon planks supported on four posts which kept the body away from wolves when deep snow accumulated. As the riverboat nosed to a landing at St. Paul, Governor Ramsey met the celebrity, invited her to his present crude dwelling, and took her to see the man-

FREDRIKA BREMER (1801–65) Novelist, born in Finland, raised in Sweden, daughter of a wealthy ironfounder. Supported philanthropies by her writings. In America two years (1849–51). Before her visit, her novels were domestic, after it concerned with reforms, especially equal rights for women. Her American impressions were published in *Homes of the New World*.

sion he was building. To further assure her that Minnesota was not devoid of refinement, he introduced her to the Norths. She wrote:

Governor Ramsey drove me yesterday to the Falls of St. Anthony. The falls of St. Anthony have no considerable height, and strike me merely as a cascade of a great mill-dam. They fall abruptly over a stratum of tufa rock, which they sometimes break and wash down in great masses.[7]

If she was not impressed by the great showpiece of Minnesota, she was impressed by the North home.

We drank tea on a considerable island in the Mississippi, above the falls, at a beautiful home, where I saw comforts and cultivation, where I heard music, saw books and pictures — such life, in short, as might be met with on the banks of the Hudson; and how charming it was to me! Here, too, I found friends in its inhabitants . . . The dwelling had not been long on the island; and the island in its autumnal attire, looked like a little paradise, although in its half-wild state.

As to describe how we travelled about, how we walked over the river on broken trunks of trees which were jammed together by the stream in chaotic masses, how we climbed and clambered up and down, over, among, and upon the sticks, and stones, and precipices, and sheer descents — all this I shall not attempt to describe, because it is indescribable. I considered many a passage wholly and altogether impracticable, until my conductors, both gentlemen and ladies, convinced me that it was to them a simple and every-day path.[8]

During the excursion, North "improved the time" by enlarging upon the opportunities of Minnesota for Scandinavians who would find the Minnesota winters little different from those to which they had long been accustomed. Miss Bremer was a ready convert. She wrote: "But this Minnesota is a glorious country, and just the country for Northern emigrants — just the country for a new Scandinavia."[9] And again, "Such as are too contracted at home, and who desire to emigrate, should come to Minnesota . . . The rich soil of Minnesota is not yet bought up by speculators, but may every where be purchased at government prices, one dollar and a quarter per acre."[10] And still again, "What a glorious new Scandinavia might not Minnesota become!"[11]

She rambled on for four pages in *Homes of the New World* about the advantages Swedes, Norwegians, Finns, and Danes would find in Minnesota, and if she did not have one of North's promotion letters before her as she wrote, she at least quoted him at great length from memory.

North had told her that a Norwegian pastor was thinking of leading his congregation to Minnesota, and in her book she exclaimed, "Good!"

In their enthusiasm to show off the falls, Governor Ramsey and North tired their visitor, for it was a cold, unpleasant October day. She had seen greater falls and rockier crags at home. What impressed her were Ann's piano, North's books, and the sentimental Victorian prints on the walls. In her account, Miss Bremer dwelt upon her nimble youthfulness in crossing the logs and blamed her fatigue upon the weather — which is literary license allowable to a young lady approaching fifty.

"Fredricka Bremer spent last Friday in town," wrote Ann to her parents, "and what is more, came on the Island and into our house, and played on my piano . . . She called with Governor Ramsey and Lady. Miss Bremer was afraid to cross the logs, and Mr. North paddled her over in a canoe. She is quite short, round-shouldered, has light hair and eyes, a large nose which was quite red as well as her eyelids." [12]

It is hard to say which intrigued Ann North more, that Miss Bremer played on her very own piano or that she shared her very own defect, an unfashionable nose. She conjectured that Miss Bremer had been writing autobiographically when in a novel she introduced a heroine with a large nose. "You recollect how much *she* suffered in attempting to make her nose less prominent." Miss Bremer showed herself "kind and good as we always imagined her, by offering herself to play a Swedish song, A Tribute to God of the Rivers, she said. It was very sweet and she plays *well*. Some one asked her to sing . . . She replied 'I never sing; only to children and to God in church — the little ones, and the Great One are not critical.' Is that not a beautiful idea?"

Had Miss Bremer waited a few days, she would have found the new member of the legislature in a house even finer than the cabin on Nicollet Island. The Norths were ready to move into the finest house in town, which had cost North fifteen hundred but was worth two thousand dollars. Pressed by Dr. Loomis to be more precise, North specified the exact cost as $1,731.27. The difference between the estimated and the exact cost was not inconsiderable; it represented enough money to keep them all winter. He owed $944.37 — $72 to Franklin Steele for the year's rent on the island house; $95 to storekeeper Wilson; $100 to William Marshall; $32 for office improvements; $131 to Uncle Gorton Loomis; $200 to his new law partner, Isaac Atwater; and $50 to the tailor who made the new suit in which he entered the Minnesota Territorial Legislature in January 1851. It was a magnificent debt. Dr. Loomis, who had helped North through his speculation, thought it ruinous. Ann, in sublime confidence in "my good husband," thought it justifiable. It troubled North himself not at all; he saw his way to solvency. His law practice would support his family through the winter; he had $100 worth of vegetables in his cellar; he would draw $200 from the legislature; he had arranged to room and board the Atwaters for the winter for $100. Altogether, he could scrape up $840 to apply to his $944 indebtedness, leaving him only $104.37 short.

Dr. Loomis as usual saw the reality behind North's great expectations. Service in the legislature would keep him from the law business which was supposed to keep the family all winter. Vegetables could freeze — and they did. And finally the Atwaters might not get along under the same roof with the Norths, as, indeed, they did not. North had known Isaac Atwater in New York when he studied law in the Jay office. When he wrote Atwater about the advantages of Minnesota, offering him a partnership, Atwater visited Minnesota, and then returned to get his wife in October 1850. North's reason for taking a partner at this time was not a rush of business, but impatience with keeping office hours and the expectation that he would represent St. Anthony in the legislature.

"The people here *almost* unanimously go for him," wrote Ann North, "but the Mill Company have found out he has a mind of his own . . . They oppose him with all their might." [13] North had brought his own followers west; he was elected by better than a two-thirds majority over Steele's candidate. North confided to his father-in-law,

I had been on the best terms with the Mill Company all the time until just before election. I chanced to incur the displeasure of Mr. Steele by opposing his brother-in-law, Mr. Sibley . . . Without any just ground of offense, Mr. Steele declared himself my "eternal enemy." Notwithstanding, . . . the people saw fit to nominate me for the Legislature by a two-thirds vote in a public meeting called irrespective of party. After the nomination was made, Mr. Steele gave out the word that my nomination "must be broken down if possible." [14]

North had packed the town against the mill company and fur company and got 121 votes to his opponent's 55. He now looked forward to the ninety-day session of the legislature, to the three dollars a day —

and to an unlimited supply of stamps! "In anticipation of this event," wrote North, "I formed a partnership a few weeks ago with a friend of mine from New York by the name of Atwater. He is a graduate of Yale College, a good lawyer, a man of literary taste and talent, and speaks the French language fluently." [15]

With his generous disposition, North did not realize that such a well-trained lawyer might set up for himself and take over the mill company business, that a man of literary taste might get into newspaper publishing on the wrong side of the political line, and that a French-speaking lawyer would naturally gravitate toward the fur company. Had he been aware of the coming rivalry, he would have been less eager to give a third of the profits of the firm to Isaac Atwater. With supreme confidence North had made arrangements with Atwater even before his nomination, at a time when he was protesting that he was out of politics — unless he was drafted. North knew that as soon as he was in the legislature he would be a power to be reckoned with and that Steele would come running. The "eternal enmity" ended with election; Steele brought North fifty more deeds at seventy-five cents apiece as a good-will token. (This was also Steele's way of enabling North to pay his lumber bill.) North wrote Loomis, "I thank you for your good advice about 'a soft answer' *etcetera* with Steele." [16]

E ARLY in 1851 North began to prosper in law, spending much of his time in St. Paul attending court and the legislature and leaving his office in St. Anthony to the care of Isaac Atwater. Close friends of the year before had drifted away, Rebecca Marshall to Catherine Beecher's school at Quincy, her mother to St. Paul. Ann looked to Mrs. Atwater for companionship, but Mrs. Atwater regarded her only as a landlady, and Atwater's loud talk drove Ann from her own sittingroom. With North spending so much time in St. Paul, nobody censored Ann's letters home; they were full of complaints: "They are very intelligent, and I suppose excellent folks [but] they are too tight . . . They furnish their own room and won't get a rocking-chair because they cost so much, so occupy ours." Atwater complained of the Norths' winter diet of salt pork, when fresh meat was so expensive — ten cents a pound! Ann wished she had her husband's charity — he had "a thousand times more philosophy" than she could have. It pained her to have to dissemble to maintain harmony, to pretend to like her boarders; she called it deception. She was distressed that the Atwaters were as trapped as she: they could not afford to set up housekeeping because prices were so inflated. A house cost Ann's Uncle Gorton Loomis the enormous rent of twelve dollars a month; food was high — eggs sold for sixpence apiece (she learned to settle coffee with codfish skins instead of eggs). Added to her household annoyances was the thought of her husband in wicked Pig's Eye.

On January 1, 1851, the second legislative assembly of the Territory met in St. Paul in a new three-story brick building on St. Anthony street. North lived close by at the home of George W. Farrington, but had only contempt for the town and for the legislature. He reported "all sorts of bargains going on, even bribery." When James M. Goodhue secured the public printing by bribery, North canceled both his and Loomis's subscription to the *Pioneer* and took the *Democrat*. Goodhue wrote an article insulting the Territorial marshal, Colonel Alexander M. Mitchell, and Judge Cooper who was absent in Washington. Cooper's brother Joseph met Goodhue on the street, stabbed him twice, and got himself shot. Almost sadly, North reported that both were recovering. Gangs of boys roamed the streets of St. Paul; a boy North thought the best of the lot was hanged in a privy. He was thirteen. To such violence was added drunkenness.

The day the legislature met, Governor Ramsey was reported so drunk on wine that he could not receive his New Year's callers. North blamed Ramsey and his brother Justus C. for supplying the distressed Chippewas with "spoilt provisions." The Indians died in great numbers, ate their children, and threatened to attack the white settlements. When Hole-in-the-Day came to see the governor, Ramsey at first refused to see him. North wrote, "I begin to think the Governor is about as corrupt as the greater part of our public officers." [1]

North was glad to leave St. Paul and return home where he could doctor himself with lobelia emetic, consult his library, now augmented by $210 worth of Atwater's books, and give an account of his stewardship to the people. The delegates from St. Anthony in the assembly were Councilor John Rollins and Representatives Edward Patch and North. They had been the conscience of the legislature and would eventually walk out of the body in protest. Their chief concern as they seated themselves about the new pine table in North's parlor was the establishment of a university. Stillwater had got the prison, St. Paul the capitol, St. Anthony nothing. The St. Anthony reform element, still weak in the Territory, now undertook to raise a thousand dollars to establish a newspaper of their own. North sent word to Burleigh that he was badly needed as editor. To raise money and to express indignation at the legislature's treatment of the town, North called a meeting. Addressing the meeting, he charged that Steele had used his influence against his own town by supporting the majority in the legislature. With the resolutions of the meeting behind him, he returned to the legislature to demand a university for St. Anthony. He wrote: "My old attachments for a 'minority' have not left me, and I had much rather stand with a minority that has some show of honesty and regard for right, than with a majority that discard all pretensions to honesty, and are governed by the present hope of spoils." [2]

North did not think it any part of spoils to locate the university of Minnesota next to his own property in St. Anthony. He introduced the bill establishing the university, and by dint of his unremitting efforts it was passed and signed by the governor. [3] The site for the university was near the old Winslow House, one of several hotels in the territory built by James M. Winslow in the peculiar style that bore his name: each had "a cupola and mortgage on top." [4] It would have been hard to put the university anywhere in St. Anthony without raising the value of some of North's property, and putting it next to North's block was less his doing than Franklin Steele's momentary generosity in providing a site. Steele perhaps gave the land to re-establish himself in the good graces of the townspeople; he later negotiated to shift the institution to land at the time less choice.

Governor Ramsey had urged the legislature to ask Congress for a hundred thousand acres of land to endow a university with. "But," said North,

no one had thought of getting such an Institution chartered at this time. There was an opportunity to locate the Institution at our place and we determined to improve it. To make matters sure I went first to the Governor and leading men of his faction, who all felt they had done St. Anthony wrong in depriving her of any of the public buildings, and they could not do otherwise than to agree to go for the measure. I prepared the bill in exact accordance with the Governor's suggestion but his followers found fault with it, and we took a transcript from the Charter of Wisconsin University and added to it a preparatory department, and it carried. [5]

By August the coolness between North and Steele ended with a call by the Steele family upon the Norths. Steele presented North with a bill for the lumber used for the academy or preparatory school. On August 5, 1851, North wrote, "We set stakes yesterday for the University building, that is, Preparatory Department, it will front on Third Street, and will be within twenty-five rods of my block." [6] Two weeks later he wrote, "We have commenced work on the academy building, and hope to have it completed this fall." [7] North started a subscription for the university, raised $3,000 for the first building, hired workmen, and made arrangements for the arrival of Professor Elijah Washington Merrill with his family in September. The Merrills stayed in the North home and were given special consideration in board — that is, they were boarded at a financial loss to the Norths. As they continued to live with the Norths for several months, the Merrills fitted into the household better than the Atwaters had done. Ann found Mrs. Merrill pleasant, but with a queer taste in dress, "so witchy." When other teachers were added to the staff, they would also live with the Norths or take refuge with them from Merrill's too close supervision. Perhaps a third of the subscription for the new university came from North's own impoverished pocket. In October, the university building was "partly shirted" and presented an imposing appearance from the Norths' sittingroom window. A month later, it was nicely enclosed, with two rooms plastered, and ready to keep school. Classes began on November 26, 1851; twenty-four scholars were in attendance on December 7, three more expected the next day.

The founding of a university required the time and talents, energies and enthusiasm of many men. At the Founders' Day convocation in Northrop Memorial Auditorium on April 21, 1932, the "founders" were honored by the university. The list of founders in the program was indeed safe: it included Ramsey, Marshall, North, Sibley, Rice, Ames, Neill, and Pillsbury. If we are to call one or another of them *the* founder, it would have to be the man whose services were unique and indispensable, John Wesley North, who, as chairman of the House committee on schools in the territorial legislature, drafted the bill for the establishment of the university, secured the university for St. Anthony, and raised money for its early construction. The only "founder" to mention a university, as far as we know, at a date earlier than North's framing of the bill was Alexander Ramsey who recommended the establishment of a university in his message to the legislature in January 1851, but Ramsey had been urged to do so by North in the interest of St. Anthony.

All the other founders carried forward the plans of J. W. North. William Rainey Marshall served on the first board of regents; Henry Hastings Sibley secured a land grant in February 1851; Henry Mower Rice was a regent in 1851; Dr. Alfred Elisha Ames served on a university committee in the 1857 constitutional convention; Edward Duffield Neill became chancellor in 1858 and prepared the reorganization bill of 1860, and John Sargent Pillsbury was a regent in 1863. Still others may have some claim as founders, but the university would have come into existence without any one of them except North. If any is to be called *the* founder it is this indispensable man with his unique contribution to its founding.

North's interest in the university did not end with its founding or with subsidizing its first teacher. His donations were liberal beyond his means. Moreover, he was soon at work helping to organize a course of weekly lectures for the benefit of the academy. Seventy tickets were sold for Merrill's lecture on the progress of science, which North thought sophomoric. The next lecturer was Chief Justice Jerome Fuller whom North had known as the editor of the Albany *State Register*. Fuller spent the night at the Norths' house (which became during this era the guest house of the university), as did other lecturers. To be married to a man of public spirit was minor martyrdom for the once more pregnant hostess, who thought that boarding the Merrills for two and a half a week should have been enough. That winter North started another subscription for the university and did not rest until he had collected two hundred and eight dollars. Said Ann North proudly, "People say, no other man could get money out of the inhabitants like him." Perhaps that was because a third of the subscription came from his own slight purse. The *Democrat* complimented North on the success of the university, giving him full credit. As time passed, the university itself would forget and neglect its progenitor, never do him proper honor, and even when grudgingly mentioning him as founder, would mistake his identity.[8] John Wesley North was alone, singlehandedly, the founder of the University of Minnesota, all campus statues and pictures to the contrary notwithstanding. A university is more than buildings raised to the donor's pride and razed to discredit of the donor's taste in architecture, but even to the university's buildings, none gave such a large portion of his means as North.

North's founding of the University of Minnesota was typical carpetbagging. He used the legislature to achieve an end desired by the reformers that was also to the advantage of the St. Anthony land investors. Public good was combined with private gain. Yet it would be oversimplification to say that North and his friends were selfishly motivated. Public good and private gain were two sides of the same coin, but a coin they did not counterfeit by impressing private gain on both sides.

A few days before the end of the session, North and six others dramatically walked out of the legislature to make a quorum impossible and prevent the passage of an apportionment bill. Those who had controlled the territory for so long now saw that control passing into the hands of the reformers. By basing the apportionment upon the census of 1850, they hoped to balance populous St. Anthony with precincts still susceptible to their control. For example, Benton county with four thousand acres under cultivation by newcomers would be given only half the representation of Pembina county with only seventy acres under cultivation. Pembina was one of the regions controlled by the fur company, seven eighths of its population was Indian, the other eighth Canadians, traders, and soldiers. Highhandedly, the legislature passed the apportionment bill even in the absence of a quorum and the Governor signed it. North found "as much dirt as glory" in being a legislator; but now what he considered dirty politics developed in the very newspaper he had urged upon St. Anthony.

Elmer Tyler brought printers from Chicago to print the St. Anthony *Express*, a weekly eight-column folio which began publication on May 31, 1851. Isaac Atwater and his Yale friend Shelton Hollister were the brains behind its composition.[9] To North's great disgust, his law partner supported Fillmore and would continue to annoy North until the paper ceased publishing a decade later with the Republican victory. By the Fourth of July 1851 it was clear that Atwater was less a partner than a competitor of North. Atwater was the orator of the day.

The partnership ended that summer, after nine months' association. One reason for Atwater's consequence in St. Anthony was that he had money to lend: friends in New York had entrusted him with three thousand dollars. North suggested to Dr. Loomis that if *he* had money to lend, he could add considerably to his business. He wrote his friend Charles A. Wheaton in Syracuse to bring out ten thousand dollars upon which they could both get rich by providing down payments to settlers. North had just made out a mortgage for a man who pledged a thousand dollars' worth of property to secure a fifty-dollar loan at four per cent a month. Having money, even three thousand dollars, to dispense, created confidence. Atwater had reason enough to wish to set up for himself, but there was also an element of personal conflict with the Norths. When Atwater would not return Ann's greeting on the street she observed in letters to her parents that he was "toady" to the mill company and shamed North by his vulgar editorials in the *Express*. North reported: "My course will be to let him have a clear track to go his own way."

New fields were also opening up. In January 1851 an officer at Fort Snelling asked North to join him in a claim across the river in the future heart of Minneapolis. He would supply the permit from his commanding officer, and North would supply the settler to hold the claim. North settled on the claim, in a five-dollar shanty, the husband of his sister Minerva, Cyrenius Finch. North also gave attention to other business from which politics had distracted him: he served as agent for the Aetna Insurance Company and also helped find lands for immigrants who arrived that summer in considerable numbers. A family of twelve arrived from Ogle county, Illinois, with four ox-drawn wagons, two teams of horses, and sixty head of cattle. (Before many seasons passed, this wealth would be wiped out by hard times and the family dependent upon North's generosity.) For the moment, North was so optimistic that Dr. Loomis (who sent him three hundred dollars to pay his debts) extracted his pledge not to buy any more land. "I am resolved," promised North, "to make no more purchases until I am out of debt." [10] Then Dr. Loomis himself came to Minnesota to check, and check on, North's speculations.

All in all, 1851 had been a good year and a year of many changes. North took into his office David A. Secombe, cousin of the Reverend Charles Secombe. The Marshalls sold their store to Upton and Green and changed residence. Joseph Marshall married Cora Patch despite his mother's disapproval and William Marshall transferred his affections from Ann to her best friend. To find a wife "just like Ann" he purposely went to De Witt, lived with her parents, and was introduced to all the eligible young ladies of Onondaga county. North also supplied him with introductions to Gerrit Smith and the businessmen of Syracuse. Marshall made the most of both kinds of introduction but did not close a bargain in either business or love. He returned more unsettled than ever, was blue about the prospects of St. Anthony, went bathing in the river and was almost carried over the falls, and, in North's new office with its French curtains, nursed the bruises the rocks had made.

North and Marshall discussed the religion of Swedenborg to which Marshall was now committed, the quality of the lands he had surveyed on the Elk River, the new Maine Law of Neal Dow which both hoped to introduce in Minnesota, Marshall's plan to open a bank, North's plan to build a steamboat, and the alternate plan of building a railroad up the Mississippi valley. The committee North met with at the St. Charles to raise thirty thousand dollars to construct the *Falls City* eventually built the boat while North built a railroad. As North and Marshall discussed these projects, however, neither saw how soon they might become realities, and out of their talks emerged an impatience with St. Anthony that finally caused both to move away.

North's defeat in the fall elections discouraged him, although the defeat was probably due to general dissatisfaction with the real estate interests he represented, for lot prices declined because of insecurity of title. He was discouraged for other reasons. Joseph Marshall had been beaten up trying to collect an old grocery bill and Stanchfield the local commission merchant had fought Godfrey over a lumber bill; David Secombe slept in North's office to be on hand when such losers turned to the law, while injuries were fresh.

North's home changed. Marshall moved in to compare his memory of Abby B. Langford, the daughter of George Langford of Onondaga county, point by point with his ideal woman. Then Preacher Harris, the husband of North's sister Eliza, moved in with two of his boys, intending to stay the winter; when he showed no signs of returning to Michigan before the annual freeze, North provided a freeze of his own: he promised his overburdened wife to get rid of him. Harris met any suggestion that he was less than welcome with true Christian resignation; in saying grace before meals he managed to imply that from their abundance the Norths ought to feed the servants of the Lord. He mentioned the barrel of Iowa pork, the ten-gallon keg of golden syrup (at sixty-five cents a gallon), the quantities of turnips, the five hundred and fifty bushels of potatoes, and the nine bushels of white beans — for all of which, dear Lord, they must be truly grateful.

CHARLES N. HARRIS (1839–?) Partly raised by J. W. North in Minnesota; enlisted in the First Minnesota, shot in the chest at Bull Run, left for dead and his funeral service was preached by Dr. B. F. Crary at Richfield, Minnesota. His recovery and imprisonment at Libby were not known until the end of the war, when he joined the Norths in Nevada. He became a district judge in Nevada.

Dealing with a brother-in-law was hard enough, but dealing with one who had the ear of the Almighty required a plain talk. North offered a compromise: he would keep his nephews Charles and John if the father would seek other pastures. A more welcome member of the family was Clarissa North who, as it turned out, spent the rest of her devoted life in the household and as "Aunt Clara" was a second mother to her brother's children. She had planned to open a girls' school in St. Anthony, but soon found herself too much involved in family responsibilities and good works.

The story of the reform frontier will never be completely told until the monumental history of the Yankee schoolmarm is recorded. Harriet Bishop, the pioneer teacher sent by Slade to Minnesota, had organized the first temperance society in 1848. To this work Clarissa North now dedicated herself. The legislature in which North sat had begun the work by requiring dealers selling less than a quart of liquor at a time to be licensed by the county in which they lived and to post a five-hundred-dollar bond. Sunday selling was made an offense. Now Clarissa joined her brother in circulating pledges and in campaigning to close the "rum holes."

St. Anthony had changed since the Temperance Fourth of 1850. Indeed, on the Fourth of 1851 Atwater had tried to borrow money from North to purchase brandy — "for his sick wife" — and though he spoke at a temperance meeting later, he refused to sign the pledge. But even as he delivered the oration so inordinately praised by his own newspaper that Fourth of July, champagne was ready to flow in Indian lands far to the south where Indian Commissioner Luke Lea and Territorial Indian Commissioner Ramsey awaited the start of the treaty-making with the Sioux. (And flow it would have, but that the local missionary spoiled the celebration by inconsiderately getting drowned while swimming.)

At Traverse des Sioux, the portage from Cannon River to Swan Lake, the commissioners persuaded the Upper Bands to give up their Minnesota lands west of the Mississippi. The Senate might not ratify the treaty: it might object to the half-million dollars given to the fur company and traders for "just debts" dating back a generation. (Never was there a statute of limitation on Indian debts to traders.) But Minnesota took the act for the deed. North's spirits rose again. "As soon as these lands are open to settlement," he wrote, "there will be a rush to these parts. . . . Send on all the good people you can induce to come here and settle." [11]

One of the difficulties in keeping settlers in St. Anthony had been the continued insecurity of titles, resulting from the disagreement among Steele and his partners, Ard Godfrey and Arnold Taylor. Late in August Franklin Steele went to Boston to see Arnold Taylor, who agreed to come again to St. Anthony, bringing along a bodyguard named Buntin. Taylor was ready to do battle in or out of court. Steele hired six lawyers and Taylor hired North, assisted by Atwater's cousin, Lucius A. Babcock, and Morton S. Wilkinson. Godfrey had a "sort of brush" with Buntin and was "whipt as usual." On December 25, an execution was issued on Steele's property for ten thousand dollars. Taylor settled himself by the stove in North's office to read Thomas Carlyle's *Life and Letters of Oliver Cromwell* while North supposedly prepared legal papers. Taylor had the puritan's contempt for Christmas, but North was in holiday mood. Instead of writing the legal drafts, he wrote to Loomis: "I have already done more than $150 worth of business for Taylor, and there is some chance for more. We have commenced two suits against Steele for $10,000 each, and have taken judgment in one of them by their default and have issued execution for $10,000, but I am expecting that they will have some excuse by which to get their default opened." [12]

In his last letter of the year 1851, North reported that his partner, David Secombe, was busy copying petitions to Washington urging that the reserve immediately be taken off lands across the Mississippi opened by the Sioux treaties. Here were new lands to conquer. North was already feeling the urge to build a community somewhat more to his liking than St. Anthony, somewhere in the Indian country. For the time being, however, he would have to content himself with reforming his town and territory by littles.

PROHIBITION YEAR, 1852

Y OUNG St. Anthony, on the eastern bluff of the Mississippi, was cradled at the falls like a huddle of spectators in an amphitheater, with all eyes of the upper and lower town looking westward to the huge empty stage of the trans-Mississippi where the great drama was now to begin between white and red men. But long before the actors entered, the people had watched the sun set over Sioux lands. In winter when ice bridged the river, they could climb onto the stage itself where later scene-shifting would create the city of Minneapolis. The early actors on this far shore were men like North, who had military friends who could get warrants for the military reserve lands. Yet the bands of Sioux riding across this vast stage suggested that in the opening act of the great western drama, they would play leading roles.

For years the Indian policy in Washington had been utter confusion. Northerners in Congress wanted to push the Indians below Thirty-six Thirty, where reservations south of Kansas would form a barrier to slavery's westward expansion. Southerners wanted to leave the Indians north of the line to prevent the increase of free states. The people of St. Anthony were too remote from Washington to concern themselves with the grand strategy of Indian removal: they were chiefly concerned with removing the Indians and military barriers from the land immediately before them. In this they had some support from the southerners in Congress, who were not yet aware how many northerners had migrated to Minnesota, and were persuaded that the new territory would continue to support the South in politics because of strong economic ties with the South formed by Mississippi River trade and traffic. On September 12, 1852, North wrote,

The Military Reserve is off, and the land is to be sold this winter to the highest bidder at Fort Snelling. This will be the finest chance to invest money that has ever happened in the Territory. The talk is that it goes by sealed bids. The treaty has been accepted by the Indians and a large payment is expected this fall. It is said to be $800,000 to the Sioux alone.[1]

Minnesota was about to break out of the triangle between the St. Croix and the Mississippi.

William Marshall was busy surveying the new lands and marking in his field notes tracts that might be profitable to North. Captain John Rollins, North's fellow politician in St. Anthony, believed that twenty thousand carefully chosen acres could make an investor a half-million-dollar fortune in ten years. Intrigued as he was by such a prospect, North was equally interested in making these lands into another Onondaga county or a second New England. To these new lands he hoped to lead friends of reform by families, congregations, and whole communities.

Some in St. Anthony, for political reasons, would be glad to see North move away, and others, staid citizens, were beginning to be offended by North's liberalism in religion. The ministers were inveighing against his Unitarianism and the ladies of their congregations looked askance at Ann and Clarissa North for taking into their home a woman of easy virtue who was down on her luck and helping her get to Galena, where she prospered by devices or vices known to herself. The woman returned in the spring with presents for her benefactors: roots of asparagus, horseradish, chives, wormwood, live-forever, gooseberry, and rose bushes. The spices and flowers luxuriating in the North yard were constant reminders to the proper ladies of the town of the spicy, floral character of the donor.

St. Paul was scarcely sober from the New Year visiting day in 1852 before North and other St. Anthony villagers descended for a temperance convention on January 2. As president of the Sons of Temperance, North accepted a banner made by the ladies, pocketed a copy of the Maine Law laboriously copied by Ann North, and set off for St. Paul with Clarissa to present to the Grand Rally a petition containing four hundred names. A procession of five hundred surrounded the legisla-

65

tive hall. To North's surprise the Protestants of St. Anthony were joined by the Roman Catholic priests and parish faithful from St. Paul under a banner which had cost seventy-five dollars. "To the astonishment of everybody," wrote North, "the French Catholics with the priests have come out actively for the [Maine] law." [2] North delivered two lectures on temperance every week that January. At midmonth a "multitude," according to the *Express*, again met in St. Paul for a liquor law convention at the court house. That St. Paul would soon be thirsty was a consolation to the hungry St. Anthony crowd barred by principle from the rum restaurants. In March the Maine Law passed the legislature with a provision for referendum on April Fool's Day.

On April 5, the bells dryly pealed the result of the referendum. But to pass the law was one thing, to enforce it another. The Mississippi flowed downstream spiked with confiscated booze, but full casks floated upstream with every riverboat. When Sheriff George F. Brott of Ramsey county (an old friend from Onondaga county now "more conceited than ever") attempted to seize a boatload of whiskey at a warehouse at the foot of Jackson street in St. Paul, the rabble resisted execution of the order, and the posse of priests and preachers of united congregations Brott had formed was stoned. A serious riot was averted when Colonel D. A. Robertson mounted a hogshead to quiet the mob. His eloquence was fruitless, his clumsiness more effective. His words carried no weight, but he did: he fell through the top of the hogshead with arms flailing wildly. All the citizens united in uncontrolled laughter, many rolling on the ground. When they recovered their composure, they were too happy to fight and left the issue to the courts.

Judge H. Z. Hayner ruled that the legislature had improperly referred its own responsibility to the people; the referendum had been an April Fool's joke. Minnesota would be wet until the legislature made it dry on its own responsibility. In St. Anthony, social pressure helped dry up the town. Pressure was brought to bear on the Upper Ten, a sewing society formed to raise funds for the Episcopal church. They were brought together more by spirit than the Spirit and only two of them were actually members of the church. "The object seemed to be," wrote Ann, "to get together once a week, to drink, play cards, and dance all night. . . . At several of their meetings, some of the male members were very much intoxicated. Garnes was carried home . . . 'dead drunk' . . . At one of their meetings two of the ladies mounted the table, swinging their handkerchiefs, and talked in a coarse and boisterous manner." North fulminated against such sewing society pastimes in a lecture, to some effect, for one of the members, Lennon, signed the pledge. But he may have been more influenced by the flight of his bride to the bosom of her family with the ultimatum that she would stay unless he sobered up.

Society was never dull. Dr. Murphy inhaled chloroform at the North house during a period of overwork, and had become an "inveterate smoker." He also sold liquor, which ruined his plan for Dr. Loomis to move to St. Anthony as his partner and open a drug store. In February, Murphy took so much chloroform that he was saved only by the arrival of Dr. Ames. Still others were addicted to opiates sold widely on the frontier. Thinly disguised references to private scandals appeared in the press. Elmer Tyler, the tailor who put up money for the *Express*, tired of his venture and Atwater found himself against his will sole proprietor. Atwater published a scandalous article about Miss Schofield and Governor Slade. She was one of the teachers sent out by Slade's National Board of Popular Education along with Electa Backus, Harriet Bishop (whose name is perpetuated in Minneapolis's Lake Harriet), and Miss A. Hosford (Mrs. H. L. Moss). The article was written by Shelton Hollister. The teacher disarmed criticism from that source by making herself "quite ridiculous" according to rumor, pursuing Hollister.

Arnold Taylor spread unkind rumors about North. North said that if he had to stand the curses of the mill company because of his client Taylor, then Taylor would be made to pay, and he thereupon presented Taylor with a bill for a hundred and seventy dollars. Both Taylor and his bodyguard Buntin went about St. Anthony accusing North of profiteering at the expense of the settlers and making capital of their distress, although he stood to profit as much as any by the settlement of property titles. North had a plain talk with them and they were "as shamed as dogs." But not too shamed to circulate an anonymous letter (North believed it was Ard Godfrey's handiwork) abusing North. Taylor wanted North to work "by the job" and not for a flat fee. "He knows as well as I do that he cannot get along without me," wrote North, "and I cannot afford to share the bitterness of the strife without good pay." [3] North brought Taylor and Steele to a temporary settlement. Taylor continued to use North's office as his own, maturing

67

wild plans to send Captain John Rollins to California with five hundred cattle and a company of pioneers. Taylor — a shy, awkward Yankee, wearing ragged pants of black mended with white and a white-bosomed shirt mended with black — was a nuisance. North hoped the litigation would be settled and he would move on. To settle with Taylor, Steele had to deposit twenty-four thousand dollars in a Boston bank within thirty days or forfeit a thousand dollars.[4] Steele went east to raise the money and succeeded; he was back in Minnesota before the opening of navigation.

In January 1852, impatient settlers had moved west of the river to new lands that would be opened by the ratification of the Sioux treaties. When it happened that their pre-emption claims overlapped and did not conform to surveys being made, North handled many of these cases. He was aware of the advantages to such pioneers and went home to Syracuse that summer to get backing for his plans. He spoke not of single homesteads, but of building whole communities comparable to those built by proprietors in the southern tier of Michigan counties, which he also visited. He needed backing because without funds himself, he could scarcely keep ahead of the calls upon him to support good works: he had given another hundred dollars to the university, fifty dollars to the Congregational church, and felt obliged to do something magnificent for the Methodists. He gave money to all the ministers who had attacked him for his Unitarian views. "You may think me too profuse in my contributions," he wrote in his accounting to Dr. Loomis, "but it is next to impossible for me to get along without it. Besides you know the 'liberal soul shall be made fat.'" He rationalized that the school and churches would add value to his property. "People suppose I am well off, and must be considered mean if not liberal."[5]

On March 3, Dr. Murphy arrived at the North home with his chloroform and easily delivered a nine-and-a-quarter-pound daughter. North wanted to name the baby after his first wife, but she was called "Betsy Trotwood" until Grandmother Lewis decided the question: she claimed the right to name the baby. After two weeks' soul-searching, Ann agreed to the name Emma, but not to Emma *Bacon*. She wrote her grandmother to use the name Emma because it would "gratify my dear husband so much."[6] She went on, "We shall call her Emma — nothing more," but the child grew up to write her memoirs as Emma *Bacon* North Messer.

Clarissa North, like many a maiden lady, was shaken by the prospect of a child in the home. Having taught French at Albion College, she now thought of tutoring in New Orleans, weighing the evils of domestic slavery in the South against her own domestic slavery to a new baby, and she got as far as St. Paul before she decided she could not leave her brother. Later that summer the Norths took the "remarkable" child to De Witt to show off its new tooth. While they were gone, Atwater persuaded Steele, from whom North rented an office on Third street, to rent it to him. Later a plain talk between North and Steele so shook the latter that he offered North the use of his counting house.

Steele was either a noble character or very practical. St. Anthony was being depleted of lawyers: Whitall had gone south "where he could keep slaves"; E. L. Hall had returned east; Warren Bristol crossed the river to Minneapolis, now taking shape on the west bank; and Atwater soon would do the same. Steele again needed North. North was a good lawyer: he beat Atwater in almost every case in which they opposed each other as attorneys (contrary to Atwater's recollection in his history of Minneapolis). Steele hired North to help Atwater in the inevitable legal complications of all the companies he controlled. Perhaps one reason for the reconciliation was the difficulty North was having in collecting from Taylor. In November, North was awarded a judgment against Arnold Taylor for five hundred and fifty dollars.

He was again friendly with Steele.

A HIGHWAY FOR OUR GOD, 1853-54

T HE year 1853 began like 1852 with excitement over temperance. Because the referendum on the Maine Law had been declared unconstitutional, pressure was now being brought on the legislature to enact a temperance law. North's abolitionist friend Messer arrived to share the temperance and reform burden. He went about town with North, who carried the new baby to display the wonderful tooth, with no idea that the baby would one day be his daughter, too. Levi Nutting, a minister from Amherst, Massachusetts, seeking a site where his congregation of a hundred and twenty families could set up a colony, joined the company living at the North home.

Messer taught singing in St. Anthony, an occupation that left him time to paint a banner for the new descent on St. Paul which would not be shamed by the seventy-five-dollar banner of the Roman Catholics. It read "ST. ANTHONY TEMPERANCE SOCIETY — TRY AGAIN" and "DRINK FROM THE FOUNTAIN." A band and glee club led the parade to St. Paul in a four-horse sleigh, followed by nine two-horse carryalls and six one-horse cutters. Charles G. Ames, one day to become a famous Boston preacher, presided over the meeting and North presented resolutions calling upon the people of St. Anthony to forget partisan politics and vote for the candidates pledged to temperance.

The fall elections were a victory: all the precinct officers were temperance men. The wets were so disgruntled that they made threats upon the life of R. S. Rust, editor of the *Democrat*, because of his editorials against them. He haled the men into court, but the charges were dismissed by a "corrupt judge." Rum-sellers celebrated the decision with an oyster supper at the St. Charles hotel. Rust had been North's fellow student at Wesleyan and his companion in abolition lectures in Connecticut. By February, the temperance people had to admit defeat even with Rust's *Democrat* supporting the movement. The legislature killed the Maine Law and the "soakers" attacked North with "hints and flings" in the *Express*. A St. Paul paper named North in a "very low and scurrilous article." The attack was joined by the Universalist preacher. It was bad enough to be a Unitarian and lead astray the Baptist preacher, Charles G. Ames, to that belief, but for the local ministers the last straw was North's taking his family to mass for the dedication of the new bell in the Roman Catholic church.

Some blamed Steele, others blamed Taylor for the insecurity of land titles, but because North was from time to time the lawyer of both, it was easy for everyone to blame him. The people of St. Anthony did not know whom to trust. Taylor's interest in the St. Anthony property was attached and sold on execution so rapidly that the Norths feared he would lose everything if he did not return at once to Minnesota. Though William Marshall purchased some of the property at the sheriff's sale, North hesitated to take advantage of his former client's distress, particularly when Steele had a lien on the property. Prodded by Loomis, he finally bought Taylor's interest in twenty-eight lots. Seven lots, bought by Marshall for North, were directly opposite the university. The lots cost North from two to seven dollars apiece; if Taylor did not redeem the lots in a specified time, they would be a "grand haul." North gave Loomis a share in the lots for the four hundred dollars he owed him. He declared he would risk no more, but he was at the sheriff's sale again on March 3, 17, and 25, and April 1. By March 15, he had exchanged some of the lots at a premium and bought more. He now had sheriff's deed to Block 13, behind the Atwater property, which he fenced for pigs. The Atwaters soon moved to Minneapolis.

By acquiring Taylor's real or supposed interest in this property, North and the purchasers replaced Taylor as litigants with Steele, who claimed that he, and not Taylor, was the rightful owner. North turned the property over to Loomis in order that he might go to court as a "disinterested person" representing the purchasers. If he retained any property, the purchasers would hold that he should fight the case in his own interest without fees from them. The case was settled in distant Washington, where Steele still had influence, by the appointment of new territorial judges, including the chief justice, Welch, a friend of the Sibley-Steele fur company. Steele moved that the purchasers be turned out of court.[1] North had a "long and plain talk" with Steele, to no effect, for Steele talked to the purchasers as if they were a pack of fools who had been gulled by North.[2] The purchasers were represented by North and the former chief justice, Hayner. At this point, Taylor and Steele lined up on the same side. With Steele's consent, Taylor got back the $24,000 impounded by the old court and Taylor in turn consented to a decree in Steele's favor. North appealed the case to the territorial supreme court and the appeal bond was signed by twenty principal citizens of St. Anthony. Steele threatened to keep the case going five years, and North admitted that Steele could do so. Steele was a reasonable man, however, and knew that a court victory over the citizens of St. Anthony might harm him in the long run. Steele began to buy up the property townspeople had purchased at the sheriff's sale, paying the purchase price and all expenses. Every person who sold his interest to Steele weakened the position of the rest. North advised Loomis and the others to come to terms with Steele. He did not want to fight their cases and antagonize Steele, for Steele was talking bridges, roads, and railroads — all things North wanted to share in.

Early in November 1853, several men representing the Illinois Central and the Chicago and Dubuque railroads called on North. They wanted his cooperation, as first citizen, in establishing a line of riverboats to connect their railroads with St. Paul. North was not much interested; he was already committed to a project for building a railroad up the west bank of the Mississippi,[3] which he thought might cost $25,000 a mile over the course of two hundred and fifty miles. He predicted that Loomis would come all the way to Minnesota "on cars" within five years. North's problem was getting into a million-dollar business without money. "I do not know that I can make anything by railroads, and yet it is an open field; perhaps there may be a chance for me even without capital to make something. My articles [on the prospect of railroads in Minnesota] are hastily written and imperfect, but you can learn from them what I think the best route . . . My letters are signed M."[4]

North probably signed his letters M because of the campaign against him in the press at that time. The initial was Marshall's, but the letters were North's, matured during their long conversations in the law office. "Mr. Marshall and myself think that if we are on hand at the beginning and manage well we can do something." [5]

Right then, Marshall had other things on his mind than writing for the press. He would soon be off to New York to raise money for the opening of his new bank in St. Paul and to get married. He had managed to find a banking partner and a wife in the same family in Onondaga county, Nathaniel P. Langford and Abby Langford. Ann North agreed with Mrs. Marshall that William was too good to marry and that no girl was good enough for him. Both felt possessive toward him. Marshall sent Ann a ballad, "Child of the Angel Wing," and notified Abby Langford of her progress in his affections by sending her the *Annals of the Historical Society of Minnesota.*

Meantime, David Secombe, North's partner, had also become infatuated with Abby Langford on one of her visits to Minnesota. So sure were they all that Abby would not succeed with Marshall that Aunt Eliza Dean Loomis again sent home for Cornelia whom she repeatedly paraded before Marshall. When Abby could not decide between Secombe and Marshall, she returned to Syracuse, followed by Marshall. He sent Ann Mrs. E. Oakes Smith's *Shadow Land* with a brief note saying that he was about to "form new relations." Apparently Secombe had ruined his chances with Abby when he appeared as counsel in an assault case and declared that it was no crime for a man to beat his wife. Secombe confronted Marshall on his return to St. Anthony to verify Abby's decision and cried like a baby at the news. North said he would have given forty great apples to have witnessed the scene. This left two broken hearts in St. Anthony, Cornelia's and Secombe's, which they proceeded to mend, together, while Marshall entered upon high finance and high felicity at the same time.

Ann North would have liked to keep her admirer of four years' standing in a state of suspended bachelorhood; his flatteries had done much to liven her dull routine. She was now the mother of another child, George, and Clarissa North had fled south temporarily, leaving the house quiet and Ann lonely. Marshall would be missed — but only as a friend of the family. Certainly Ann's whole affection was centered upon "my good husband." He filled her life. "You can hardly know how good he is," she wrote her parents, "and some things may look to you like

extravagances which, if you could look as we do, might not seem so." [6]
One day in November when Ann had got up at three to start her wash-
ing and was not done until six thirty; when she had the care of two
children, a sick husband, and had prepared the usual meals for his
temperance, religious, railroading, university, and political friends; she
nevertheless closed her day writing,

I believe I hardly know how to appreciate what a treasure I have in
my husband . . . Such efficient help he renders and with such cheer-
fulness . . . I believe if I do now improve at all, I shall owe it in a good
measure to his constant good example. No one can know the real beauty
of his character till they have *lived* with him and see him under all
circumstances.[7]

Perhaps the proud grandparents of Emma and George were convinced. North had done well in Minnesota for himself and for Dr.
George S. Loomis, who was now the owner of a considerable estate in
St. Anthony lands. Taking his property at its lowest estimated value,
North said that he believed he was now worth not less than five thousand dollars. "Owing to your liberality to me," he wrote Loomis, "I have
succeeded in accumulating more property than I had dared to hope for
when I came to the Territory." [8]

Men were forcing money upon North for investment at the going
rate of five per cent a month. Dr. Thomas S. Williamson, missionary to
the Indians, gave him three hundred dollars. Israel Smith of Syracuse
followed North home to force money upon him; if North would not
start a bank, he threatened to turn the money over to Atwater and
Steele. North had a Methodist conscience about usury, especially when
there was a great work at hand which better conformed with his ideals.

In the Minnesota of 1854 railroading was a faith curiously confused
with the Christian. Edward D. Neill preached a sermon on railroads
and religion, claiming that railroads were antidotes to bigotry, idleness,
and profligacy. Railroads would promote "pure and undefiled religion"
by encouraging immigration from the East to outweigh the heathens,
roughs, and nominal Roman Catholics in Minnesota. Bigotry — at least
the kind God and Neill objected to — would end when steam carriages
could whisk the ministers of the Gospel to distant parts. Neill took his
text from Isaiah 40:3 — *Make straight in the desert a highway for our
God.*

In essence, this was the carpetbagger's faith, a combination of the ideal and the practical, advocating the moral improvement of a country by immigration of the right sort of people in such a flood as to inundate the wrong sort. The faith appealed to North, and during the next five years he would do his best to exalt every valley, make every hill low, the crooked places straight, the rough places plain — but he could not get the iron rails on the highway before all hell broke loose. Isaiah gave no instructions about strap iron, bridges, and locomotives. On January 1, 1854, North wrote,

We are looking for an appropriation of lands from Congress to build a railroad to Dubuque and another to Lake Superior, which will bring us within the range of the circle of travel from Lake Superior to the Valley of the Mississippi, or to speak in the more classic language of Dr. Ames, we shall then be within the range of the "periphery" which "now lies like a faint line on the sea of the mind!" [9]

When the legislature met, the only important business was the incorporation of the Minnesota and North-western Railroad. The bill, introduced by the retiring editor of the *Pioneer*, was not passed during the session, which closed by law at midnight on the ninetieth day of the session; it was passed instead after midnight and all were surprised when the new governor, W. A. Gorman, signed it. Gorman had been a congressman from the sixth district of Indiana before he was appointed governor of Minnesota Territory by Pierce, and he should have known what a furor the railroad's incorporation would cause in Washington. Nor had he any reason to suppose that delegate Henry M. Rice would defend his action in Congress, except that all differences of political opinion in Minnesota were forgotten as the rough places were made plain, even though all crooked were not made straight. The Moccasin Democrats — the party in power — had split: Henry H. Sibley was aligned with Gorman, and Rice was supported by Ramsey and by Daniel A. Robertson of the *Democrat*. For more than a year, until the organization of the Republican party in Minnesota, North was a Rice supporter. The railroad articles published under *M* had brought North to Rice's attention. Although North had said at the time of Rice's election in the fall that he had won by a $1,500 majority, he was completely won over to the delegate three months later. The Rices called socially on the Norths when in Minnesota and sent them packets of flower seeds and publications from Washington. This was one of the strangest associations of men who should have been political enemies and were instead brought together by common interests in Minnesota lands and railroads.

In early February two railroads were formed and Rice was hard at work in Congress getting land grants for them. "All the leading influences in the Territory and all the *hostile elements*, are harmoniously combined for this purpose," wrote North.[10] From Washington Rice wrote that as soon as the land-grant bill passed Congress, he would return to Minnesota and help North promote the railroads. "Expectation is on tiptoe," reported North, "I get a letter from Mr. Rice every mail and he keeps me thoroughly informed . . . This is all a confidential matter here, and is not fully understood except by the initiated. The railroad bill was introduced in the United States Senate by Mr. Shields on the 17th of January." General James Shields was among the "initiated." The senator from Illinois would soon come to Minnesota, also to help promote railroads, and to challenge North, as he had Lincoln, to a duel.

The Minnesota territorial legislature, in anticipation of the Congressional land grant, passed a law vesting the lands in railroad companies. The Minnesota bill was written by "the great financier Robert J. Walker." Finally, North confessed, "I have ventured to take $5,000 stock in each company. Of one company (from St. Paul to the Southern boundary of the Territory) I am a director and Treasurer."

As originally written, the Congressional land grant specified that lands could be used for railroad companies "constituted or organized." Those not among the "initiated" in Congress, or who had been left out of the deals, surreptitiously changed the word "or" to "and." On August 3, 1854, Rice wrote from Washington, "This morning the select committee reported that the word 'and' between the words 'constituted' and 'organized' had been substituted for the word 'or,' but exonerated General Stevens [Michigan member of the Committee on Public Lands] and the clerk of the House [Forney] — and recommended that the word 'or' be reinstated."[11] The conjunction made all the difference in the world. The Minnesota companies were constituted, but not organized. Substitution of the word "and" meant that they had to be both. The surreptitious change in the bill had been part of southern tactics to defeat the land-grant bill; the investigation into who had changed the wording gave the opponents time to rally support, and then, under the leadership of Letcher of Virginia, the House repealed the Minnesota land grants completely. If railroading in Minnesota had a holy end in view, it had an unholy beginning. In the House a Congressman had drawn his gun on a colleague from Tennessee during the debate.[12]

While the land grant was still in doubt, and perhaps to gain popular support for the bill, numerous celebrities and prospective investors made an excursion to Minnesota in five steamers superintended by Farnam of the Chicago and Rock Island, who had some hope of connecting his line with the railroads in Minnesota. The excursion celebrated the Rock Island's reaching the Mississippi.[13] In Lake Pepin, the lagoon of the Mississippi, the five boats were tied abreast to form one great convention hall. Among the famous visitors were former President Fillmore; the historian George Bancroft; Professors Silliman, Gibbs, and Larned of Yale and Parker of Harvard; Edward Robinson; Charles Sedgwick; and many more. After cursory inspection of the capital, they rushed to see the Falls of St. Anthony and quite emptied the stables of St. Paul. They returned to dance in the Senate chamber and visit Fort Snelling, but a great many who were friends of North stayed in St. Anthony. General Lawrence and his two daughters spent a week. While North "improved the occasion" by talking investments, Ann took the ladies to see the wild flowers. She wrote:

The prairies are now covered with wild flowers. There seems to be a color of flowers peculiar to each month. Our first Spring flowers are light blue, which grows deeper as the season advances, and passing through several changes, are displayed the most gorgeous tints, gold, orange, and red, by late Summer. The prevailing colors are now a deep rich blue, a light crimson and blue, although there are flowers of other colors. Wild roses are in bloom, too.[14]

No excursion however large could bring enough capitalists to Minnesota to suit North. He wrote Gerrit Smith asking him to take an interest in the territory; what he really wanted was Smith's vote on the railroad land grants in Congress. He wrote in the reformer's language that Smith could understand, "There is a great deal to be done here in the laying the foundations of our institutions aright . . . in correcting evils of longstanding." [15] Minnesota Territory was then the asylum for the most bigoted and servile politicians, he said — meaning Governor Gorman and Chief Justice W. H. Welch who had been sent out by Pierce. He asked if Smith had become acquainted with his personal friend, Rice. Rice did not sympathize with all Gerrit Smith's views or with all

North's, but North thought Smith would find him a gentleman and a friend of temperance. North regretted that he had less time himself for "benevolent effort" than he had had in New York.

North did not mention that his health had failed as it had in New York. During one temperance convention he had to sit silent, too weak to speak — a frightful punishment for a man with a golden voice. Dr. Murphy prescribed wine, and a little later beer, and must have been amused when North followed his directions religiously. Eventually it dawned upon North that these were strange remedies for piles. Unable to walk or ride, he attended to law business from his sofa. His improvement was marked when Francis Morrison began to plan a bridge over the Mississippi between St. Anthony and Minneapolis. Morrison was president of the company, North one of the investors, and Steele was rapidly taking control. A ferry at the same point had cleared two thousand dollars the past summer, and the toll bridge company capitalized at twenty-five thousand seemed sure to make money. North subscribed for five hundred dollars' worth of stock and had another eight hundred dollars' worth to sell to friends. Steele tried to get the stock out of North's hands "for Sibley" (as he said). He predicted that the stock would rise two hundred per cent in two years.

The North family was using stationery with a picture of the completed bridge long before it was ready for traffic. The actual construction of the suspension bridge was begun in May 1854 by T. M. Griffith, just back from surveying in Panama, who was paid seven dollars a day for his services. No sooner was the bridge completed than a tornado threw the planking onto the ice. In December the new Territorial road was completed from St. Paul to St. Anthony, past the North property to the end of the bridge.

North now assumed a neutral attitude toward everything; he said he was going to sleep until after the elections. Ann tried to take up his "benevolent efforts," even toying with the idea of becoming associate editor of a new temperance newspaper edited by Charles Gordon Ames. But North remained impartial and neutral. He gave fifty dollars to the *North Western Democrat*, but when it was sold and moved to Minneapolis, he provided another fifty dollars for the *Republican*. In view of such benefactions, it is difficult to understand why he was puzzled about where all his money went. That summer he was worth eight thousand dollars, and in a year or so he expected to be worth ten thousand. He took pride in being able to borrow a thousand or two on his signature alone.

As the year closed, the Norths gathered friends around them. The future botanist of California seas who would follow North west, Dr. Charles Lewis Anderson, returned to St. Anthony with his wife. The newly wed Leavitts from Toledo rented the front chamber. William and Abby Marshall came to celebrate Thanksgiving on the New York date, not on the date proclaimed by Pierce's pliant tool, Governor Gorman. Ann's letters were full of what she called "emptyings." North was kicked by his cow, everybody had boils as usual, the children were saying or doing remarkable things. The spiritualists held a meeting at the North home and the medium preached a sermon calculated to convert North to a belief in the possibility of communication with the spirits. Everyone was prosperous and improvements in the upper town would soon make North's lots worth a thousand dollars each. North was offered a waterpower claim extending seventy-two rods along the west bank of the river below the falls, together with an undivided half of twenty-eight acres adjacent to the claim, on condition that he build a grist mill with a run of two stones in eight months. It was not lack of business sense or vision that made North turn down this offer which would have made him a multimillionaire. When the offer was made, Dr. George Loomis had just given him one of his periodic lectures on avoiding visionary schemes.

"You may think me visionary," wrote North, "and yet I need rapping over the nose a little . . . as you have a right to do." [16]

Like the spirit rappings, Dr. Loomis's rapping this time should have gone unheeded.

I have the pleasure of writing you on my fortieth birthday," January 4, 1855.

That was how North began his first letter of the new year in which he would found two cities and the Republican party in Minnesota. The honor of establishing the national Republican party is claimed by Michigan, New York, Wisconsin, and Iowa, and in all four places some of the founders were friends of John Wesley North. The party itself dates from 1854, but North did not organize his temperance and abolitionist friends in the Minnesota Territory until the end of March 1855. As first organized, the Republican party was the political expression of a religious belief in a whole series of reforms. John Wesley has been credited with founding not only Methodism but the British Labour party, and it is no less true that the Republican party was founded upon evangelical humanism. The early Republican platforms and resolutions might be footnotes to the works of Wesley in such matters as abolition, temperance, and education. Republicans were not conscious of their identity as part of the evangelical movement springing ultimately from the Church of England because the evangelical reforms had already become secularized by such agencies as McGuffey's readers, tracts, pamphlets, and the press; except for home and foreign missions and schools and colleges, evangelicalism had been secularized into humanitarian reforms in the United States, where less than a quarter of the people were members of any church. The evangelical reforms in Great Britain, particularly the abolition of slavery in the Empire in

1833, had produced demands for abolition in the North and had steeled the South to declare slavery a positive and permanent good.

The South had cut itself off from the humanitarian spirit. There, planters had long controlled the local churches: though the colonial commissaries of the Church of England represented the Bishop of London, in reality priests could be hired or fired by the parish, paid or cheated of their tobacco incomes. In congregational kinds of church, the planters had even more direct control over the clergymen. None was called if he had expressed any preference for reform, none remained if tainted with abolition. Association between preachers North and South had to be prevented at all cost as soon as the evangelical reforms became widespread. The Presbyterians split. Among the Methodists, the slaveholders tried first to capture the conferences, and when this was not possible, the Methodist Episcopal Church, South, seceded. Publications of evangelical reformers were barred from southern mails; pulpits, press, and platforms were closed to northern men. Except in the border states, there was no evangelical reform base upon which to build a Republican party committed to humanitarian reform. Republicanism was a northern phenomenon. What a historian says of J. W. North's meetings in Minnesota could be said for all: "The meeting at St. Anthony and the convention at St. Paul [were] governed by a set of men the majority of whom were very radical and might be called purists; they attempted to build a political party upon the lines of a church organization." [1]

All Republican meetings had this religious fervor, sometimes called fanaticism, through the nomination and campaign of Frémont for the presidency in 1856. Reform cannot win without substance, and the Republicans were not men of wealth; but when the election of 1856 demonstrated that a great number of people, committed severally to particular reforms, could combine in one party to seek common goals, the politicians became interested and provided the practical framework on which a party could be built. By 1860, the idealists were joined not only by the practical politicians, but by their employers, the men of wealth looking for railroads, contracts, tariff, cheap labor from immigration, Indian trade, and so on. These two sections of the Republican party were not mutually exclusive. Certainly in Minnesota the men who supported the Republican party as idealists in the 1850's were foremost in making economic demands in the 1860's.

In March 1855, nine months after the Republican party was organized under the oaks at Jackson, Michigan, North and his friends organized the Republican party in Minnesota. The call for a meeting, prepared in North's office, was signed by North, Marshall, Ramsey and others. Two hundred met in the Congregational church at St. Anthony in this first Republican meeting, called to order by John Wesley North; the invocation was given by Charles G. Ames whom North had persuaded to leave the Free Will Baptists and become a Unitarian. North's friend Messer sang the "Marseillaise," and William Marshall took the chair to let North present from the floor the resolutions he had prepared.

The North resolutions adopted by this first Republican organization on March 29 called for the abolition of slavery in the District of Columbia, in all territories and new states. One resolution called for repeal of the Fugitive Slave law, another demanded complete prohibition of alcohol. Still others demanded free land for settlers and reduction of postal rates. North closed the resolutions with a battle cry: "Man and Morals first; interest of property, afterwards."

Charles G. Ames presented the consensus of the meeting in a *Circular Address of the Territorial Republican Convention to the People of Minnesota*, published April 11, 1855 — the first great document in the history of the Republican party. Both North and Ann assisted in its preparation. In fact, the whole Republican campaign in March and April 1855 centered in the North home, where the front room became Minnesota's first Republican headquarters.

North helped plan a festival to raise a hundred dollars for the convention expenses and Republicans from a distance stayed with the Norths during the meetings on March 29 and 30. Ann wrote that it seemed like old times being at an anti-slavery meeting, but she could attend but one session, for there were guests to feed — President William Marshall and Abby, secretary H. P. Pratt, vice presidents Eli Pettijohn, A. P. Lane, and members Moffet, Sewell, Whitney, Draper, Babbit, and Jenkins.

The chief work of the St. Anthony convention was to call a Territorial Republican Convention in St. Paul July 25. This convention met with ninety-four delegates under the chairmanship of a former St. Anthony lawyer, Warren Bristol. William R. Marshall was nominated as Congressional delegate. The Democratic ticket was split between Rice

and David Olmsted, and if the Republicans had been better organized
at the polling places against fraudulent Moccasin Democrat votes, it is
possible that Marshall would have won. The returns gave Rice 3,705,
Marshall 2,493, and Olmsted 1,746 votes. Democratic strength was in
St. Paul and on the frontier, where precincts were not policed and
where administration leaders and the local Democrats could freely vote
lumberjacks, half-breeds, soldiers, and fur-trade employees. North's
opposition to Rice cooled their friendship, but while it lasted, it had
been profitable to North.

Rice had pressed through Congress a bill to secure the rights of
claimants on Sioux lands, and he promised to telegraph North how the
reserve lands would be sold so that North could have as early information as anyone.[2] It would have been to North's advantage to support
Rice in the subsequent election, but when public interest and private
gain conflicted, North followed his ideals. By January 1855, he was
ready, at forty, to start a new life on the Sioux lands. Traveling over
the country with Marshall, North waxed almost poetic about the Cannon River valley.

"The whole valley of this River is beautiful and very fertile. . . .
The part I visited is on the route to Iowa, and new villages are springing up all along the route. It is forty or fifty miles South of [St. Anthony]
and the seasons are said to be two weeks earlier. The crab-apple and
wild plum grow there in abundance and furnish fruit to the settlers." [3]
In the Cannon valley Dr. Loomis might realize his ideal of owning a
farm of a thousand acres. Soon, said North, flourishing towns and cities
would mark the line between St. Anthony and Dubuque, Iowa, and
one day there would be a railroad connecting them all. It would take
months to get patent for the land, but North began to develop the area
along with the Faribault Townsite Company lands. General James
Shields, former senator from Illinois, took an interest in Faribault and
made it his home. On his next trip to the Cannon valley, North took
along Thomas Hale Williams, a surveyor, who described the journey in
his minuscule handwriting.[4]

Faribault was an old Indian village selected a couple of years before
by the Reverend Levi Nutting as the place for his Methodist congregation from Massachusetts to settle. "It would not be the most remarkable thing," declared Williams, obviously under North's inspiration,
"if in five years a railroad should go thro' there from Dubuque to St.

Paul." Along the hundred-mile course of the Cannon, he saw black walnut logs three and a half feet in diameter.

The party consisted of ten persons in two sleds, including North, his brother-in-law Finch, a millwright named Moffat, and the Nutting brothers. Each sled, drawn by two horses, had a long box. Williams and Finch crossed the Mississippi on the ice to pick up North and Moffat at Mendota. Winter sleighing was slow and cold, and by nightfall they had only reached the Laird house on the Vermilion. The Lairds were the once-prosperous family from Illinois (p. 37). Now four adults and four children lived in a six-by-eight-foot cabin, and it seemed impossible that ten more people could be accommodated, but there was no other habitation within fifteen miles and the party could not go on. The mother of the family smoked her pipe in silence while a daughter baked hoecake and the father talked of giving up. Depressed, the whole family would have preferred going to Stillwater to winter with friends. The idea of the Lairds moving away was preposterous. "Mr. North said that would not do, they must not give up now." The family protested that they had no choice — that their horses were nearly starved and so weak that they could draw only small loads of firewood. They might soon be out of fuel; they were already out of provisions. The long recital of the Lairds' problems undoubtedly made North conscious of the barrels of apples and hundredweights of butter in his own cellar. The guests agreed to leave a big bag of oats for the horses and to send provisions for the family. "Mr. North offered to lend Mr. Laird enough money to support them until warm weather. . . . They began to brighten up. Mrs. Laird said we had done her five dollars' worth of good already." At least she would have tobacco for her pipe.

Supper consisted of flour hoecake, fish, fried pork, tea and molasses; such was the animation that they enjoyed themselves as much as if they had been stopping at the Tremont. About ten, preparations were made for sleep — eighteen people in the six-by-eight-foot room. The chairs and the box used as a table were moved outdoors, and Mrs. Laird and her three daughters lay on the floor between the stove and the door while the men slept between the stove and the wall. There was no need for ventilation, for the wind blew freely through chinks in the logs. At five in the morning, North kindled the fire and they ate. "Mr. North gave them five dollars and promised to bring them more oats on our return," wrote Williams. Then in a snowstorm that covered the track through the wilderness, the party set out again into the Minnesota winter. "I had a pair of overshoes lined with fur, two pairs of mittens, a comforter and my shawl. I sat down on an old bed quilt by the side Mr. North, which was pulled about us, and covered our feet with a horse-blanket. . . . We looked very much like . . . the French returning from Moscow."

They reached Alexander's — "Northfield," as it was soon to be — about noon and found a large log house, neat, orderly, and quite a contrast to the Laird cabin. There they dined on venison, potatoes, excellent bread, doughnuts, pumpkin pie, butter, cheese, and crackers. Williams went no farther, but North and Finch set off again with the millwright Moffat to find a millsite on the Cannon River. They returned "having engaged a man to erect a log house for the workmen on the mill, and he having already commenced chopping. It is a word and a blow here." Such was the beginning of Northfield, but in North's mind's eye it was already there — mills and town, colleges and library, churches and bank. The next day the party went on to Faribault. The weather was bright and pleasant as they moved along the narrow road overhung by great trees of a forest that stretched nobody knew how far. North said it reminded him of the Vale of Tempe he had read about in college. In the deep forest there were Indian wigwams, and a squaw with two papooses stood by the road to watch the visitors pass. Williams hoped that the Indians would not pitch their camps on the Cannon for long; what he could not guess was that they would massacre several hundred Minnesotans before they left.

There was a ball in Faribault on January 23, 1855, but North and his party had no time for frivolity. Williams and North set off to find a claim for an Englishman named Crump who entertained them with his reminiscences of seeing Czar Nicholas review Wellington's troops. On returning to Faribault, they went to the Morris house to get a map of the town; North had purchased Morris's interest in Faribault. The map was locked in a trunk and the son of the house was at the ball with the key. The proprietors assembled for a meeting. "So after supper," said Williams, "the City Council had another session." They agreed upon exchange of property; North was given power of attorney to manage affairs. "I could not wish for anything better," said Williams, "Mr. North offered me the eighth part [of Morris's property] that Mr. Porter Nutting was to have at the same price, seven-hundred dollars. . . . So

there is a possibility of my owning a part of a city instead of one lot."
Williams was at a loss to understand why he had been so favored by
North. The Quaker Welles told Williams, "Friend North likes thee,"
but perhaps it never occurred to him that North needed someone near
him he could talk with about such things as the Vale of Tempe. North
wanted only the right sort of people: Williams and the Nuttings — Tru-
man, Porter, and Levi.

Back at the millsite on the Cannon where Northfield was taking
shape,

Mr. North requested that Mr. Alexander call a meeting of the neighbors to see how much work they could do on the mill. . . . Mr. Moffat
sat down at the table, and in about half an hour had a bill of the timber
drawn out. Then each was requested to state what he could do or would
do, and in a short time a plan of operations was agreed on for building
the saw mill, a grist mill, and a bridge — the two mills are to be on
opposite sides of the stream.

Cyrenius Finch expected to start the next day with four men to score
and hew the logs. Williams added with obvious surprise, "I think I get
a pretty good idea of the New England settlers an hundred and fifty
years' ago. . . . Men and boys work as if they were alive."

With all its business accomplished on Cannon River, the North party
returned to St. Anthony. "It was delightful to get into Mr. North's
warm dining room with a mahogany table, clean cloth, and an astral
lamp, and everything comfortable and convenient, with plenty of
room." It was not until after North returned tired and cold that Ann
North broke the news to Dr. Loomis that North talked of moving to
the Cannon, though Loomis may have suspected as much when North
described the river's beauties and sold his lawbooks. Loomis would
come to recognize this signal, for North sold several sets of lawbooks
before he died. Nothing was yet said about the extent of North's com-
mitments, nothing about the sawmill or gristmill. How could North
explain the force that drove him from the comforts of his home to
pioneering in a hard country; how could he explain his longing for
an ideal community without street fights and staggering spendthrifts,
without litigation, where every man could enjoy in time a mahogany
table and an astral lamp? All North need do to get rich was stay at
home in ease and comfort and watch his twenty-thousand-dollar property appreciate to twenty millions. He might have done so.

That spring John Sargent Pillsbury arrived in St. Anthony. For a year he had looked into opportunities in the West and now in 1855 he opened a store; soon he would be one of the original proprietors of C. A. Pillsbury and Company. North was writing off St. Anthony too soon: it was not that he could not foresee the tremendous increase in land values about to take place, for he pointed these possibilities out to Dr. Loomis in his letters. He was confident of St. Anthony's future — but on the Cannon River he and not Franklin Steele would be the squire.

To understand a man of vision, one must see the vision. Today we can stand in the shadow of "A" Mill at the falls of the Mississippi, walk along the banks of an island now ill-kept and divested of its sugar maples, and look out upon the great and thriving city that has so befouled its cradle. We can assess the present value of North's property on both sides of the falls. That is not enough. We must see the other vision realized at the falls of the Cannon: trees still shade the Cannon at Northfield and arch over its streets, the great woods have given way to rich farms and prosperous houses, and by the sound of their bells we can count the churches and two great colleges. Minneapolis was the dream of Steele and Pillsbury, but Northfield came from the heart and mind of J. W. North. Settlers followed North to the Cannon — mostly Republicans committed to temperance, abolition, and education. "Brother" Walter Bacon came from Connecticut, Sarah North brought her savings from New Orleans. Miss Mary L. Knight, who resigned from the University Academy to sew and make her home with the North family, entered a claim; when it was jumped Clarissa North gave her half of hers.

The Cannon River valley filled up fast. North went to Syracuse for money and to Rock Island for machinery for his mills. With lumber selling at twenty dollars a thousand, North was in a hurry to complete his sawmill. George Loomis invested in the mill, but the cost ran a thousand dollars beyond North's estimate. North wrote Dr. Loomis that young George thought North should have a greater share of the mill returns and that he was willing to pay the difference out of his profits; then North carefully crossed this out of his letter — but not so carefully that it cannot be read a century later. Keeping the books, young George had to bother with only one side of the ledger. Every day's delay meant great loss. Fifteen thousand bushels of grain waited to be ground, and North could not even get one run of stones, without a bolt, in operation by January 1856. Double shifts and all the expedients to rush the mill to completion cost money. North considered hiring a thousand dollars for ninety days at fifteen or twenty per cent interest. The grist mill was not completed on schedule, but the millwrights had both mills ready to receive the spring flood and all destruction. Dr. Loomis called his son home to get a firsthand report and urged him to curb North's runaway speculations. In the expectation that George would return with more money, North went to Chicago to see about buying more machinery. George returned with the money and with grandmother Lewis to care for the new baby, John Greenleaf North. On his return, George helped surveyor Iddings plat the town, and North pushed the sawmill to completion early in December 1855.

North had not planned to bring his family to the new town until spring, but he spent so much of his time on the Cannon that Ann insisted on moving earlier. After renting his house on Third avenue to the Chutes and his farm to Seth Fielding, North could by January 6, 1856, address his first letter of the year from Northfield. "We are here comfortably settled in our new home, which you may have heard before this bears the euphonious cognomen of Northfield." A meeting of the new settlers had insisted upon honoring its founder.

KEEPING up her correspondence was impossible for Ann North during the week after arriving at the new home, because her ink froze. Her new dwelling was a house eighteen by thirty feet with a ten-by-thirty lean-to. The house fronted west, with a fine view of the mill, the river, and the woods on its opposite bank. The walls were made of muslin tacked on the studs; roaring fires were needed to keep warm.

It had taken a day and a half to come through from St. Anthony with a four-horse team drawing a sleigh covered like a prairie schooner with a feather bed and comfortables in the sleigh box for the children and a rocking chair for Ann North and the new baby.

The discomforts of the new home did not discourage visitors. Three stoves plus a dumb stove (a drum around the pipe in the upper chamber) kept them warm. North held a public meeting to which everyone interested in building a schoolhouse that might also be used for religious services was invited. Twenty men came, subscribing nearly three hundred dollars. The next morning a building committee called on the Norths to discuss selecting lots and stayed for dinner: the nine men filled the first table, emptying it of the turkey; the women and children at the second table had to make do with beefsteak — one of the hardships of the frontier. Elder Cressy preached in the North home to twenty people, and the next evening a Methodist quarterly meeting convened and lingered until the late hour of ten, with Ann playing and singing for the meeting. Life took on an interest that it had not had since the winter on the island as new friends and business associates were drawn into their circle.

From the first, the sawmill was a paying proposition, though all the income from the mill had to be spent upon improvements after the drum of the circular saw, ready for its first trial in mid-February, flew to pieces. In two weeks North would have to meet a two-thousand-dollar payment on mill machinery and all the earnings of the sawmill would fall short of paying for the gristmill, the frame of which was up and half enclosed, and the cogs dressed. In due time the gristmill would make money, but right then North urgently needed five hundred dollars to complete it. North was again experiencing the shortness of a shoestring.

Northfield prospered. In the spring of 1856 there had been built a forty-foot store as well as shops for two wheelwrights, a cabinetmaker, joiner, and a blacksmith. And an icehouse was built by J. W. North, according to his incontrovertible logic: in summer Northfield would need ice, the time to cut ice was winter, to keep ice one must have an icehouse, in an icehouse the packing was sawdust, sawdust was the waste product of the sawmill. Nothing could have been clearer than that he was the logical person to build the icehouse, and the logical time to build it was then. Dr. Loomis might have been philosophical about North's eagerness to invest in everything at once if he had had any assurance that North would give all his time to private enterprise. That would never be. In the letter advising the doctor of his new projects, North also said:

In addition to what I have written, we have a charter for a railroad which I think must pass through this place. We also have an Act to establish a Territorial road from Iowa through our place and I am one of the commissioners named in each bill. I am also appointed one of the viewers to lay out the road from Faribault to this place. All these things count in directing attention to our Town.[1]

All these things counted also as distractions that would eventually get North into trouble. Crosby, the miller, came to live with the Norths when the gristmill began to operate and the whole household sewed sacks. When Ann North had "nothing to do," she was pressed into writing promotion letters copied from North's correspondence to the *Republican*. The rooms in their new house were already so crowded that the Norths strolled along the banks of the Cannon to select sites for their "mansion" and for the American House, the finest hotel west of the river. North wrote what he called puffing letters and could hope soon to mail them under a Northfield postmark, for Rice was busy in Washington getting the post office transferred from Fountain Grove to Northfield.

On April 3, 1856, teams still drove over the ice in the millpond, but on the night of the fourth the ice went out and it was feared that the mills would go with it. When the water rose up to the saws both mills were shut down for a month. The mills normally closed on Sundays so that church services could be held in the gristmill with a congregation of a hundred and ten. Now there was another attraction at the mills, an unexpected treasure: fish could be pitchforked from the stream into wagons.

In the summer of that year the Norths returned to Syracuse for the marriage of George Loomis to Kate Ashley, a fateful match for the Norths, since it brought into the family circle Kate's brother-in-law Charles N. Felton, later senator from California and a capitalist whose money North would use in founding two cities. The newlyweds returned with Ann to Northfield (she said she felt like "a fifth calf" on the honeymoon) and North returned alone. Coming up on the same boat with the Loomises and Ann was "our brother" Steuben Bacon, the second of the family to arrive in Minnesota, to look over Northfield and perhaps escape the scandal of his father Nathaniel Bacon's marriage to a girl younger than his children.

Political meetings in Syracuse had revived North's interest in national affairs, and he matured a plan for Kansas during these meetings which approximated his later carpetbagging plans for the South. He proposed that the Kansas Committee call upon each of the northern states for men and money — for immigrants and the means to maintain them in Kansas. State committees in the free states would apportion the tax and the soldier-settlers from each county and town. The result would be ten thousand well-equipped anti-slavery men in Kansas by spring.

The second winter, as soon as the new schoolhouse was built, the Northfield lyceum was established according to North's usual plan:[2] in November the residents drafted a constitution for the lyceum providing for a reading room, a circulating library, and a debating society. At the meetings a choir sang and the president introduced the topic. Since the citizens were of one mind on the major topics of the day — temperance, anti-slavery, free education, and Republicanism — it was hard to organize a true debate; the situation became humorous when North was delegated to defend slavery or Ann to attack the Maine Law. In May 1857, she wrote, "We have enjoyed the past winter more than any part of our lives before and it has totally unfitted us for separations." [3] She said this knowing full well that long separations lay ahead while North lobbied the legislature, attended the constitutional convention, and managed the affairs of the Minneapolis and Cedar Valley Railroad, though it's true that she often accompanied her husband. In April they stayed in the Fuller House in St. Paul where she had the satisfaction of moving among the "elite and polite." She met Gorton Loomis's nearest neighbor, George A. Nourse, who had been prominent in the St. Paul Republican Convention and who would follow North to Nevada and become famous. She met the new territorial governor, Samuel Medary, and that strange and exciting politician, General James Shields.

North was in St. Paul in that April "to take care of the Legislature. You know," advised Ann, "they need much supervision." In effect, he was representing Faribault and Northfield, for the "miserable member" from Rice county had gone off to California. The Republican Convention in Faribault nominated North's friend, Dr. Charles Jewett, and planned to send North as delegate to the Minnesota Constitutional Convention if he did not do something before the convention "to render him so unpopular as to prevent it." North enjoyed a new reputation in Minnesota as the squire of Northfield.

The Norths moved into their new "mansion" on the hillside, from which they could watch the endless line of teams carrying grain to the mill; North built a new office; the whole town was booming. The Norths donated lots to worthy institutions, including one to the Methodists for a new church.[4] In her new house, Ann was thankful "for such a husband, who took me when a mere child, and continued so well the education already commenced. . . . I believe there is not another man in the world who would have made so much of me. . . . He has true Christian charity and patience with all my faults and failings, and encourages all the good. You cannot wonder I think him so nearly perfect." [5]

This rapture was not inspired by the magnificence of wardrobe North provided. She never had a costume that was all new; when she had a new basque, her skirt showed wear. She had no time to sew and no room for a seamstress in a household of nine adults, three children, and an endless stream of visitors. People were coming to Northfield by armies and all were deficient in commissary. Exchange of property was kaleidoscopic. Frost of Oneida Depot came out from New York with his partner Sewell and bought the sawmill, but there was not enough waterpower to run both mills, so North bought back the sawmill to give him control of the water for the gristmill. He raised money to buy steam engines to run the mills if water failed and to build a four-thousand-dollar block of stores by the liberty pole. In the spring of 1857 floods carried out the millworks; in March the boilers arrived for the steam plant by ship at Cannon City, hauled overland by a four-horse team. The arrival was celebrated with an oyster supper at the North mansion.

The North house was imposing only in the context of Northfield's haphazard architecture. A typical New York State house of white clapboard, its interior was, unlike other houses in the region, plastered. From a piazza high above the ground one had a view of the valley, the mills, the American House at Third and Washington, and the block of stores at the liberty pole. There North could sit and watch his industries working night and day: see the burning refuse in the millyard cast shadows on the long line of waiting teams; hear the whine of the saws, the whinny of plunging horses, the rattle of harness and whippletree, the shouts of teamsters and lumberjacks on the log drive. Hammers rang through the valley; night and day the work continued, interrupted only by the quiet of the Sabbath. The hours were marked only by the passing of stages on the new road.

Early in 1857 the stage line built stables in Northfield and the American House became a dinner stop. North wrote, "We have a railroad line surveyed through here a few days ago from the Iowa line to St. Paul which the Engineer tells me is the best yet found." [6] He did not bother to mention that this inside information was his because he was a director of the railroad. He was frustrated still by having to realize his big dreams by littles. But littles grow, and his family grew up with his ideals. The children played behind the North house on the present Carleton College campus and at night watched weird Indian dances in the camp by the river, a spot still dedicated to wild contortions: it is now occupied by the college stadium. North's hotel would one day be a college residence hall. Old men and small boys still fish at the mill dam and along the shady banks of the Cannon, where walking in summer through the haze of mosquitoes is like a plunge in piranha waters. Travelers still follow the stage road and pause at the narrow bridge to view the fall of water; it is no Niagara, but it has the charm of a fountain in the green farmlands. The traveler may wind north from the Cannon valley to see the distant skyline of the Twin Cities, or pause by the monument to war heroes in the town square, and think of Northfield as a place made famous by outlaws who tried to rob its bank. Forgotten is the man who created this lovely valley town and who, sickly again at forty-two, brooded over its destiny, deceiving himself that with all his investments he was gaining on his debts in the depression year of 1857.

TWO CONSTITUTIONS FOR
MINNESOTA

C ONGRESS passed the enabling act authorizing Minnesota Territory to organize as a state in February 1857. Governor Willis A. Gorman convened the legislature in special session three months later and his successor, Samuel Medary, addressed the legislators. Qualified voters were summoned to the polls on July 1 to elect delegates to a state constitutional convention which would meet in the capitol at St. Paul on Monday, July 13, 1857, the seventieth anniversary of the Northwest Ordinance.

The political division in that year was still into fur and anti-fur parties, now organized as Moccasin Democrats and Sowbelly Republicans. Republicans constantly increased as settlement grew in the farming, or "sowbelly," areas. Democrats increased only as the administration in Washington packed the territory with Indian agents and their employees, land offices and their staffs, customs officials and territorial officers, and military establishments at two forts with their sutlers and contractors. The Democrats were interested in sending to Congress a constitution that would please the administration and not arouse the ire of the southerners in Congress, thus keeping the Minnesota statehood from being tied into the struggle then going on over Kansas. The Republicans, on the other hand, were determined to bring Minnesota into the Union as the North Star State in politics as in geography. As before, the Democrats controlled the frontier polling places in the July 1 elections, whereas Republicans were stronger in the settled regions; the result was a number of contested seats in the constitutional convention.

The sort of constitution that Minnesota presented for admission might have far-reaching results. A Democratic constitution and redistricting of the state could result in sending Democrats to Congress to bolster that party in national councils. A Republican constitution and redistricting could send men to Congress from Minnesota to help the North in the great struggle going on in Kansas. Party strength in Congress rested to a degree on thirteen contested seats in the Minnesota convention. It was possible that St. Anthony could decide the national issue of slavery in the territories.

In St. Anthony North's friends claimed four seats for the Republicans, Steele's friends four for the Democrats. When county clerk Charles G. Ames ruled in favor of the Republicans on a technicality arising out of the careless wording of the Democratic ballots, Governor Samuel Medary removed him from office. The Republicans immediately reinstated Ames by action of the commissioners of Hennepin county. Returning boards of the two parties granted certificates to all eight for the contested four seats, leaving the decision to seat or not to seat the delegates up to the constitutional convention. Republicans in the convention would even admit one delegate who was not certified by anyone. In short, both parties tried to pack the convention. The two parties caucused in St. Paul, each trying to outmaneuver the other before the convention met.

The enabling act passed by Congress did not specify the hour at which the convention was to meet on the designated Monday, saying merely that it would meet at the usual hour. If the Republicans gathered at the usual hour of high noon, they feared they would find that the Democrats had met at the usual hour of eleven and have the convention organized and the delegates seated by twelve. No agreement could be reached between the Republican and Democratic caucuses as to what the usual hour was. North proposed that the Republicans meet in the capitol at midnight on July 12, in order to be on hand at any hour the Democrats might decide was usual on July 13. Several of the delegates objected because the twelfth was a Sunday. They were reminded that it was a most fitting time to meet, since it was the anniversary of the battle of the Boyne when William of Orange defeated the Roman Catholic adherents of James II, just as the Republicans now hoped to defeat the

Loomis home, De Witt, New York

North's office and buildings, St. Anthony Falls, Minnesota, 1850

Ann and her "good husband" at the time of their marriage, 1849

Mills on the Cannon River at Northfield, Minnesota, 1860's

*Washoe City, Nevada Territory, 1864 (above); Riverside, California, 1870; wing
at left was office of Southern California Colony Association*

North's house in Oleander, California, 1887; left to right: Ida Moody Russell; Mary North (later Shepard); Ann North; J. W. North; William Prior Russell; Charles L. North (third son of North)

Democrats and their Roman Catholic adherents in Minnesota. One of the delegates arrived at the capitol near midnight on Orangemen's Day riding a white horse, the traditional mount of King Billy at the Boyne. Others waited as late as possible and then took a Sabbath stroll which happily ended at the capitol at the stroke of twelve and then in good conscience took up Monday's business. North spent the hours after midnight urging the Republican delegates to put away the pistols they had primed for Democrats and committing them to a united plan of action when the Democrats appeared on the scene. It was a long, weary night, and one by one the Republicans nodded over their newspapers or spread blankets on the floor of the chamber. Others kept guard as if waiting for attack. Morning came, the forenoon passed. Sleepy eyes in unshaved faces looked with chagrin upon the quiet town. North rallied his forces to new alertness, and they signed a paper directing him to act for the entire Republican body as soon as the Democrats entered the unfinished capitol.

The Democrats lounged and laughed in the saloons, confident that they held every advantage. The secretary of the territorial government, whose responsibility it was to call the constitutional convention to order, was a Democrat. They went to mass, lingered over breakfast, lined up in barber shops, and did casual business in perfect confidence that nothing would happen until Secretary Charles L. Chase started for the capitol, and only he and they knew when that would be. At 11:45 by Republican watches and high noon by Democratic timepieces, Chase entered the capitol, followed by the entire body of Democrats, elected and self-appointed. He was met at the door by J. W. North, who, by Republican arrangement, fell in step and strode with him to the rostrum. Chase turned to the milling assembly and said above the roar, "As Secretary of the Territory of Minnesota, I call this Constitutional Convention to order."

Waiting only for the verb "call," North interrupted in his orator's voice, according to the written agreement of the Republicans: "I nominate for temporary chairman Thomas J. Galbraith!" Well-rehearsed Republicans responded with one voice. "All in favor," North went on, "say *Aye*; all opposed say *No!*" The Democrats had been caught off guard; the ayes shook the room. "The ayes have it," declared North with a ring of triumph. "Mr. Galbraith will please take the chair!"

The Democrats later complained that they had not voted because of the irregularity of the proceedings; but even if they had voted by secret ballot at that moment, they would have lost, for Republicans duly and provisionally certified as delegates outnumbered them in the chamber. Belatedly, former Governor Gorman moved to adjourn until Tuesday noon. The Democratic strategy apparently was to delay the work of the convention until the Republicans yielded on the question of seating the eleven Democratic delegates, four from St. Anthony. The Democrats filed out of the hall, leaving the Republicans behind, uncertain as to what they should do, but all looking to North. He persuaded them that they must proceed upon the assumption that the vote placing Galbraith in the chair was valid, and that since Galbraith had not recognized Gorman the motion to adjourn was out of order and the convention was still in session: they continued the business of the convention.

The Republicans foresaw that when the Democrats returned Secretary Chase would announce the list of delegates properly certified to him, which would mean accepting the Democratic slate. Then with the territorial machinery in their hands, the Democrats could rig the convention to suit their purposes. At the hotels and boarding houses, word was passed among the Democrats that no official recognition would be taken of the Republican meeting at the capitol or of their presiding officer, the newspaper man, St. A. D. Balcombe. At noon on the fourteenth of July the Democrats again stormed the Bastille, to find the Republicans still holding the fort as an organized convention. Secretary Chase entered the room, then went back outside to address the waiting Democrats: "A meeting of citizens has occupied the hall of the House of Representatives and refuses to give up the chamber. I direct the members of the Constitutional Convention to assemble herewith in the Council Chamber."

Gorman led the "convention" to the other chamber, which was not yet completed. The Democrats quieted the hammers and saws and sat on planks and saw horses while Henry H. Sibley was voted temporary chairman of the "Constitutional Convention." They then adjourned until the chamber could be put in order for regular meetings a few days later. From that point on the Democrats and Republicans met as two separate conventions and each began to frame a basic law for the state of Minnesota. Remarkably, both bodies adopted nearly the same provisions from the start. Both had before them the same models, the New York, Wisconsin, and Iowa constitutions, and some members had taken part in the constitutional conventions of one or more of those states. Lawyers had discussed privately the changes they wanted to make in these models when Minnesota's turn for statehood came. The radical changes desired by North and his friends were modified by the more practical Republicans who hoped to avoid a fight in Congress over the acceptance of Minnesota's constitution.

As time went on, party was forgotten in the serious work at hand. When the press and people of Minnesota were stirred to anger at the lack of a sense of responsibility in both parties, and when newspapers began to arrive from the East with articles expressing serious doubt about the prospect of statehood for Minnesota, the more sensible members of both conventions began to meet together unofficially to come to some working arrangement. A lawyer framing a proposal for his own convention would quietly pass the same provision along to a lawyer in the other body. One convention would occasionally observe a moment of silence to hear the outcome of a vote in the other body. At last, official committees were appointed to harmonize the work of the two conventions. No doubt the two conventions were more efficient separately than they would have been as a single body subject to the animosities and bickerings of a bipartisan convention. Minnesota may have discovered a device by which two irreconcilable groups can act in concert with due speed, free from partisan irritation.

The question of the state's borders, for example, might have disrupted a full convention, for this was a party issue. The proposal to make an east–west state instead of a north–south state was fraught with political difficulty. A state extending west to the Missouri would have cut off northern Minnesota, where the Democrats had much of their strength and would have embraced farming lands where the "sowbellies" would in time have a Republican majority through the immigration of still more farmers. North very wisely committed the Republicans to accept the present boundaries of Minnesota on the first day of the convention when he presented a resolution saying "That it is the wish of the people of the proposed State of Minnesota to be admitted into the Union at this time in accordance with the provisions of the act of Congress. . . ." [1] Said North: "It seems to me that insurmountable difficulties will arise and multiply in our path, if we attempt to step aside from the plan laid down for us, and change the boundaries. . . . I have ever been opposed to carving out States for the success of this or that political party." [2]

When the Republicans yielded to the aggravations of St. Paul to condemn Democrats personally and the wicked city in general, North checked these ungenerous outbursts as he did his wife's.

Such remarks, it seems to me, are not desirable, are injudicious, and inexpedient. We are all aware of the circumstances under which we meet . . . Our course is the proper one, the regular one, and the right one. Let us be satisfied with that and go straight forward in the discharge of our duties, without turning around to charge wrong upon those who differ with us. . . . We have assembled in this Convention for a more dignified purpose than that of passing encomiums or censure upon the people of any place. St. Paul, like other places, has its good and bad men. The good are not responsible for the bad, and some of whom we may call bad, may not be as bad as we imagine.[3]

On July 17, he went further and offered a resolution inviting those delegates "known to have been elected to this Convention who are now in the city and apparently undecided" to take their seats among the Republicans "on terms of perfect equality." Another delegate suggested that the invitation should mention the need for the "combined wisdom and experience" of the "absent members." Clergymen in the convention objected strenuously to Christian charity and North chided them: "It is refreshing to me to see . . . even our clerical friends nerve themselves in so war-like a manner, [it] is a little gratifying . . . But it seems to me there is nothing lost in showing courtesy in this matter." [4]

In the discussion of the judiciary, the question arose whether a jury was competent to decide both law and fact in libel cases. Lawyers began to display their erudition in an attempt to overawe the laymen in the convention. "I tell you," said North, "common-sense people sometimes know law better than the judges." He cited the famous judges who had tolerated slavery's existence in England while the common people declared repeatedly that the air of England was too pure for a slave to breathe. The people won, and even Blackstone was forced to revise his *Commentaries*. North wanted the convention to be guided by common sense — to give equal rights to women before the law and to give suffrage to the negroes.

North felt more strongly about the issue of negroes' voting in Minnesota than about any other problem before the convention; it is ironic that his efforts to bring the two conventions together were frustrated by this very insistence upon negro suffrage. The committee working to keep the two bodies in harmony reached a crisis in its labors on July 24 over the question;[5] there was thereafter no hope of getting the two conventions together. " 'Nigger suffrage' was the rock the committees split upon,"[6] said a St. Paul paper. Minnesota had few negroes — the issue was purely a matter of North's principle. Even the Republicans saw so little practical advantage and such great political disadvantage in trying to get a constitution granting negro suffrage accepted by Congress at that time that they voted against negro suffrage thirty-four to seventeen. Voting with North were his old abolitionist friends: Baldwin, Bates, Cleghorn, Colburn, Davis, Gerrish, Hayden, Holley, Mantor, Messer, Phelps, Perkins, Putnam, Peckham, Secombe, and Sheldon. The best that North could elicit from the convention was a promise that the people of Minnesota could vote upon the question of negro suffrage when they voted upon acceptance of the constitution. The committees harmonizing the two conventions' documents agreed on a proviso that nothing in the constitution would prevent the legislature from extending the right of suffrage. The Democratic draft was accepted as amended by some language from the Republican constitution. The Democrats had their way because they were being paid three dollars a day, since the territorial officials were sitting with them, while the Republicans sat at their own expense. The people of Minnesota accepted the constitution by a vote of 36,240 to 700. North went home to Northfield poorer in pocket but richer in heart, convinced that it was only a matter of time before the people of the state would rally to Republican ranks.

At the end of the Civil War, North's view of negro suffrage prevailed in Minnesota. He then wrote, "In 1857 (against the well-meant remonstrances of many personal friends,) I ventured with a few others, to ask the Constitutional Convention of Minnesota to give the colored people the right to vote. One strong reason which I relied upon in my argument in favor of this measure, was that they had fought for our liberties in the Revolution. . . . It was not strange that at that time this measure of simple justice did not carry in Minnesota. No one expected it would. . . . I am delighted that the Legislature of Minnesota [in

1865] has taken a noble stand in the matter, and passed a proposed amendment to the Constitution . . ." [7]

The people of Minnesota approved the amendment of 1865, and William R. Marshall, then governor of Minnesota, wrote, "We are indebted to J. W. North more than to any other man for this victory." [8]

W HEN Congress granted railroad lands to Minnesota, the legislature named commissioners for a line south to Iowa, among whom were Steele and Sibley. The shareholders demanded that the leading writer on railroads in the state, J. W. North, be added as director of this line, the Minneapolis and Cedar Valley Railroad. On Lincoln's birthday in 1857, the shareholders met at Mendota, long the center of the fur trade, where the houses of Sibley and Faribault were surrounded by warehouses and docks running down to the edge of the river. Here gathered the stockholders to select the directors. They quickly elected Franklin Steele, Henry H. Sibley, and Alanson B. Vaughn, all of whom were commissioners, unanimously, added the name of J. W. North to the board. Then, after a brief contest, they elected commissioner William F. Pettit, Ezra Abbott, and General James Shields who, as senator from Illinois, had helped push railroad and land bills through Congress. While the stockholders and prospective investors wandered about the parklike Mendota, eating their picnic lunches under the trees on the riverfront, the newly elected directors met in the Sibley mansion. Shields was elected president, Steele secretary, and Sibley treasurer. North was appointed to a committee to confer with engineers about the route and about connection with railroads from the east. The president and directors were authorized to receive subscriptions to capital stock.[1] The next meeting took place at President Shields' house at Faribault on April 22. There the board formally voted to apply to the legislature for the

grant of land donated by Congress to aid in the construction of a railroad from "St. Paul and St. Anthony, via Minneapolis to a convenient point of junction West of the Mississippi River to the Southern boundary of the Territory in the direction of the mouth of the Big Sioux River with a branch via Faribault to the North line of the State of Iowa West of Range 161." [2]

The directors adjourned to meet in St. Paul to lobby the legislature. Shields wrote, "The Legislature is now in session to dispose of the railroad grants and never in my long life have I witnessed such a struggle of interests — town against town, company against company, even man against man. I am persuaded now that these grants are more of a curse than a blessing. I am president of a company from St. Paul and St. Anthony to the Iowa line." [3]

Shields, then but half-way through his remarkable career, was already a romantic figure. Leaving Ireland as a youth, he was wrecked upon the coast of Scotland where he taught the classics learned from Jesuit preceptors in Ireland until he could work his way across the Atlantic. In America, he served in the Mexican War and settled in Illinois. When he took offense at a lampoon written by the Misses Todd and Jayne, Abraham Lincoln gallantly assumed the responsibility for the indiscretion of his future wife, accepting Shields's challenge to a duel on the banks of the Mississippi, and, it is said, selecting broadswords at two paces. A look at Lincoln's long arms told Shields that his honor could be satisfied by an explanation. Later he was elected senator from Illinois on his record as land commissioner and as a hero in the Mexican war.

After a month of lobbying, Shields and the directors met officially at the Central House in St. Paul and appointed a committee to go to Chicago to consult with the Chicago and Galena Railroad, and with the Chicago, Iowa and Nebraska line, about possible connections with the Minneapolis and Cedar Valley Railroad. The engineers making initial surveys diplomatically recommended connecting the towns in which the directors had property interests.[4] The meeting of the board on May 22, 1857, followed within a few hours the legislature's approval of the land trust created by Congress for railroad construction. Shields estimated that the railroad would be completed in three years,[5] but he was not present to fulfill his prediction, for the legislature elected him United States senator from Minnesota. He would serve Minnesota as he had Illinois, and as he would one day serve Missouri. In his place, North was elected president of the railroad.

North's chief function was selling railroad stock. He opened the books for a million-dollar subscription, but as usual he was his own best customer. At first offices had been wherever Shields or Sibley happened to be, but now that Shields was senator and Sibley governor, the railroad headquarters moved to Northfield. North rented office space to the company. Engineers worked out of Northfield, and plans were underway to set up railroad shops there. Grading was started at three points along the line by chief engineer Laurence Kellett. Edward Murphy gave the company twenty acres in Minneapolis for a depot. The railroad from St. Paul to Minneapolis, which took, for a ten-mile stretch, the optimistic name of Minnesota and Pacific, was to meet the M. & C. V. Railroad on Seventh street. North talked with such financiers as John G. Forbes, but capitalists had little faith in the railroad as an investment. North, on the other hand, was ever optimistic and sold as many of his other Minnesota investments as he could to bolster the railroad and keep the construction workers fed and on the job. By June 1858, the shares of stock were held largely by Shields, Sibley, Steele, and North.[6]

Governor Sibley soon sensed a conflict of interest between his official position and his directorship of two state-subsidized railroads. Early in 1858 he would have resigned as director of the Minneapolis and Cedar Valley if President North had not prevailed upon him to remain on the board:

I hope you will not be in haste to decline a reelection as Director in our Company. I do not see the difficulties that need embarrass you in acting as Governor and Director at the same time. Yet I have not given as much attention to the matter as you must have done; and therefore am not as well prepared to decide. But I do not like the idea of your leaving the Board.[7]

Sibley was quite right in trying to avoid all appearance of conflict of interest. Though as governor he often acted against the best interests of the railroads, he could never convince his critics of his honesty. His connections with the railroads defeated him politically and seriously damaged his reputation. North's view was typical of the carpetbaggers'. The railroads were needed by the state of Minnesota; North therefore saw nothing wrong in the governor's using his executive position to advance the interest of the railroads as long as in doing so he also advanced the interest of the state. He was confident that when the interests of the state and the interests of the railroads were in conflict Sibley would protect the state's interest even at the risk of losing money on his railroad investments. This is exactly what Sibley did do when the time came. North could not imagine any conflict, but when it came, it was too late for Sibley to wash his hands of the railroad grime. The transfer of his stock to his brother-in-law, Steele, fooled nobody.[8]

It soon became clear that the railroad could not be completed without assistance from the state, and the constitution would not permit a loan. In their eagerness to get a railroad the people of Minnesota voted overwhelmingly to amend the constitution so that a loan was possible. As a railroad president, North should have welcomed such a loan, but his carpetbagging instincts would not stretch far enough to risk state credit for private gain; he opposed it:

I do hope our Company can commence work on this Rail Road this Spring, *without the aid of the Five Million State Loan, and then I think* we shall prosper. Some people think they see great benefits resulting from that loan, but I do not believe in the principle that "the end justifies the means"; especially when the interests of so large a number, must be sacrificed to that of so few.[9]

North conceived of government as the partner in any undertaking in which public good and private gain could be achieved together; but he opposed even his own private gain at the expense of public interest. He stood with the Republicans in opposition to the state loan to railroads because he knew that such a loan might endanger the public credit of the new state. When it seemed certain that in the election the people of Minnesota would follow the Democrats and amend the constitution to make a loan to the railroads possible, North bowed to the inevitable. Indeed, he had reason to be actually relieved, for the loan to the M. & C. V. Railroad might save his private fortune. He had invested and mortgaged all he owned to support the railroad. Its failure would mean his own bankruptcy. Ann North wrote, "This is the week of the election on the State loan. I am still opposed to it, but I believe Mr. North got partially worked over when he was in St. Paul. Some of his objections were answered in such a way that, I believe he is not so positively against it at least, as he was." [10] North preferred to finish the railroad with private subscriptions, but once the people had expressed the desire to have the railroads at the risk of state credit, he went along with the plan against his convictions. The loan took the form of state bonds which could be exchanged for railroad bonds when the railroads had "completed construction." Nobody was sure what that meant; it could mean when the railroads had completed grading, or it could mean when rails were laid, or when the first engine traveled over the route. The loan of state credit to aid in this construction amounted to $2,275,000 in bonds of the state bearing seven per cent interest, maturing in twenty-five years, or on December 1, 1883. Bonds were issued to four land-grant railroads. North's road received $600,000 in bonds, but state credit declined and the bonds never sold at face value. All four railroads forfeited their right to further aid from the five-million-dollar loan by failing to pay the interest due on the bonds. The law authorizing such aid was repealed.

By October 27, 1858, thirty-five miles of roadbed had been graded. To continue work at this rate, two new issues of bonds would be required. North proposed that Governor Sibley take the bonds to New York to raise money for construction "at once." [11] Reluctant to go to New York in his mixed character as governor and railroad director, Sibley put the matter in the hands of his old friend of fur-trading days, Charles W. Borup of the banking firm of Borup and Oakes in St. Paul. But Borup's New York banking connection could not sell bonds of the M. & C. V. Railroad because of the way the Minnesota press had criticized the loan. Railroads had become a political issue. If anyone was to go to New York, it would have to be North.

North arrived in New York in November 1858, and succeeded in getting $20,000 for railroad construction, but he found the bonds were not up to par and were selling slowly. [12] New York papers were very critical of the Minnesota state loan. The *Evening Post* carried headlines such as THE GREAT FIVE MILLION DEBT, BANKRUPTCY OF THE STATE OF MINNESOTA. "Plaindealer," writing from Minnesota on November 24, 1858, recited the events which threatened the state's credit. He claimed the railroads had graded the easiest parts of their routes, such as the prairies, neglecting the costly grades and bridges, and had then applied for the state loan bonds at the rate of ten thousand dollars a mile for work that had cost but three or four hundred dollars a mile. In these circumstances Governor Sibley refused to turn over the state bonds in exchange for railroad bonds. Even if other railroads were guilty as accused by "Plaindealer," North knew that the M. & C. V. Railroad could justify its claim. He applied to the state supreme court for a mandamus forcing the governor to turn over the state bonds for the work completed. Regarding this as a put-up job, New York financiers believed that Sibley's refusal had been public deception, and that he knew full well that the supreme court would force him to do as governor what he wanted to do as railroad director. He was urged by New York friends to resist the court order and become another Andrew Jackson. Hudson's Bay Company agent Ramsay Crooks wrote Sibley, "The attempt of the Rail Road Companies of your State to coerce you into exchange of their bonds for those of the State, *before the Iron is laid* upon their roads, is looked upon here as nothing less than an attempt to defraud and swindle the State and has already had the effect of throwing suspicion upon her Credit. . . ." [13]

"Plaindealer," writing from St. Paul, had done great damage to railroad investment and state credit. North answered one of these letters published in the New York *Tribune*. Then, faster than he could reply, other attacks upon the railroads developed in the New York *Times*, *Evening Post*, and *Courier*, and *Enquirer*. North replied to each and wrote several "extra articles."

It was clear to North that the situation could be saved only by Governor Sibley's coming to New York to assure the financiers that the bonds were good and state credit above reproach. This was hard to do with only six cents in the state treasury. North wrote:

You know that I have been looking for you every day since I have been here and waiting with the greatest impatience. . . . I took it for granted that you were on your way. I telegraphed to you nearly two weeks ago . . . asking you to *come on immediately*. . . . Almost all the papers of the City have attacked us, and *nothing but a statement from the Governor can put matters right*. The bare idea that there is a fight between the Companies and the Governor ruins the credit of the State.[14]

But such letters to Sibley, going through Borup's bank, were not delivered to the governor. As a banker in Minnesota, Borup was not eager for North to succeed in New York now that the bonds could be used by Minnesota banks as the basis of expanding currency issues. Borup had even held up transfer of the $20,000 North had raised to pay the starving construction workers. North was filled with indignation at Dr. Borup and equally put out with Sibley. "*Now when you get this, if you have not started already, if you do not jump into your boots and travel day and night till you get here I will never forgive you. And I* shall charge upon *you* and *you alone the ruin of our company.*" [15] He signed the letter "Indignantly yours, J. W. North."

Sibley jumped into his boots and was in New York a few days later. He found things ten times as bad as he supposed.[16] He had left a Minnesota paralyzed by depression; the people who had voted for the railroad loan in overwhelming numbers were now complaining that the railroad "swindle" had reduced them to desperation. Senator Shields wrote, "Minnesota is in a deplorable condition. . . . No money — all in debt — people who wish to live extravagantly. They will not work as long as there is a chance to borrow, beg, or steal, but their resources are exhausted. The State bonds are the only chance for stealing now — and it seems hard to raise money on them." [17]

North, blaming all on Borup and his bank, told Sibley that his delay in coming to New York had spoiled everything. Sibley, North contended, had let Borup direct railroad affairs which were none of his business except in anticipation of having the bonds deposited with his bank. But Sibley had had no choice in the matter: he owed Borup and Oakes $2,150 which was guaranteed by Steele. Borup had refrained from collecting the debt either from Sibley or Steele "for old time's sake." In North's absence the director Ezra Abbott tried to raise money to feed the hungry workers and keep construction going, but Borup and Oakes refused to advance funds.[18] Six weeks later, Franklin Steele managed to place half a million in bonds with R. M. S. Pease of the Minnesota banking house (Pease, Chalfant & Company) for their use in banking, in return for construction money.[19]

The inflation resulting from the use of bonds selling far below par to back bank currency completed the general ruin of the railroads and the state's credit. Once more North put the public interest ahead of private interest, and opposed the bankers. He led the fight against this inflationary procedure with such vigor that the Republicans began talking of North as their candidate for governor.[20]

There was some hope for the railroad as long as it could raise money to pay the interest on state bonds. Failure to pay this interest meant that the state would take over railroad assets and North, the chief investor, would be bankrupt. Interest was due Dr. Borup, who held the M. & C. V. Railroad's state bonds, and North cautioned Sibley, "When the Doctor is kind beware!" [21] North needed money to continue work on the railroad; the banks would accept the remaining bonds only at a discount — ninety-five cents on the dollar, which, under the circumstances, was a generous offer. Governor Sibley was reluctant to admit the depreciation of the state bonds on the eve of an election campaign. "But I saw no other way [to continue construction] and so I went at it boldly [to persuade Sibley]. It was a hard try for half an hour, but I succeeded," wrote North.

Nothing could really help, and the effort put North in bed. When J. Jay Knox wrote an article against the use of the bonds for banking purposes, North sat up in bed and wrote a reply printed in the *Minnesotian*. He agreed that the use of the bonds for banking was bad, but the main thing was to finish the railroads so that they might begin earning money and redeem the bonds, or at least pay interest on them. "It proved a good hit," reported North, "and was hailed with delight by the people. I became all at once quite a hero in vanquishing the hostile Bankers." [22] Even Knox was convinced and his next article in the *Minnesotian* was "unexceptional."

When the board of directors of the Minneapolis and Cedar Valley Railroad met at Northfield in mid-April, 1859, North controlled the company. The railroad offices and shops were in Northfield. His brother-in-law, George Loomis, was treasurer at a salary of two thousand a year. North could outvote the other directors with his 334 shares. His investment in the railroad was $3,340, with $30,060 due.[23] To raise the amount due, he would have to mortgage or sell everything he owned in Northfield. He brought out from Syracuse his old friend Charles Augustus Wheaton to take an interest in the railroad, and to purchase his interest in Northfield. Wheaton became the leading man of the town, in due course one of the leading editors of the state. He had been a carpetbagger investor in Tennessee railroads in the 1850's and was regarded as a valuable addition to the M. & C. V. railroad company.

June 1859 began with renewed hopes for the railroad, and ended with disaster for North. For one thing the location of the railroad shops at Northfield had created jealousy in towns all along the line, and North made a series of talks to "pacify the people" who resented the railroad's becoming a one-man company.[24] The bankers who hoped to take over the railroads were angry at North's success in drawing in private capital. Even the directors were ready to rebel against North's control of the road. He had hoped to have the cars running between Northfield and Mendota by the fall of 1859, but by the end of July, he had failed.

The reasons for his hope of success in early July and for his despair late in July were summed up in a letter from Minnesota that month, "Capitalists are visiting here to some extent and investing in land," and then, "General Shields has been elected President of the Minneapolis and Cedar Valley railroad in place of J. W. North." [25]

Capitalists from Syracuse had come too late. Wheaton became secretary of the railroad at a salary of three thousand a year, but his guidance was also too late. At the annual meeting the changes in the board voted by North as controlling stockholder did not please Sibley and Shields, and they immediately resigned from the board. So much depended upon public confidence that the news of this resignation would have been disastrous; but when North urged them to reconsider, *all* the directors resigned. All were angry and insisted that the old board be re-elected — in other words, that North forgo his right to name the officers. He agreed to the re-election of the old board, if they would let him resign and make Shields president. Either North would run the road, or the rest must; he was tired of divided counsel. Shields was "very blue" and had no confidence in the railroad, but as president he could no longer undermine public confidence by wild criticisms of North. Shields was elected president; though North thought nothing had been gained by the change [26] he justified it thus: "This takes a great load off my shoulders and is really a great relief. Do not think that I was put out of office against my wishes, I urged the change and am heartily glad it has taken place." [27]

General Shields had criticized North as extravagant, pointing to North's salary and Loomis's. He maintained that the president should get no salary, a contention accepted to his own disadvantage when he was elected president. At the meeting in Northfield on July 5, the difference between North and Shields caused the general to challenge North to a duel. North did not respond, nor did he take the challenge seriously; it was soon passed over and forgotten as incidental to heated argument. Because of North's ill health, the July meeting took place in his hotel, where he could lie on a couch. The General "faced up to Mr. North in a very courageous manner, when Mr. North was lying on the sofa, and declared that he would not receive from any man such language as Mr. North used to him." North's talk had been unusually "plain" and in the Methodist manner calculated to be for the good of Shields's soul. But Shields was no Methodist, and instead of taking thought of his errors and mending his ways, Shields took thought of his honor. "Mr. North continued to talk, looking him in the eye, and the Governor stepped between them and pressed the General back." [28]

Under the guidance of General Shields, the railroad went from bad to worse. By August the railroad was effectively in the hands of Selah Chamberlain, who held onto the bonds for many years until the state of Minnesota finally established its credit by redeeming them on March 2, 1881. The railroad became a political liability to Sibley. W. F. Pettit reminded Sibley that the railroad construction men were all good Democrats and should be paid before elections because their votes were needed.[29] Sibley advanced $600 from "personal kindness," and Ezra Abbott wrote him that the token payment had had good effect. The results of the election in fall 1859 showed that Sibley could not straddle two horses in the political circus when the gubernatorial and the iron horse cantered along divergent paths. On December 6 he resigned from the boards of the Minneapolis and Cedar Valley and the Southern Minnesota railroads, but by then Republicans had won on the issue.

Early in 1860 the former opponents of the railroad loan, who would now run the Republican state government, came out in support of their own railroad bill. Backed by the *Minnesotian,* a bill was printed to put all the railroads in the hands of Chamberlain and make good his bonds, whereas all bonds in the hands of the Democrats (and North) would be put down to twenty-five cents on the dollar. North threatened to stump the state against any such bill. The new Republican legislature in its 1860–61 session rechartered the M. & C. V. Railroad as the Minneapolis, Faribault, and Cedar Valley Railroad Company.

Selah Chamberlain had worked closely with Franklin Steele in getting control of the railroad. Most of their schemes would have saved North's investments in the road at the sacrifice of public interest. Wrote Ann of her husband,

Thus far his integrity stands firm. During the last week he had an offer, that was really a tempting one, in his state of health. Mr. Chamberlain of Cleveland is very anxious with Mr. Steele to get control of this railroad. He would give Mr. North one-hundred dollars an acre for his land surrounding the town [of Northfield] and take enough unimproved lots at Mr. North's prices to amount to $50,000.[30]

North could have solved all his difficulties if he had accepted this bribe, disguised as it was in a business deal which would have passed public scrutiny. Instead, he held on to his nearly worthless bonds until they were redeemed twenty-five years later. Ann said, "He would not do it without the consent of the Directors; and all came to the conclusion it would not be for the general good, and he has decided not to do it." Thus, when the Republican legislature rechartered the railroad, North continued on the board of the new road. Associated with him were some of the most famous American capitalists and railroad builders: Erastus Corning, Dean Richmond, James F. Joy, W. Brooks, Walter L. Newberry, Elliott Anthony, William Osborne, Roswell B. Mason, Platte Smith, William H. Dyke, Thomas A. Harrison, J. Jay Knox, John H. Abbott, and William G. LeDuc. Here were some of the best brains in the nation's railroads combined with some leading citizens of Minnesota, but they did not do much better than the old board.

On February 1, 1864, the name was again changed, this time to the Minnesota Central Railway, which put in operation a line between Minneapolis and St. Paul Junction at Mendota, a distance of 9.66 miles. In 1865 it was extended 22 miles; in 1866, 60.99 miles. The Minnesota River was bridged for the railroad in 1865. By 1870 the railroad was completed, with 87.19 miles of track, at a cost of $24,489 per mile. In 1865 the city of St. Paul provided a $50,000 bond issue to bridge the Mississippi to get a railroad connection. In 1867 there was a sale to McGregor Western by which the road was controlled and operated by the Milwaukee and Prairie du Chien Railroad Company. In 1874 it passed to the Chicago, Milwaukee, and St. Paul which was sold in 1926 to the Chicago, Milwaukee, and St. Paul and Pacific.[31]

The impossibility of North's ever having completed the railroad and bridges with the financial backing at his disposal is indicated by the gratuities received in the course of its completion, altogether $1,873,-628.24.[32] It is plain that North might have put part of the road into operation if public lands could have been sold during the depression years, if the press had not undermined confidence in the railroad and in the state credit pledged for its completion. North and Sibley went deeply into debt to achieve their goal, which was the greatly desired goal of all the people of the state. That they failed is perhaps less surprising than that they avoided the graft in contracts and the financial manipulations which characterized contemporary railroad construction.

North had to live with the railroad "scandal" the rest of his life. He, along with his Democratic associates, was blamed by the Republicans.

On the one hand, he was the man the Republicans wanted to nominate as governor or elect as senator, but since he was the leading railroad man of the state, they could not put him forward consistently when the great local issue of the 1859 campaign would be opposition to railroads. His failure to receive political preferment forced North into other fields which in the end gave purpose to his life. The railroad "scandal" was used against him when he tried to become Indian Superintendent in 1861, thereby saving him from any responsibility for the Sioux War of 1862. The "scandal" was used against him in Grant's administration when he sought to be Commissioner of Indian Affairs, thus saving him from any responsibility for the greater Sioux wars of the West. Perhaps he was right when he wrote, "It seems to me as though I was driven along, by a kind of destiny."

L INCOLN was accorded a ten-thousand-vote majority by Minnesota in 1860, a victory possible only because the Republicans had reversed the tide of politics in Minnesota in 1859. In 1859 they defeated the long-entrenched Democratic party on the railroad issue, won six national offices, and achieved a two-thirds majority in the legislature, which assured their electing a Republican senator, possibly two, in the next year. Patronage passed to the Republicans.

Early in the spring of 1859 the political leaders in the eastern states promised the Minnesota Republicans $5,500 for the campaign. Eastern Republican speakers promised to canvass the state. This concentration of men and money was necessary to overcome the Democratic patronage and control of elections. Republicans had for some time claimed a majority of the voters in Minnesota, but the majority never appeared in the election returns. The reason was clear. The Democrats voted Indians, half-breeds, Canadians, and foreigners who were often not residents of the state; they harvested votes in the distant polling places along a thousand-mile frontier which local Republicans had had neither men nor money to police.

Democrats long in power in Washington had appointed sutlers and officials at two forts, an Indian Superintendent, two Indian agents, several customs officials, two surveyors of the Land Office with receivers, registers, clerks, and other employees. These Democratic appointees disbursed half a million dollars a year in the state, quite sufficient to control the votes of a numerous group looking to them for contracts and favor. This captive vote had been determining in past elections.

The Republican need for campaign funds was obvious, yet Cameron of Pennsylvania promised a thousand dollars and sent nothing; Massachusetts Republicans promised a thousand dollars and sent a few hundred. The campaign was well under way before the Republican National Committee came to the rescue.

Zachariah Chandler of Michigan came to speak in Minnesota and wrote Edwin D. Morgan, the chairman of the Republican National Committee, of the pressing need, whereupon Morgan sent his personal check for a thousand dollars. In their desperation, the Minnesota Republicans rashly drew upon Morgan for another thousand dollars without his knowledge. When Morgan objected, they promised that if the Republican candidates were elected to Congress the new congressmen would make the loan good from their salaries. Morgan apparently did not think them a good risk and refused to honor the draft. Everything seemed to go wrong. Free campaign literature was sent from Washington by slow freight; Minnesota Republicans had to pay for a second lot and have it sent by express. When it reached Minnesota it had to be translated into Scandinavian languages and German. The greatest expense was the cost of sending Republicans out along the thousand-mile border to police the polls. These men had to be paid traveling expenses and living costs, for most Republicans in that depression year in Minnesota were too poor to pay their own way.

Nationally, the Republicans stood for aid to western railroads, but in Minnesota the Republicans won by protesting against federal land grants and state loans to railroads. North was in harmony with the national party, but temporarily out of step with Minnesota Republicans. Only after the election was won did the Minnesota Republicans forget North's railroad affiliation and welcome his leadership in the party again. With all the paying positions disposed of in the election, North had to be content with honorary posts. The Republicans sent him to Chicago with the Minnesota delegation to the Republican National Convention of 1860, but did nothing for him in 1859. Not even Ann, who thought her husband deserved every honor, took seriously the talk of making North governor or senator. There were too many candidates in the new party to consider a railroad man, and most of them needed office as badly as he did. Eastern Republicans had little conception of the handicaps and poverty of the Republicans in Minnesota in 1859.

The Republican counties, where men had invested in land and its

116

improvement, were the hardest hit by the depression. It was said that people were actually starving in Faribault.[1] Meals in Northfield were something less than banquets. Dr. Loomis had to send North and his son George money to pay their grocery bills. Those who could raise fifty dollars were joining companies to go to Pike's Peak. All North's friends were in financial difficulties. Marshall and Company, Bankers, of St. Paul had not been able to live up to their letterhead promise, "Collections Made and Proceeds Promptly Remitted," and Marshall and his partner, N. P. Langford, closed their doors. Marshall tried to sell his fine cream-colored house, the showplace of St. Paul, to Sibley.

The Minnesota economy, and to some extent the Republican party in Minnesota, were saved by the distant Chinese. As cranberries had seen Minnesota through the difficult winter of 1850, so now the lush growth of a curious plant in the Big Woods found eager buyers on the far side of the globe to carry Minnesota through the depression. Minnesotans couldn't spell it, they had no idea what Chinese herbalists wanted with it, but the aromatic root ginseng provided ready money. Whole families went to the Big Woods for the harvest of riches. Wrote a resident of Hastings:

Pike's Peake is left in the shade by the discovery in the big woods of an inexhaustible quantity of Gensing [ginseng]. The excitement is great — everybody in the vicinity of the Big Woods is digging the root. They average two to five dollars a day. . . . Some estimate the probable value of the trade this season in Minnesota as high as $2,000,000.[2]

Ginseng, selling at ten cents a pound, was a godsend. Debts that North never hoped to collect were now paid. Hundreds who thought they could not contribute to the Republican cause now did their part. Unlimited quantities of ginseng in the Big Woods and unlimited Chinese in China raised hopes high until August, when it was reported that ginseng was in oversupply. "The gensing trade has fuzzled out, but it aided some poor people in obtaining bread while it lasted," wrote one observer.[3]

It would have taken stronger medicine than ginseng to cure the malady North's affairs suffered from. He had spent time on railroad matters to the neglect of business in Northfield. He had pledged his property to raise money to prevent a halt in the railroad's construction, and with the failure of the railroad, his ruin seemed inevitable. With his personal affairs in such desperate straits, he could not give as

117

much time as he would have liked to politics. Alexander Ramsey and George A. Nourse came with other Republican leaders to persuade North to run for governor, but he positively refused.[4] Nourse said that if a Republican legislature were elected, that it in turn would draft North as senator, and that he would be "shut up if he offer[ed] one word of objection to being U. S. Senator."

Ann North discouraged her husband's political ambitions. Their worn carpet, a constant reminder of their poverty, Ann mentioned in a letter to her parents and then was embarrassed when North asked to read the letter before it was mailed. She had been caught making one of her few complaints. A few days later, North managed to send home a new carpet — just in time for the arrival of Syracuse friends, Charles and Ellen Birdseye Wheaton. The carpet may have been the result of the ginseng prosperity, for it was at this time that Ann reported, "We think it is almost equal to a goldmine in our country. . . . There are very few people idle now. There is work for all and with the best of pay." [5]

Minnesota's economic plight affected the outcome of the election in still other ways. Professional men closely associated with the Democrats in Minnesota were disillusioned. Isaac Atwater wrote, "I cannot get money enough to buy provisions for my family." [6] Long tied by trade to the Southland, the Democrats now found that southerners were reluctant to pay their debts. Half a million dollars' worth of lumber sold on the lower Mississippi on tick had to be written off as complete loss.[7] Many who had been Democrats were ready for change. Frustration was general.

None was more frustrated than North. As the American House, the sawmill, the gristmill, the railroad, the Northfield town lots — as all these slipped from his control, he became an invalid. When he went to St. Paul he had to receive his visitors lying down. Ann wrote from the Fuller House there,

Mr. North is very tired and is unable to leave our room today, and lies on the lounge most of the time. . . . He is talked down almost every hour. . . . Mr. North has visitors almost constantly, on business or politics. You see they will not leave him out entirely unwell as he is. He seems just now to be exceedingly popular — perhaps only for a day however. He does not wish political preferment — still, an appreciation of his labors is very gratifying.[8]

118

North could provide only half what the politicians wanted. If he was to stay out of the race for political office so as to attend to his business, then they wanted him to use his influence in their candidates' favor. That he could do. They also wanted money for the campaign; a substantial contribution from North would have guaranteed his election as senator by the new legislature in the event of Republican victory. Like everyone else he was too poor. Zachariah Chandler reported that the Republicans in Minnesota were all *"poor, very poor* but ardent." He wrote,

They can beat their enemies at a fair game — but the Federal Treasury supplies the funds for fraud and violence and it is to meet this illegal Indian vote, scattered God knows where, that they demand aid [from the Republican National Committee.] We need the two [Minnesota congressional] votes in the organization of the House and very much desire the vote [of a Republican] in the Senate. But more than all and above all we want Minnesota as a permanent Republican State and the election this year will settle the point for a quarter of a Century if we carry it.[9]

Chandler was right, but the national committee did not know he was a prophet. They could only promise to send to Minnesota in 1859 such minor figures as C. M. Clay, Lyman Trumbull, and a certain "Abram" Lincoln. Lincoln did not keep the engagement, though he would have been welcome, for he was better known in Minnesota than in most other places. Ten years before, his name had been important in the territory. When North arrived in Minnesota it was customary for lawyers to give references in their cards in newspapers. Naturally, the lawyers listed only those persons whose reputations would reflect creditably upon them. Attorney Morton S. Wilkinson in the St. Paul *Chronicle and Register* of 1849 and 1850 gave as reference Abraham Lincoln of Illinois. For ten years the name of Lincoln had been known and respected in Minnesota.

Belatedly, the Republican National Committee realized the importance of Minnesota's congressmen in the next Congress. The secretary wrote that "The organization of the next United States House of Representatives may depend upon it."[10] With this encouragement, the Minnesota Republicans began to cast about for the strongest men to send to Congress and the best man to run for governor. A popular gubernatorial candidate might carry the whole slate into office. Inevitably, the name of North was again put forward, despite his refusal to run for office. Ann sent one paper to her parents to let them see how North was touted for governor, but did not send the Faribault paper which opposed him. North went to New York to help raise campaign funds for the Republicans, and returned upriver with General Shields and his old friend John P. Hale of New Hampshire, who had come west to address Republican rallies.

North was welcomed back cordially by the Republicans. Alexander Ramsey was the Republican candidate for governor, but they now urged North for senator. Ann wrote home:

Some of Mr. North's friends are very urgent that he should be in St. Paul at the time of the election of U. S. Senator [by the legislature] but we feel as though there was no possibility of success, and he does not *wish* to undertake it. However, some are making such desperate efforts for him, that he thinks it might seem ungrateful to do nothing, and he will probably go there — though with no hope of election.[11]

North went to St. Paul, even though most of the delegates from his own Rice county were against him. His principal occupation while there was "cleaning up his character" from railroad smears, and on his return to Northfield he reported that he received only eight votes. "Most of the members said that personally I was their first choice for Senator, but as the Republican Party had carried the State on the anti–Rail Road issue, it would not do just now to take the most prominent Rail Road man in the State and make a Senator of him. Though they had the highest opinion of my integrity, it was too short a corner to turn."[12] North would have to be satisfied with being president of the state convention which instructed its delegates to vote for Seward in Chicago.

In the spring of 1860 all eyes were on Chicago and its convention hall, the Wigwam. N. B. Judd wrote the Republican National Committee that some citizens proposed to build a temporary hall for ten thousand people. "They propose to give us [Republicans] the use of the hall and complimentary tickets to the extent of one thousand, and then charge all others."[13] Judd did not add that this would allow him to pack the hall with a thousand Lincoln boosters.

Lincoln was as much talked about in Minnesota as Seward. In March Governor Ramsey noted that he saw a concerted movement in the Northwest to bring out Lincoln and that Thurlow Weed, who was touting Seward, must look to his laurels.[14] As delegate to Chicago, North decided to go first to New York and enter Chicago with the Seward forces from his native state. In Syracuse, the papers that had recently recounted his financial failure in Minnesota now lionized him as a local boy who made good. The Syracuse *Journal* hinted broadly that he be drafted for a political address.[15]

Two railroads raced to Chicago from New York, and North, then in New York, would not have missed the race for anything. "I took the Fast Train at Buffalo at six o'clock Monday Morning . . . and came through [to Chicago] in little over fifteen hours; notwithstanding two Engines gave out and had to be exchanged for others, which, of course caused considerable delay. We travelled considerable of the time at the rate of fifty miles an hour and beat the Michigan Central nearly half an hour." [16]

In Chicago the Minnesota delegation waited impatiently for him at the Richmond House. He arrived "at a very late hour" but the delegation was still assembled. They were David A. Secombe, his former law partner; Stephen Miller, the future governor; S. P. Jones of Rochester; A. H. Wagerner of New Ulm; Aaron Goodrich, the former chief justice; John McCusick, a proprietor of Stillwater; and Simeon Smith of Chatfield. They knew North was riding to Chicago with the Seward forces, including the founder of the Republican party (according to New York reckoning), Vivus N. Smith of Syracuse. When North arrived, the Minnesota delegation elected him chairman. North did not get to bed until one o'clock and then could not sleep because of three noisy men in the "back room." The next day he arranged to stay in a private home. "The Hotels are overwhelmed with people. I never saw such a crowd," he wrote. Streets were conduits to the overflow of the hotels; crowds poured out of the hotels as if spouted up by popular eruption.[17]

On the day the convention opened in the Wigwam, North had all he could do to hold the delegation to Seward. "The electioneering for the different candidates has become intense," wrote North, "but Seward is still strong. One of our Delegation became shaky; but I talked to him and have appointed a daily meeting of our delegation 'to confirm the feeble knees.'" [18] Thurlow Weed, Seward's manager, turned his charm and flattery on North, but it was not needed, for North intended to carry out the mandate of the Minnesota convention. Weed, as always, was "so gracious, so assuring, so genial and friendly" that he charmed everyone into discounting all the bad they had heard of him; he reminded one Republican of Byron's Corsair, "the mildest mannered man that ever scuttled ship or cut a throat." [19] Weed did not know that he and his New York crew were about to be scuttled. North said, "Thurlow Weed told me he had been looking anxiously for me, to keep our men right." [20]

Lincoln said that he was most too much of a candidate to go to the convention, and not quite enough of a candidate to stay at home.[21] Had Lincoln come to the convention, it might now be said with certainty what can only be said with reservation: that the men assembled in the Wigwam constituted the greatest moral force ever assembled upon this continent. Leaders were consummate politicians, skilled in presenting their own candidates, but knowing when the favorite sons must yield to the more favored candidate. Seward was nominated, North seconded the nomination for Minnesota. The first day of the convention passed before it was apparent that the choice was between Seward and Lincoln. New York, Michigan, Wisconsin, Minnesota, and Kansas supported Seward from first to last; [22] these were the states in direct westward bearing from New England, the Yankee vote. They did not hold decisive power in the convention — Minnesota had only four votes. Power was held by the more populous states in the tier just below — New Jersey, Pennsylvania, Ohio, Indiana, and Illinois — all supporting favorite sons. Four of them caucused and found that the only man all could agree upon was "Long Abe." They rejected Seward because of the "unreasoning infatuated idea abroad in the land that Seward [was] the monster embodiment of all fanaticisms, and that his accession to the presidency would be but a prelude to so radical an anti-Slavery administration, that Dissolution of the Union would be inaugurated at once." [23]

With the lower tier of populous states for Lincoln, the upper tier of Yankee states had to follow. Indeed, Lincoln apparently had foreseen this outcome and had gone out of his way to lecture in the Seward territory, from New England to Kansas. Only in Minnesota had Lincoln failed to speak, but there he had strong friends. In the Wigwam, the greatest word in our history was born in an instant with the shouts of *Lincoln*. All wanted to see this man or monkey, magistrate or monster. North was one of the few to have an immediate opportunity.

After the Convention was over, being on the committee to notify Mr. Lincoln of his nomination, I went to Springfield to see the next President. The [Illinois] Central Railroad gave us an extra train and paid all expenses. It was a long ride, more than two-hundred miles. We arrived in the evening and started back at midnight. We had a pleasant call on Mr. Lincoln.[24]

The delegation with some forty or fifty joyful citizens walked to Lincoln's house and the delegation was received at once into parlors thrown together by the opening of folding doors. It was the home of a successful railroad lawyer, and not unlike the North house in its furnishings. In the corner was a low-backed mahogany sofa upholstered in horsehair, and red upholstered side chairs were formally arranged against the walls. A secretary — a drop-leaf desk with three drawers below and four shelves of books above — stood in another corner, a low horsehair rocking chair by the window. A table with curved ends and a white marble top held a candelabrum and a sewing box, and a three-shelf whatnot of carved mahogany displayed treasures of the house. After the delegates had crowded in, there was a moment of confusion and embarrassment as they looked at Lincoln and he at them. Standing at the rear of the ordinary back parlor, bowing in jerks, pale, with compressed lips, he seemed an extraordinary man. The delegates shifted uneasily and nervously looked around for Ashmun, who was urged forward to make the official notification. Lincoln heard him with folded hands and inclined head, his eyes so deep that they might have been closed. Then he stepped forward, accepted the nomination, shook each by the hand, and harked to each name, all with an attentive ease and grace that surprised some of them. He led them across the hall to another parlor, where Mrs. Lincoln received them as if she were already a "distinguished ornament" of the White House.

Delegates got supper, heard several speeches in the state capitol, saw a most brilliant display of fireworks, and at midnight boarded the cars for Chicago. The I. C. Railroad might pay all expenses, but there was a limit to its generosity — there were no sleeping cars. North arrived in Chicago jaded, but with a Sunday of rest before him. Monday he took the cars for Prairie du Chien, riding all night in a day coach to catch the Tuesday riverboat that would get him to St. Paul in time for Wednesday's ratification meeting. North plunged into the Lincoln campaign with all his heart. After whipping the St. Paul meeting to enthusiasm, he went home in a lumber wagon to plan the speaking campaign he and John P. Hale were to conduct in Illinois. He went again to St. Paul to introduce Senator William H. Seward to the largest gathering in Minnesota up to that time. Seward spoke on a Tuesday, North returned to Northfield on Wednesday "very much fatigued"; but on Thursday, in spite of a cold September rain, he shared the platform with Governor Ramsey at Faribault, and even so prejudiced a listener as Mrs. Ramsey said his speech was "much the best." He came home hoarse, coughing, and lame, with severe pain in his chest and arm — and in a day or so he was off for the State Fair at Fort Snelling with his sister Clarissa to deliver the opening address.

The Republicans were turning the tables on the Democrats by corralling the soldier vote. Republican officers at the forts were telling the soldiers that the Democrats, now out of office in the state, had introduced a bill to keep the soldiers from voting. In one company there were a hundred Republican votes. On October 16, North answered the call of the Illinois Republican Committee and arrived in Chicago to stump the state. Two weeks later, he wrote, "I have just closed my term of campaigning in Illinois, and start for home this evening . . . It has been a severe test of my ability to speak by the side of John P. Hale; but I have lived through it and have not been disgraced." With the election of Lincoln certain, North asked his father-in-law, "What think you of the propriety of my applying for some office?" He did not wait for an answer. Governor Alexander Ramsey suggested that he ask for the Superintendency of Indian Affairs, which paid three thousand a year. Ramsey urged him to go to Springfield to see Lincoln before returning home from the Illinois speaking tour, but North decided to wait for the results of the election. In the meantime he returned to Minnesota to hold conference with Ramsey, who aspired to become Secretary of the Interior.

After the election, North set off again downriver full of confidence. He stopped in Chicago to pick up letters of introduction from Norman B. Judd and the Illinois Republican committeemen before joining the parade of office seekers to Springfield. Lincoln had infinite patience with office hunters, for while there were the selfish and undeserving among them, they were mostly men eager to serve the new nation in the political revolution ahead. When North arrived, Springfield was still celebrating Lincoln's election, with a "splendid illumination" and speakers Trumbull and Yates. Senator Lyman Trumbull was conciliatory to the slavocracy and North wrote, "I have given him and Mr.

Lincoln a plain talk in reference to all this twaddle of giving the South assurances of good behavior." [25]

Lincoln was so plagued with well-wishers and office seekers that he could not talk with North in his temporary office in the capitol at Springfield, but invited him to his home the next day. "I called upon Mr. Lincoln at his room in the capitol," North wrote Governor Ramsey. "He received me very cordially, as much so as was possible in such a crowd. Seeing that there was a constantly increasing crowd coming to call on him, after a few minutes conversation I took my leave. As I left, he said he would see me again at his house at eight o'clock the next morning." [26]

On November 21, North called at Lincoln's house and had "a pleasant and satisfactory conversation with him." Even as they settled down in the parlor to discuss the recent campaign in Illinois, North wondered how best to present the aspirations of himself and Governor Alexander Ramsey.

"Mr. Lincoln, Minnesota is considerably interested in the Indian and Land departments, more so than any other state."

"Those agencies come under the Interior Department," noted Lincoln.

"We feel like doing all we can for Minnesota, and considering what we have done to make Minnesota the strong Republican state she is, we feel we have some strong claims for consideration of our people for positions in the department of Indian Affairs and the Land office."

"It certainly would be appropriate," agreed Lincoln, "for a state like Minnesota, which has the greatest interest in these agencies, to have control of them."

"The one thing that would most gratify the Republicans of Minnesota, would be to see Governor Alexander Ramsey made Secretary of the Interior in charge of these departments."

Lincoln nodded encouragement and North said, "And perhaps I should let you know that I intend to apply for the position of Superintendent of Indian Affairs."

Lincoln then inquired about politics in the state of Minnesota and North described at length the rise of the Republican party, the emigration of temperance and abolition people from New York and New England, and the struggle they had had with the Fur Company and the administration appointees. The radical expectations of Minnesota Republicans turned the conversation to national policies, upon which Lincoln had been silent publicly and would remain silent until he got to Washington. Seward and Charles Francis Adams had been "making policy" for Lincoln, urging conciliation of the slavocracy; Charles Sumner had been "making policy" by declaring that Republicans must stand firm and resist any compromise of their great moral principles. Lincoln, with amazing self-control, held his tongue. The newspapers that day speculated that Lincoln would desert the radical Republicans to favor a conciliatory policy toward the south. Lincoln made no statement at all, but his treatment of North may suggest that he had no idea at all of deserting the radicals. He knew North had been a pioneer in abolition; he knew about the campaign in Minnesota and in his own state of Illinois during which North had declared the importance of not retreating from radical ideals. And there could be no doubt left in Lincoln's mind where North stood after his "plain talk."

"I told him," said North, "if the statement in the papers was correct that he was going to 'throw the radicals overboard,' that I wanted him to understand that I was a radical." [27]

Abraham Lincoln dismissed North's fears. When North was about to leave the Lincoln house, the president-elect put his arm about his shoulders in the confidential manner he reserved for friends, and said, "Mr. North, I will tell you a secret. The Missis and I are going up on the same train with you, to meet Hannibal Hamlin by appointment in Chicago. I have kept the fact from the public so that we will not be overrun by crowds, but I tell you because I know you would like to meet Mr. Hamlin, and think you should stop off in Chicago to do so." [28]

The stopover in Chicago meant the painful stage ride up the river for North, because he would miss the boat; but he quickly consented, and joined the Lincolns and their party on the train to Chicago. On the train were Judge and Mrs. Lyman Trumbull and several "other notables." The first day in Chicago Lincoln and Hamlin were closeted in secret council, and North did not see them until the next evening at supper, when Chairman Judd of Illinois' Republican Committee invited North at Lincoln's suggestion to "tea." North reported, "There was a pleasant gathering there, among whom were Mr. and Mrs. Lincoln, Mr. Hamlin, Mr. and Mrs. Trumbull, Mr. Schenck of Ohio, Mr. Piatt and

---

ROBERT CUMMING SCHENCK (1809–90) Ohio lawyer and diplomat. Strongly antislavery, he was an early supporter of Lincoln for the presidency. Lincoln commissioned

Lady, Mr. and Mrs. Arnold, [Governor Wood,] and many others. When
Mr. Judd gave me an introduction to Mr. Hamlin, he received me with
much cordiality." [29]

"I have known Mr. North well for a number of years," said Hamlin,
reflecting upon North's abolition work in his state. Hamlin urged North
to come the next day to his hotel. "He seemed to appreciate the fact that
our state is largely people from Maine," wrote North, "and that hundreds of our men are his old personal friends." Hamlin promised to do
what he could for North and the North Star State.

If Lincoln had been noncommittal about Ramsey's becoming Secretary of the Interior, despite the "appropriateness" of the appointment,
it was because he wanted to give the place to an old friend, Caleb Smith,
who had helped his nomination in a crisis and who had the support of
Lincoln's manager, David Davis, and others. North learned at the Judd
supper that cabinet posts would be given Indiana, possibly Pennsylvania, and that there would be a post for Bates of Missouri. Hamlin
enlarged indiscreetly upon these appointments at his hotel and North
reported all to Ramsey, adding a word for the governor's lady: "Tell
Mrs. Ramsey that Mrs. Lincoln came out with jewelry last evening,
showing good taste; and that she appeared remarkably well." [30]

Lincoln and Hamlin would support North for the superintendency,
he believed. "Yet much depends upon our [Minnesota] Congressional
Delegation. And two of them I am confident are against me. Yet to balance that influence I have the Governor and nearly all the State Officers on my side." [31]

The problem now was to get to Washington for the inauguration.
Lincoln had no idea what the expense of the trip would mean to North
when he extended the invitation. North sacrificed some of his railroad
bonds, then selling at thirty cents, to buy new clothes. Although he
would never have thought of it in those terms, the Indian Superintendency was a gamble. If he got the job at three thousand a year, his

---

him general and in 1862 gave him charge of the radical army reconstruction in Balti-
more. Late in 1863 he entered Congress as a radical. While he was minister to Great
Britain, his name was used to sell shares in Utah's Emma Silver Mine to his discredit.
He was an authority on draw poker.

DONN PIATT (1819–91) Ohio judge and journalist, friend of Schenck, celebrated for
his invective and humor. Lincoln commissioned him and he became Schenck's chief
of staff, causing consternation by recruiting slaves for a colored brigade. After the war,
he was correspondent for the Cincinnati *Commercial* and editor of the *Capital*. He wrote
an essay about Lincoln.

family would eat that winter and he could even provide a clerkship for young George Loomis. But if he did not get the appointment, his family might well go hungry. When he returned to Minnesota, North found he had formidable rivals, including C. C. Washburn; whose brother in Galena, Elihu B. Washburne, North wrote reminding him what North had done for him in the recent campaign and suggesting that he reason with his brother. North had letters of recommendation from the governor and the state officials, the Episcopal bishop and all the missionaries, from Lovejoy, Fell, and Judd, and many more in Minnesota and Illinois. In New York North got the unqualified endorsement of every leader of the missionary and reform movements; only Horace Greeley would "not meddle with it." [32]

North waited in New York until Lincoln had departed for Washington and then followed on the train with Hamlin. In Washington North called on his old friends Chase, Sumner, Wilson, Burlingame, and Jay and received their letters of recommendation. Washington was overflowing with visitors and he could not get a private room. He was also running out of money, so time was of the essence. "Things are in a

---

ISRAEL WASHBURN (1813–83), ELIHU BENJAMIN WASHBURNE (1816–87), CADWALLADER COLDEN WASHBURN (1818–82), and WILLIAM DREW WASHBURN (1831–1912) Governor Israel W. of Maine may have suggested the name "Republican" for the party. Elihu, who added an "e" to his name, had seen seven years' service in Congress when he advised his friend Lincoln in Chicago. He continued in Congress as a radical in reconstruction and promoted the interest of his fellow townsman Grant. Cadwallader, from Wisconsin, joined his Maine and Illinois brothers in Congress. Lincoln commissioned him a general. He became governor of Wisconsin and owner of water rights at the Falls of St. Anthony, where his brother William became secretary of his Minneapolis Mill Company. William arrived in Minnesota in 1857 as a lawyer and was made surveyor-general of Minnesota by Lincoln. He later founded the milling company, W. D. Washburn & Company, the M. St. P. & S. S. M. Railway Company, and the Pillsbury-Washburn Flour Mills Company before being elected to the United States Senate.

OWEN LOVEJOY (1811–64) Rededicated to anti-slavery beside the body of his martyred abolitionist brother Elijah Parish Lovejoy, for seventeen years he led the state anti-slavery movement from his position as pastor in Princeton, Illinois. He was the earliest and most constant supporter of Lincoln both in Illinois politics and in Congress, where — first among radicals — he held many to Lincoln's policies. Lincoln called him "my most generous friend."

HENRY WILSON (1812–75) Historian, senator from Massachusetts, and vice president. Like Burlingame, he was challenged by Sumner's assailant. As chairman of military affairs, he was foremost in arming the nation and in urging Lincoln to proclaim freedom for the slaves.

ANSON BURLINGAME (1820–70) In Congress he revenged the assault on his colleague from Massachusetts, Sumner, by holding the assailant up to ridicule. When he was defeated in 1860, he was appointed Lincoln's minister to Peking, where he began a brilliant diplomatic career.

whirl," he wrote, "and I must grind out something in a week." The day before the inauguration, Ann wrote that if he did not get the appointment, she did not know what would become of them; they would face poverty.

North attended the inauguration in his new clothes and was relieved when Lincoln did not desert the radicals but put the responsibility for disunion on the shoulders of southern leaders. He was less happy with the disposition to wait and watch what the South might do. North still thought that his appointment would come through within hours, little realizing that there would be delay in private as well as public affairs. Inauguration day was a happy one for him and the small group listening to Lincoln. The weather cleared as Lincoln stood on the crude scaffolding to deliver his address, the clouds parted, and a star shone in daytime above his head; this common though often unnoticed apparition was given mystical significance. On March 7, North reported that he had called at the White House and seen Lincoln again. The president was courteous, but said the papers all so impressive with the names of the great Republicans would have to come to him through channels. North took his file to the Department of the Interior and waited.

In the meantime he had several meetings with members of the Minnesota delegation and it was quite clear they did not want him as Indian Superintendent. They had nothing against him and would like to see him well provided for, but not in *that* office. They were not about to cut themselves off from lucrative patronage and perhaps graft by allowing the appointment of a man of North's principles if they could help it. When they learned of the recommendations he had secured, of the personal assurances of Lincoln and Hamlin, the Minnesota delegation was troubled. They tried to bargain with him. If North would forget about the Indian Superintendency, they would all support him for any other office he wanted. If he insisted upon applying for the job, they would oppose him, which might mean defeat. "Wilkinson and his friends have become somewhat concerned and are now trying to buy me off with another office. I tell them that if they will make the thing secure before I let go this [application], that I will be satisfied with something else as good or a little better." [33]

It soon became clear that the Minnesotans in Congress would like to see North made governor of a distant territory where his criticism and competition for political office would be removed from Minnesota. "They are all three, Wilkinson, Aldrich, and Windom, going to see the President tonight and their first object is to get me provided for." [34] At the White House the Republican delegation found they had less influence than North did. They returned bitter, complaining that North had not told Lincoln that he had withdrawn his application for the Indian Superintendency. Lincoln had assured the Minnesota men that North was still in the running for the important post. The whole delegation now united against North as one man. "Our delegation are *all* against me. If I fail I am humbled, if I win it is a triumph." North's friends tried to see the busy president, but not even Trumbull could see Lincoln on North's behalf. North watched the appointments Lincoln sent to the Senate for confirmation, and his name never appeared. Toward the end of the month he was out of money and out of spirits. "I suppose that all is lost and I am defeated. I had fairly whipped the delegation and all my opponents, and had the promise of the Secretary of the Interior that he would send my name to the President for the appointment I asked. It was also brought up in the Cabinet meeting, and agreed on by the President and the Cabinet." [35]

The trouble had come from Wisconsin, where the men Lincoln wanted to appoint were also opposed by the Wisconsin delegation. Lincoln knew that he would need the support of Congress and he had no recourse but to put aside his personal preferences and follow the recommendations of the state delegations. He made this a general rule, but when he applied it to Minnesota, he found that North could not be appointed. He would have to find something else for his radical friend. Lincoln wrote Secretary of the Interior Caleb B. Smith, "Please make out and send blank appointments for all Indian places, to serve in Wisconsin, in favor of the persons unitedly recommended by the Wisconsin Congressional delegation. And in like manner, all in Minnesota, in favor of the persons unitedly recommended by the Minnesota Republican delegation in Congress." [36]

WILLIAM WINDOM (1827–91) Arrived in Minnesota, 1855, elected to Congress, 1858–69, as a radical. As head of Indian Affairs, he differed with Lincoln on the necessity of hanging all the captured Sioux after the 1862 war. Contended for the presidential nomination, 1880; twice Secretary of the Treasury. When Minnesota failed to re-elect him senator in 1883, he turned his back on the West and became essentially an eastern conservative.

"So my case is in defeat even after I had gained a victory," wrote North.[37]

North's strongest advocate was Lincoln. On the same day that Lincoln closed the door on North's appointment as Superintendent of Indian Affairs, he had North in mind as governor of "Dacota" or for some other job. Then the friends of Nathaniel G. Wilson urged his appointment to Dakota, and Lincoln considered both North and Wilson until his Illinois friends insisted that he appoint William Jayne. Lincoln then wrote North's name on a memorandum concerning Nevada, along with that of Rufus King of Wisconsin, as governor. Secretary Seward insisted that Lincoln do something for General James W. Nye, who had accompanied Seward on his campaign through the West. Bates of Missouri insisted that Lincoln find a place for an unsuccessful newspaperman of his state by the name of Orion Clemens. With Nye governor and Clemens secretary, the position of surveyor-general of Nevada was open; Lincoln wrote in after that position the name of the radical friend he had no intention of dropping, J. W. North.

This juggling of men and jobs is clearly indicated in Lincoln's memoranda [38] — but North never knew how hard pressed Lincoln had been to find something for him. He mailed the letter announcing his defeat on March 23 and started to walk home from the post office to his cheerless room, when he met a man who congratulated him upon his appointment. "What appointment?" asked North. "Why, it was sent to the Senate today by the President — you are to be Surveyor-General of Nevada."

"I could hardly believe it," said North. He hastened to the capitol to see if it was true. He went to the office of his old friend Rice, the only Democrat now in office from Minnesota. Senator Rice put out his hand and said, "*General* North, congratulations!" Rice then suggested that there was not an office in the gift of the president that afforded a better opportunity to make a fortune in a shorter time. Although North had many misgivings about accepting so distant a position, his relief was great just then at receiving anything, so he hugged his bad bargain

RUFUS KING (1814–76) Grandson of the famous Federalist. Editor with Thurlow Weed of Albany (N.Y.) *Evening Journal*; later editor of Milwaukee (Wisc.) *Sentinel*. Lincoln appointed him minister to the Papal States, but when war came commissioned him (as a West Pointer) general; led the Iron Brigade. After the war, while minister to Rome, he took in John H. Surratt who fled there after Lincoln's assassination.

tightly. "It is in the region of the Washoe Mines, and is filling up faster than any spot on Earth. The salary is $3,000 a year and office, rent, fuel, clerk hire, etc. I shall be confirmed by the Senate on Monday."

He had yet to learn what terrible trouble he would have over each of the items mentioned — salary, office rent, fuel, hire for a clerk, and the *et ceteras.*

The *et ceteras* most of all.

GENERAL NORTH

B ARE maintenance of the nation was not what the Chicago platform committed Lincoln to, but rather the development of the West. "Upon the plainest grounds of good faith, one so elected is not at liberty to shift his position." [1] These words were struck from the inaugural address, but not from the mind of Lincoln. Two days before his inauguration, Congress organized the Territory of Nevada, placing the keystone in the arch of the West between the amorphous Utah Territory and California.

Nevada Territory looked all right on the map, but it was all wrong on the ground. Now out from under the uneasy jurisdiction of Utah Territory, the lawless men of Nevada reverted to primitive force, each man a law unto himself with jurisdiction limited by the trajectory of his bullet. David S. Terry and other secessionists who had been flushed out of California reigned briefly in Nevada under rebel banners. Lincoln must establish the rule of law.

None was better qualified to bring Nevada into the Union as a loyal state than the man who had helped create a Republican Minnesota in ten years. In Nevada he would have three. The most important man in the territory would not be the genial governor, but the man with authority to settle disputed boundaries and embattled claims: General North. The act of organization provided that the eastern part of California would be added to Nevada if California agreed. Thus the ingenious Congress hoped to avoid the cost of surveying along the high crest of the Sierra by moving Nevada's border westward to more accessible terrain. California refused to give away an inch of its eastern slope, citing the prohibition found in the state constitution. The real reason was the view from the crest of the Sierra.

Californians by the thousands had stood on these heights and seen in the near distance the richest mountain in the world rising to a bare pinnacle from the alkali desert of the Carson sink. The wealth of that mountain might extend beyond its shadow, and the rising sun cast that shadow across the disputed border. To withdraw from the present border would mean at least giving away the timber of the eastern slope so necessary to the mines of the Comstock, to say nothing of the importance of the neighborhood of the wealthy Washoe mines.

Californians had quickly filed claims upon the slope of the rich mountain; a lawless lot, they were already contesting the claims of the Mormon pioneers. General North could bring order out of chaos with his land surveys and rally Republicans to the radical cause, but he was ill fitted to deal with the miners. That was a job for Governor James Warren Nye, who could riptail and snort with the miners as he had with the rough-and-tumble in New York politics. The governor could be persuasive and firm, and then, on the verge of contention, would call for a round of drinks with a practiced voice; by the time he sobered up, dissension would be long forgotten. His greatest ability has made more than one politician famous: the faculty of doing nothing at all and doing it well. If one did nothing, one made no enemies. Governor Nye would be one of the best-loved men in the country. By waiting for the course of events to shape every decision, he could always appear to yield to the inevitable. In his campaign in the West with Seward in the fall of 1860, he had earned his keep for the next four years. His wit and waff were legend among overly serious Republicans. When Seward sat on his hat, Nye had exclaimed, "I could have told you it wouldn't fit before you tried it on!"

Three more impecunious men never set off for the far west than Nye, North, and Clemens. Orion Clemens had not a cent, but he had the next best thing, a brother on the riverboats, who in a moment of indiscretion had joined the secessionists in Missouri. Orion Clemens solved both the financial and the family problem by offering Samuel Clemens the job of secretary to the Secretary if he would finance the journey overland.[2] Meanwhile Nye scouted around to find free transportation overland for himself and General North. Secretary of War Cameron promised a military escort west — until it became obvious that the great need was for soldiers to come east, not go west. Though both North and Clemens had tried to get advances on their salaries to pay their way, North had to borrow from a Syracuse friend and Clemens had to undertake the journey described in *Roughing It*. Nye arranged to go by sea with North, but he could not get away from his friends in the New York police department who were intent upon celebrating the great honor that had come to their commissioner. As each sailing date approached, the send-offs began, and by the time Governor Nye was decently sober, the ship had sailed. It took him weeks to develop sea legs adequate to the walk up the gangplank. Finally North gave up and left without him, and Nye's friends carried him aboard the next ship, forgetting only his baggage.

On March 28, North wrote that his nomination as surveyor-general of Nevada Territory had been confirmed by the Senate and that he hoped to receive his commission the next day; he was mistaken. Commissioner James M. Edmunds of the Land Office informed him that *if* he accepted the position to which the Senate had confirmed him it must be with the understanding that Congress had appropriated no money for his salary.[3] With a war at hand it might never do so. Nor would the salary that might be appropriated begin to accumulate until North arrived in Carson City, the place selected for his office by the commissioner on the advice of one who had been there "in person," J. C. Birdseye — the man who paid North's way west.[4]

From the very start, complete lack of understanding developed between North and Edmunds. On April 13, the commissioner wrote North, "Should you elect to enter upon the discharge of your duties as Surveyor-General of Nevada with the understanding that you must depend upon the future action of Congress to provide for the payment of your salary . . . signify your choice to this office."[5] This was a surprise to North, who had visited the land office and made arrangements to receive his instructions and outfit. He had not, however, taken account of the red tape: he had not formally accepted the job, in writing, and Edmunds, the typical administrator, held up the preparation of instructions until North did so. Edmunds thought a man a fool to "elect" to be surveyor-general of a distant territory on such terms and he treated North with ill-disguised contempt. Instructions for North were submitted to Secretary of the Interior for approval on April 29, but Caleb Smith did not get around to approving them until May 9, two days after North completed arrangements for himself and his sister Clarissa to sail (the rest of the family would stay in De Witt until North could afford to send for them) — and again Edmunds wrote to North to "signify his choice."

By this time North was beginning to wonder if going to Nevada was not a mistake. The condescending orders from Edmunds hurt his pride. When North and Nye missed the boat on May 11, and again on May 21, Edmunds lost patience. North forgot his plans to sail with Nye and promised Edmunds to leave "with all possible promptness"; [6] he and his sister sailed on the *North Star* at the end of May, 1861.[7] The delay had done nothing to calm the stormy Atlantic — both suffered the agonies of sea travel — and it made the passage through southern waters dangerous. Off Cuba they sighted a ship which all feared might be a rebel raider, but they reached Aspinwall safely. Cuba's terra firma was welcome until North and Clarissa discovered that they had descended into a Hades where wine flowed and people sang all the night. With some relief they caught the train to Panama, which dragged from one banana plantation to the next until all the passengers reached the Pacific shore in happy confusion. At Panama the steamer *Sonora* gave some promise of a return to puritanical life, though they still had ahead of them a sea voyage as long as the passage from New York to London. Aboard the *Sonora*, North wrote, "We have already seen several schools of small whales from fifteen to thirty feet long — spouting and rising partially out of the water, as you have seen them in pictures. The vessel has a gentle undulating motion; nothing like the roll and pitch we had on the Atlantic." [8]

North spent his time learning something about California from books and concluded that the most striking characteristic of the Californian was his love of women. The Californians aboard spent their time paying attention to what he called "a certain class of women" and to indiscreet young girls with simple and unsuspecting mothers. But the wild California boys settled down on Sunday to give good music for the services conducted by North, who read a sermon from a volume of Dr. Edwin Hubbell Chapin's discourses just published,[9] selected for the edification of the "guitar-playing wild girls" to whom even the captain took exception. By the time they had reached Acapulco, North was sorry that he had not come "over the plains" by stagecoach — rather thoughtless of his sister, whose boils continued "prosperous as usual."

The ship arrived in Acapulco at one thirty in the afternoon and lay at anchor while Clarissa, North, and five hundred other passengers went ashore. Water taxis did a thriving business, but the boatboys were unfriendly. Trouble was started by John C. Birdseye, North's friend from Syracuse and Lincoln's collector for the port of San Francisco. On a trip to shore he had a dispute with a boatboy, who followed him, hit him over the head knocking off his gold spectacles, and drew a knife. When the time came for all passengers to return to the ship, the boatboys raised their prices from the usual quarter to a dollar. Several ladies who had ventured ashore unattended found themselves adrift halfway between shore and ship with a rowers' strike on their hands. The women expressed Yankee indignation at the forced fare increase, and the boatboys drew knives more convincing if not sharper than the women's tongues. The extra fare was paid and the ladies were rowed to the *Sonora* in frightened silence. Boatboys in another skiff demanded more pay before they would draw up to the side of the ship and Captain Dall argued that two bits had always been the accepted fare. One of the boys hit him over the head with an oar and the captain grappled with his near-naked assailant. Knives did not settle the argument in this boat, but Captain Dall was wounded in the scuffle. Passengers on deck of the *Sonora* had a good view of the fracas. One of them, something of a marksman, fired into the crowded boat tossing on the swells and hit one of the boatboys, who fell into the water. None knew if he was killed or not, but the shot persuaded the boatboys to bring the passengers alongside. When all the excitement was over, it was discovered that four men were still ashore. The *Sonora* fired her cannon, the men returned to the ship, and all steamed away toward the Golden Gate, arriving in port at ten o'clock on the night of June 13, 1861, eight days out of Acapulco.[10]

North and Clara registered at the American Exchange Hotel and wandered through the San Francisco markets to behold wonders of substitute and makeshift. North noted that a thousand barrels of murres' eggs from the Farallon Islands were consumed every year, and described these seagull eggs as blue and larger than a turkey's. The course about town in search of a sewing machine for Clarissa brought North face to face with General James Shields, who was delighted to see him.

General Shields was still full of blarney and very uncomfortable in his political position in California, having started off supporting the secessionists, and then being obliged to "fetch around in favor of the Union." [11] Shields blamed men like the Reverend Thomas Starr King for the war. Shields wrote, "The whole preacher world here with few exceptions is for guerre à la mort." [12] North got Dr. Grover to take him to see Starr King.[13] They talked of friends they had in common and of reformers in New England, thus beginning a friendship which would last until King's death. North called on all the ministers and leaders of the Union sympathizers in San Francisco; Starr King went with him as far as Sacramento, where North attended a Republican convention before moving on to Nevada. Then, in a light Concord covered wagon with a good span of horses to carry them in style over the Sierra Nevada, North and his sister set out.

They followed the course of the south fork of the American River, keeping to the sides of the mountains on a road a thousand or two feet above the water. From Strawberry they ascended six or eight miles to the Sierra summit and looked down on Lake Bigler, named for a California governor who was then in such disgrace that the lake would be renamed Tahoe. There they stopped at a house kept by "Mr. Mac" who provided all the comforts of an eastern hotel — a good carpet, sofa, and chairs, and an "elegant" piano. In the morning they traveled eight miles to the next summit and looked down upon Nevada.

I could not call it "the lovely Carson valley" as some have done, for it seemed composed of marshland contrasting with surrounding sterility and barrenness. The road down the mountain is really a fine one, of easy grade, but the most crooked zig-zag line, down the steepest mountainside you can imagine. It was really frightful to look down from one bend of the road to another, and then to another, until we were almost discouraged in looking for the bottom.[14]

North and Clarissa were fortunate in having taken a private wagon. One woman who took the stage with her Irish servant had cramps on the descent and the maid had to be held in the stage by force. But all

---

THOMAS STARR KING (1824–64) Unitarian minister called by the California legislature "the man whose matchless oratory saved California to the Union." After his father, the Reverend Thomas Farmington King, died, Starr King, then sixteen, supported the family and educated himself. After a time as preacher in his father's Universalist church, he came under the influence of Theodore Parker and became minister of Hollis Street Unitarian Church in Boston. He was prevailed upon by Henry Bellows to accept a call to the San Francisco Unitarian church, where, through the influence of parishioners, he became wealthy from mine stocks. He died at forty. His farewell to the East was a volume on the White Mountains published in 1860.

arrived safely at the Penrod House in Carson City, where North found comfortable but close quarters for fourteen dollars a week. Money was his first thought in Nevada. Money in San Francisco was put out at two and a half per cent a month and North said he could not think of running into debt at that rate. "I think there are fine chances for making money here," he added, "I have written T. B. Fitch and through him to T. T. Davis and Captain Myers to come out at once. I think that George had better come out at once." North, the carpetbagger, was at work again — the only governmental official in Nevada.

Nye found landing in San Francisco as convivial as departure from New York. He had friends, friends, everywhere, all with a drop to drink. North's clerks set off over the mountains, and Nye celebrated their departure, explaining that he must wait for the baggage left behind on the docks of New York. North was already established (and drawing salary) by the end of June when John F. Kidder and Butler Ives arrived to assist him. A committee from Carson City called on North to invite him to a Fourth of July celebration. There, he was paid the honor due the first territorial official to arrive in Nevada. In San Francisco, Nye and his friends celebrated the arrival of his impedimenta, but not to the impairment of his oratory. He disclosed why Lincoln had sent him to Nevada: to create a free state.

Nye celebrated his departure from San Francisco and his arrival at Sacramento; he was given a send-off from Sacramento that would carry him happily over the Sierra Nevada, oblivious of all danger, to the hilarious celebration of his arrival in Carson City. On July 11, the town went out to meet him, a large company of horsemen, office seekers, contractors, speculators, and curious miners — all armed to the teeth with corkscrews. No monarch was ever welcomed home from exile with more feeling than Governor Nye was welcomed to his shanty capital. Among those horsemen, and among those who could not afford a horse, were heirs to princely fortunes; men who would reign as kings of the Comstock; men destined to wealth that would buy and sell crowns, start revolutions, and present their wives to Victoria herself. Nye would be ruler of princes with veins of silver.

Only North stayed home. Nye came to him with a sobering question: how were they to live on salaries that had looked so large in Washington but diminished to insignificance in the shadow of the limitless treasure of Sun Mountain? A house that would cost them a thousand in Syracuse would cost three thousand here. Interest rates were double in Carson what they were in San Francisco. Freight over the mountains added thirty cents a pound to the cost of goods in California. Nye solved his immediate problem by moving into the office with North.

"I have not yet decided to engage in outside business," wrote North in self-deception, "but I am making diligent inquiry." [15] Already he had an opportunity to take an interest in a lumbering venture, in a quartz mill, and in a water-power project to run the stamping mill. North and Nye made cross-country junkets to inspect opportunities for becoming wealthy. In the office they received old friends from New York, each with a plan, a project, a mine, or a mill to promote.

North's surveyors, Kidder and Ives, went to work as soon as they arrived. They were on hand when one of the legendary bad men of the territory came to his bad end. North wrote,

The gamblers and murderers are a little cross about the establishment of law, but they will soon find their place and keep it. One of the worst desperados and murderers in the Territory was shot the other day to the great joy of all the people. His name was Sam Brown. He was here in Carson City some ten days after we arrived here, though I did not see him to know him. Last Friday morning he was at the Hotel where I board, but on that day he started to leave the Territory for fear that when the Governor came he would be arrested. On that day he boasted that he was just thirty years' old, and had killed eleven men, which was true. He went from here to a stage house a little South of Genoa, [a hotel] kept by Mr. Van Syckle, and there he drew his pistol and chased Van Syckle through the house to shoot him. The man escaped him and [Sam Brown] went out and got on his horse to leave. Van Syckle and a few other men armed themselves with guns and pursued him about ten miles South to Olds Hotel (about twenty miles from here) where Mr. Kidder and Mr. Ives were stopping overnight. There Van Syckle shot him before [Sam Brown] got off his horse. It was about eleven o'clock at night and as Van Syckle discharged both barrels of his shotgun loaded with pistol balls full in his breast, they say Brown gave a most unearthly yell, turned his horse and rode across the street and fell dead. The whole people in California as well as in Nevada, are rejoicing in his death as they would in the destruction of a wild beast, only more so, as he was more dangerous. [16]

Kidder and Ives had set off, as soon as Clarissa had sewn their tents, to find the terminus of the second degree standard parallel run from California, which was to be the starting point for all surveys of Nevada

Territory. North had nothing to do while they collected data but scout the country with Governor Nye and his friends. Coldwell of St. Paul took North to Washoe valley to find a site for a quartz mill, and North decided to take an interest in the project, if he could do so without money. It was here in Washoe valley that he would build in time the Minnesota Mill, one of the finest in Nevada. Here North would found the thriving Washoe City. A branch of the Carson River had a fall of three hundred and twenty feet in four miles in this valley, and North's experienced eye could see the commercial possibilities of the site.

There are nine very reliable men who have formed a joint stock company calling the stock $500,000 — they have already expended about five thousand. They wish me to be a member of their company and have this morning offered me a chance to come in. I informed them, to start with, that I could not pay money. They therefore offered to let me have one-twentieth part of the stock, which shall be receipted as paid up as far as they have gone, and for the future, I am not to be called on for money but my share shall be paid by my law services.[17]

North was inclined to accept. He was too much a carpetbagger to see any impropriety in engaging in law and speculation while he was surveyor-general. Indeed, he would have been a man out of his time if he had discerned any conflict of interest. Senator Rice had hailed his appointment as a chance to get rich, Governor Nye urged him to practice law; in fact, he could not live in Nevada on his salary alone. On the other hand, North was no fool. He knew the "nine very reliable men" wanted his name on the board because he *was* surveyor-general.

"It is becoming understood that I am more confided in than any one else, by the Governor, and my influence at [the gubernatorial] court is being sought for, even by some whom the governor brought with him from New York." North enjoyed this prestige and added a hundred-and-twenty-five-dollar desk to his office furniture, partly to accommodate the governor. Nye attended to territorial business in the land office and hastened North's plans for a more commodious law office. "He advises me by all means to open a Law Office at once," wrote North, "and I am going to do so." [18]

North had his own house built in Carson City by July 22; Clarissa took in boarders (the chief clerk John F. Kidder and draughtsman Julius E. Garrett) and was expecting Dr. Craig. Samuel Clemens would soon join surveyors Kidder and Ives in their attic room. Carson City

141

was crowded, despite the building boom, and the capital was growing in loyalty as well as in numbers. There were now seven liberty poles, one of them a hundred and sixty feet high surmounted by a golden ball and eagle. Secessionist flags had disappeared like the outlaws, at the coming of the territorial officials and at the prospect of territorial law. One midnight, William Morris Stewart, later to become senator and the chief lawyer for the mines, routed North out of bed to use his influence with Governor Nye to call an election. A legislature was needed to pass a mining law which hopefully would settle conflicting mining claims on the side of Sun Mountain.

After a month in Nevada Territory, North had put a party of surveyors in the field, planned to develop a quartz mill, paced out the townsite of Washoe City, built a house, gained two prospective law cases, and become the right bower to King Nye. Five days later, admitted to the Nevada bar and sharing an office with the governor, North was for the moment the most important lawyer in Nevada. His break with the genial governor was sure to come, but right now he not only exerted influence upon Nye, but wielded power in his own right. He was final arbiter in land disputes, he could grant or deny the right to cut the timber upon which the mines' development depended, he could point out the best millsites for crushing ore; only the mining claims themselves were as yet outside his jurisdiction. To Nye, North was a convenience and at times a necessity — but just another subordinate officer. Nye found North too serious and hardworking, though a good companion for sober moments and an appreciative audience for his wit. But North was touchy and not diplomatic.

Late in July, Nye urged North to join a party of the governor's friends on a visit to the Indians of the Walker Lake, Truckee, and Pyramid Lake reservations. Four hundred Piutes received government gifts, with North supplying all the answers to the Indians' questions and making Indian policy for the governor. With his knowledge of

---

WILLIAM MORRIS STEWART (1827–1909) Left Yale for the goldfields in 1850, where he struck it rich. Studied law in Nevada City, California, wrote the first quartz-mining code, and was elected attorney-general of California. His law partner and father-in-law was ex-governor Henry S. Foote of Mississippi. Stewart made millions in fees on the Comstock and was president of the Sutro Tunnel Company. He was senator from Nevada from its admission to 1875, posing as a radical, and head of the silver lobby in the Senate (1887 to 1905). He published a silver newspaper in Washington and supported Bryan, then McKinley in 1900. He is credited with writing the Fifteenth Amendment, but opposed the Lodge Force Bill in 1891.

Minnesota councils and his study of Indian affairs in preparation for the superintendency he did not get, North was well prepared to advise Governor Nye in the conduct of his ex-officio duties as Indian administrator.

At Fort Churchill, the officers made as elaborate preparations to receive the governor as the means of their desert post would allow. In the confused introductions, the governor neglected to present North; the desert crossing had been long and dry, and the governor's mind was no doubt on the cup that cheers so constantly at lonely military outposts. Knowing that North would not accept this hospitality, Nye left North to his own devices while he refreshed himself — becoming so refreshed as to forget all about North. Taking their cue from the governor, the officers ignored North completely. It is also possible that Wasson, the Indian agent at the post, had told the officers about the time North had threatened to report Wasson for drinking too much brandy. Whatever the reason, North was provided with neither food nor bed. Deeply hurt, his pride offended, North had a long "plain talk" with the governor in the morning as the carriages left the fort. Nye, astounded that North had been so neglected, expressed indignation at the officers' discourtesy. "Not at all," North told him, "*you* were at fault." North had been Nye's guest, not the officers'; Nye should have made sure that the surveyor-general was looked after.

The governor bore many burdens that day, not merely the weight of a hangover and North's plain talk, but the incompetence of an officer-guide who took them twenty-eight miles astray in the burning sun. When they approached Pyramid Lake, one of the women, wanting, in opposition to the other women of the party, to be the first white female to reach its shores, insisted upon North's accompanying her by moonlight. They were lost for hours before they stumbled upon the camp.

The governor was less cordial to North after the trip, but officially they united to achieve Lincoln's goal of a new free state of Nevada. On August 12, they addressed the Union Club, consisting of Copperheads and pro-slavery men, at the New Orleans theater. "On the slavery question," said North, "they are at least a quarter of a century behind the age. I thought they needed the truth, and gave it to them, charging upon slavery the war and all our National troubles." [19] When North concluded, Nye spoke against secession and carried the day against the Copperheads, who had been jubilant over the news of Bull Run. Privately, North felt a new independence now that he was estranged from the governor. He could manage his public and private concerns without regard for the governor's opinion; he had only to contend with Edmunds'.

His instructions from Commissioner Edmunds were to run the Mount Diablo line from California into Nevada, and to run the base, principal meridian, and standard parallel lines. He was to survey the valleys of the Walker, Carson, and Truckee rivers; mark out the township lines; and, in areas of actual settlement, subdivide the townships. He collected a vast amount of information about the old Mormon land claims, talked with people who claimed vast grazing areas against the law and with small farmers struggling on irrigated lands adjacent to the strange rivers that lost themselves in desert dust. At the end of six weeks, North had spent most of the appropriation and was ready to go beyond his instructions and survey mining lands, new towns, and timberlands in order to put a stop to unauthorized cutting; break up the vast areas illegally held under Mormon grants; and establish one-hundred-sixty-acre homesteads in the valleys. Faced with this supererogation, Edmunds quietly vetoed every suggestion from his surveyor-general. North had only ten thousand dollars to spend on surveys, and had spent a third of it before Edmunds knew he was in Nevada. Why had North contracted at twenty dollars a mile when surveys in Oregon cost only eight? Why had North not invited bids from California surveyors? The implication in Edmunds' letters was that Butler Ives had imposed on North; but North replied that Ives had been approved by the General Land Office while he was in Washington, and that he had not invited bids from Californians because neither he nor Edmunds had thought of it. Moreover, a million dollars had been wasted in California in paying incompetent surveyors. North expressed confidence in Ives, his friend from Syracuse, and pointed out that two per cent of survey costs had been reserved for checking Ives's surveys according to regulation. Edmunds replied that this would never do, that regardless of what regulations might say, he regarded the two per cent as graft. Edmunds objected to the office costs in Nevada, pointing to lower costs on the Pacific Coast. North explained that between the Pacific and Nevada there was a range of mountains over which every necessity had to be freighted. Nye had just paid twelve cents a pound to get his office furnishings over the Sierra.[20] The governor also wrote Edmunds, but the commissioner was not convinced.[21] North cited regulations for every expenditure by rule and section, but Edmunds brushed aside all the regulations, saying that however proper they might be in peace, this was war.

It was a difficult job to remain a great man in Nevada with Commissioner Edmunds constantly cutting him down to size from Washington. North's office was the center of government. Nevada people stopped to get the latest news from Washington. To keep abreast of administration policy and trends, North subscribed to newspapers and periodicals. Edmunds refused to allow such office expenses. He also demanded to know how, in the warm desert, North could burn seventeen cords of wood costing $167.[22] North explained about Washoe "zephyrs" that swept down from snowcapped mountains, the benumbed state of his draftsman's fingers, the makeshift construction of office walls, the necessity for both a stove and a fireplace, the consumption capacity of each, and the tinderlike quality of desert wood. Edmunds said that even though it was justified he would not allow the bill because it had not been submitted according to form. North replied that no wood dealer in Nevada would wait two or three months "according to form" and then accept payment in government drafts discounted five per cent in Nevada.[23] North was obliged to assign one of his clerks to the job of cutting wood — until he was deprived of the clerk's services by Edmunds.

Unfortunately, in an excess of zeal, North had called the commissioner's attention to the fact that all wood in Nevada was on government land, and that it was being pirated by lumbermen who supplied the posts and headers to the mines. He urged that timber lands be surveyed and the lumbering and woodcutting rights sold by the government. As long as the cutting was done on the public domain, lumbermen wastefully felled the largest trees, making no use of the branches; the cutters of firewood, on the other hand, used only the small branches, leaving the logs to rot. Edmunds used this report against North when the firewood bill came to his attention. "There is a feature in this transaction which has not escaped observation," wrote Edmunds. "Your communication dated October 9, 1861, shows that not an inch of timber can be had except what is public property — The timber thus afforded and obtained becomes the ground of charges against the government by one of its own officers." This memorandum [24] was too caustic to be copied into the commissioner's letterbook and appears only as his com-

145

ment on North's letter; but there is no doubt that North received it, because he replied to it.

North was not alone in being attacked for thriftlessness, but letters to other surveyors-general are models of brevity, whereas Edmunds' letters to North are exceptionally long, beautifully written explanations and discussions of land-office policy. These lengthy essays gave Edmunds opportunity to indulge his sarcasm; the care he took to justify his decisions suggests that he feared North would appeal to Lincoln, and that he wanted his own sweet reasonableness spread upon the record.

Perhaps Edmunds suspected that North was planning to get into the lumbering business himself. He soon would have a sawmill, financed by C. N. Felton and operated by young George Loomis. The distinction between carpetbaggers like North and the exploiters cutting on the public domain was that North would pursue his own interest, and use his office to promote his own interest, but only if it was in national interest. He would not stoop to theft from the public domain. The men then lumbering in Nevada had some show of title, however faulty. Everywhere settlers had cut trees from public lands to build cabins, barns, outhouses, and movables; this was considered a legitimate part of homesteading. In Nevada, the settlers did not much need wood for these purposes; they needed not rail fences but mine supports. When the mine posts and headers caved in, the miners were forced to adopt a system of square-set bracing of heavy timber like underground skyscrapers. The demand for heavy timber threatened quickly to denude the mountain sides. As early as the summer of 1861, North could see the damage to the public domain and warned that timber was being "rapidly removed and destroyed by parties claiming to hold possession of large amounts by virtue of grants under the old Mormon laws." [25]

Edmunds agreed that Mormon grants were invalid and that every tree felled under this pretense was stolen. The only valid claims in Nevada were mining claims. Informed of this, the lumbermen forgot about the Mormon grants and began staking out timberlands as mines.[26] Recommending that the timberlands be surveyed, North toured the forest in the company of honest capitalists ready to make claims on the public domain and buy the government lands. Instead of approving this timber survey, Edmunds sent North an old 1853 circular placing upon the surveyor-general the responsibility of stopping

146

logging on the public domain, which in turn would have meant stopping all deep mining in the Nevada Territory. North was forced to publish over his name a "notice to trespassers" invoking an 1831 law.[27] He wrote, "The notice to trespassers on the public lands, is being published as directed, but I confess myself at a loss to understand my duties in the premises." [28] Edmunds replied that he expected North to warn the lumbermen and to turn the thieves over to the attorney general for prosecution.[29] North suddenly became very unpopular, for there could be no mining without timber, and the only timber in Nevada was on the public domain.

It was soon clear that Edmunds was doing all he could to frustrate Lincoln's intentions in sending North and Nye to Nevada. North knew that he had no authority to survey the mineral lands, which were an utter chaos of overlapping claims. He did, however, have the authority to survey townships. Since the towns of Virginia City and Gold Hill overlay the mineral lands, he wanted to settle the mining claims by surveying these and other towns. Edmunds rejected the suggestion, contending that the mineral lands were the heritage of the whole nation, *including the rebellious South,* and that a "sectional" Congress could not deal with them.[30] Such a Copperhead view was incomprehensible to North and Nye, who could not regard themselves as custodians of rebel interests. It was not for this that Lincoln had sent his radical friends to Nevada Territory. He had sent them to Nevada to produce treasure from the mines to help finance the war against the rebels; he had sent them to assist in bringing the region into the Union as a free state. To do this, all the resources of the territory must be developed to attract not only transient miners, but a permanent loyal population.

Governor Nye, soon after landing in San Francisco, had addressed a ratification meeting of Republicans at the Music Hall on June 29 in which he declared Lincoln's purpose. "Hail California!" he began. He apostrophized San Francisco as a Magical City without an infancy, sprung full-grown. He went from "Hail California" to giving the secessionists Hail Columbia. He did not blame the South for the war: even the angels in heaven seceded when their leaders, like the southern congressmen, decided they would rather rule in hell than serve in heaven. The reason Lincoln had sent him west, he said, was to shape the destiny of the country by calling into being free states to redress the balance of Union.

I am going to climb, if I live, the summit of the Sierra Nevada and I would like to see on my journey the valleys and hill-tops vocal with songs of freedom. I am going across the mountains to make an earnest effort to add another State to the constellation, [to help create] a chain of liberty-loving States that shall stand with one foot on the Atlantic and the other on the Pacific, in glorious, loving brotherhood, until He, who stands with one foot on the sea and the other on the land, shall declare that nations shall be no more.[31]

North expressed the same view in less highflown language in the reform and religious press, urging settlers to come to Nevada. He pointed to the good farm land along the river bottoms. He wrote Edmunds to see if the pre-emption laws might be applied to Nevada. The answer was no. Still holding the territory in custody for the "whole" nation, Edmunds ruled that there could be no squatting in Nevada.[32] The best farming lands of the territory had been settled under Mormon laws which allowed the acquisition of all the land one could fence. North reported that now great stretches were held without fencing, however — held at gunpoint against the encroachment of small farmers. He urged Edmunds to establish a land office in Nevada to redistribute these lands as homesteads.[33]

North's objection to the Mormon holdings was a legal one, but Nye's was emotional. The governor gave some of Brigham Young's "destroying angels" twenty-four hours to get out of Nevada or be hanged. He visited Salt Lake City and told Young, "Brigham, I come to advise you as a friend that it isn't safe to send any of your angels into my Territory, for I have more devils in my jurisdiction than you have angels in yours, and if they come in contact there will be a hell of a row." [34]

North managed to survey 147,584 acres before his appropriations ran out, and asked for $100,000 for the next year. Edmunds reduced the appropriation in the budget to $10,000.[35] So poor a representation did Edmunds make in behalf of Nevada that Congress concluded there was not enough surveying needed to warrant continuing the office of surveyor-general; the Nevada duties were turned over to Surveyor-General Beale in California, leaving North stranded in Nevada with part of his salary still unpaid. Edmunds wrote on April 12, 1862, to tell North that his office had been consolidated with California's, giving a terminal date of July 15. The wisdom of opening a law office was now apparent. Had North not been admitted to the bar, after informing Edmunds of his intention to open a law office, he would have been cut off without fare home.

North wrote his old friend S. P. Chase, now Secretary of the Treasury,

My office of Surveyor-General of this Territory terminated . . . Though my salary was cut off just as I got my family into the Territory I have not troubled the President or any of my friends with complaints. Being accustomed to rely on my own energies, I have done so here, and with success. My law practice is now worth much more than my salary as Surveyor-General. I stand in no need of an office. But the late election of one of our Judges as Delegate to Congress creates a vacancy which I am desired to fill.[36]

His three-thousand-dollar salary had been so small by Nevada standards that he had been unable to indulge his usual benefactions. "I have been so economical that I have not yet given a dollar for the suffering soldiers," he confided to his father-in-law, "I am really ashamed of this; but I hope soon to be able to contribute without feeling the loss so much as I should now." [37]

North was about to develop the garden spot of Nevada, Washoe Valley. When Ann and the children arrived, they moved to Washoe City, where Clarissa had just opened, a few rods from the new North house, a twenty-by-thirty-foot schoolhouse that had cost a thousand dollars. "General" North was about to become "Judge" North, one of the most controversial figures in the history of Nevada.

J UDGESHIP of the First District was the temptation that, in the fall
of 1862, the lawyers of Virginia City started placing before North. To
a man, the Nevada bar said they wanted him. North was conscious of
the honor, but not unconscious of the salary — three thousand dollars.
He had found that he could not live on a federal salary in Nevada, and
as judge of the First District he would have no time to augment his
income. With every mine in Nevada in litigation, his would be the
busiest court in the United States.

The lawyers would not let North decline. They promised that the
legislature which they controlled would increase the salary to five
thousand dollars or more, and on November 11, 1862, Governor Nye
urged the legislature to raise it to five or six thousand.[1] North wrote
that the more he thought about the offer, the more he thought he could
do without the honor. "I can easily do five-thousand dollars' worth of
law business the next year without spending half my time away from
my family, at considerable additional expense. And then in the practice of Law, I am not cut off from outside speculations." [2] When North's
opinion was known, the lawyers in the legislature raised the salary to
six thousand dollars and even promised to raise it to ten thousand if
North would consent to become a judge.

The appointment would have to come from Washington, of course,
but the lawyers were certain that their united appeal in North's behalf
would influence Lincoln. North had no doubts as to his favorable consideration by Lincoln, he simply did not want to leave his garden city
for the gun-toting, knife-throwing, slambang salooning of Virginia City.

Today, Washoe City is a dematerialized ghost of a former ghost town, but during North's residence, it was the chief town of the Washoe Valley. The Gold Hill *News* wrote,

This Valley is the garden spot of [Nevada], literally so. Three towns stand within the space of as many miles in the western portion of the valley. Each town with its streets, and stores, saloons, and shops, and its droves of moon-eyed Celestials. In Washoe City is a large brick Court House, the finest and the most substantial in the Territory, a building showing the inhabitants of the country to possess an amount of public spirit not to be found in some of the more populous and wealthy counties. Fine farms and farm houses are everywhere met with, and one is seldom out of sight of the tall smoke-stacks of steam quartz and saw-mills or beyond the reach of clattering stamps of water mills. . . . The many long trains of teams engaged in hauling timber out of the valley and returning with ores for the mills make trade lively . . .[3]

While Virginia City thrilled to performances of such artists as Adah Isaacs Menken, a quadroon convert to Judaism, who rode in naked-looking pink tights across the stage in *Mazeppa*, the Norths entertained Thomas Starr King and read Darwin, Huxley, Spencer, Tyndall, and current books about the war. The sober lyceums and family gatherings of Washoe City were in distinct contrast to the masculine society, secessionist cliques, and hell-bent Hibernians of Virginia City. No wonder North preferred peace in his happy home to honor in the neighboring mining town.

That winter North was away from home more than he liked, attending meetings of the legislature which met in a makeshift building at the edge of Carson City. North's friend, the schoolteacher Miss H. K. Clapp of Ypsilanti, and Mrs. H. A. Ormsby were given the privilege of the floor by the legislature for having furnished the members with the uncommon luxury of chairs.[4] The gallery stood around in various conditions of sobriety, and bottles passed with the laws.

After such legislative victories as the enactment of mining laws for Nevada (mines had been until then incorporated in California), the legislators celebrated with such flow of language and liquor that no quorum could be formed the next day because of the mass hangover, the most conspicuous casualty being Governor Nye. On December 21, Dr. Charles L. Anderson, the scientist who had come from Minnesota to live with the Norths, wrote, "Last night I remained up until after midnight to see the Legislature adjourn. They were nearly all *foolishly* drunk. The Band was out to discourse music, and after adjourning they serenaded Governor Nye. He was *foolishly* drunk, I understand, and sung *Dixie* to the crowd." [5] Singlehandedly, the governor "captured" the rebel tune three years before Lincoln claimed it.

Even the legislature sobered up to hear Methodist Bishop Matthew Simpson, but there was no Sabbath in Nevada. "Stores and shops are open," reported Anderson. He agreed with North that Nevada was no place to raise children, that it was devoid of refinement, and he said he heard no good music except in the North home (music consisting of such selections as *The Old Sexton, We Gather Them In,* and Hood's *Unfortunate*). "About all the music I hear [in Carson City] comes from a negro saloon near my office. They have a guitar and poor John Brown is executed in all styles. Poor old man, the soul finds no rest there." [6]

When the sporting population got drunk in the capital, bonfires, anvils, processions, illuminations, and firecrackers were the order of the day and the disorder of the night. Still, Nevada had its quiet beauties, too. "I can look from my office to the summit of Washoe Mountains which overlook Mr. North's place. They are covered with snow. Mrs. North says she intends climbing to the snow some day." [7] Anderson had failed to reach the snowline, but Ann North would succeed before leaving Nevada.

Among the Minnesotans came George and Kate Loomis. He had lost his job in Northfield when the sawmill was sold, and he now came on to Nevada to begin another sawmill with North, using the money of his wife's brother-in-law, C. N. Felton, the San Francisco capitalist. North also raised three thousand dollars with which to start his quartz mill, soon valued at a hundred thousand dollars. By July 1863 the frame was nearly enclosed and amalgamating pans were on their way over the Sierra Nevada. The Minnesota mill would be the best, rather than the largest, in the territory. Mineowners backed North's mill because they could not trust high-grade ore to mills accustomed to crushing poor-grade ore. To understand the troubles that developed later, it is important to understand that the Minnesota mill was designed to handle only high-grade ore [8] and that the mineowners had promised they would reserve such ore for the specialized Minnesota mill.

By September 1863, not only was North's mill ready but he owned part of a sawmill and a thousand feet in various ledges. "And now the news has come," wrote Ann North, "that he is appointed Judge for this District! . . . We care very little about it, except that it will take him from home too much." [9] North had been drafted. The legislature and the Nevada bar had petitioned Abraham Lincoln to appoint North to the bench as early as December 9, 1862. Both petitions were worded by the same person, both petitions signed unanimously by those present in the legislature and in the meeting of the Nevada bar.

The undersigned members . . . understanding that a vacancy will soon occur in the office of Associate Judge of the Supreme Court of this Territory, by the resignation of the Hon. Gordon N. Mott, Delegate-elect to Congress, beg leave most respectfully to suggest to your Excellency, and most earnestly urge the appointment of General J. W. North, one of our own citizens as the successor of Judge Mott. We regard General North as possessing in an eminent degree those qualifications and attainments which befit him for the position and have confidence in believing that such appointment would reflect infinite credit on the appointing power and at the same time give us a Judge who would render satisfaction to the Bar and people generally within the Territory. [10]

Signatures to the petitions read like a California and Nevada legal hall of fame. Most curious, in view of later assertions, is the prominence of the third signature on the Nevada bar's petition — William M. Stewart. Lincoln did not have to be influenced in favor of his radical friend North. On the envelope containing the petitions, which he sent to the attorney general, Lincoln wrote, "John W. North to be Judge of Nevada — when a vacancy." In other words, Lincoln had provided North with a judicial office several months before North himself had made up his mind he wanted it. It was not until April 9 that Governor Nye could notify Attorney General Edward Bates that North would accept the position for which his name had been urged four months earlier. "Sir, I am pleased to have it in my power to say our late Surveyor John A. North is willing to accept the office of Judge of the first Judicial District of this Territory. The office is of great importance and his appointment is most earnestly desired by our Best Citizens." [11]

On the same day, E. B. Dorsey telegraphed Bates that "J. W. North authorizes me to state that he will accept the appointment of Judge of the first Judicial District Nevada Territory vice Mott resigned. I am thoroughly satisfied that no other appointment would give so general satisfaction to all who desire Justice. No one stands higher than him for Integrity or capacity."

The later contention by North's enemies such as Senator Stewart and by Nevada historians that North was appointed to serve special interests is not supported by fact. He was universally acclaimed and drafted by the entire Nevada bar and the entire Nevada legislature. Most distinguished citizens in California as well as in Nevada backed his appointment. Senator Milton S. Latham of California wrote Lincoln urging North's appointment, saying, "He is recommended by the entire Bar of the Territory, is a fine Lawyer, a Republican, and in every respect worthy and competent." [12] Latham spoke for the San Francisco stockbrokers who were interested in quick settlement of mining cases on the crowded docket of the Nevada court. John H. Kinkead and Governor Nye both went to Washington to secure North's appointment.

Nye sailed from San Francisco on New Year's Day 1863 after celebrating both his own and the old year's departure. Knowing the temptations en route, North telegraphed a copy of the petition Nye carried "signed by every member of both Houses of the Legislature." When news reached New York that Governor Nye was on his way home, friends began to prepare a "handsome reception." [13] At the Astor House, Nye was hissed by the Copperheads whom he would put in Fort Lafayette "until their heads and heels stuck out the windows." [14] What the war needed was "a few *happy deaths*." [15] Nye then went on to Washington to support North for the Nevada court.

North was now eager to have the appointment. All his affairs were well in hand and he was ready to undertake the job that everyone said only he could do — he had been mercilessly flattered. On June 2, 1862, District Attorney Dighton Corson sent him a petition signed by all the members of the bar at Virginia City "with the exception of two or three . . . absent from town." [16] All signed it willingly and nearly all prefaced their act with "*very* complimentary remarks." [17] Corson went on for two more paragraphs to overcome any objections North might have to the job. Never did the office more clearly seek the man.

North was more restless than persuaded. He wanted to do something important in the war effort or for his country. His sawmill would turn out mining timbers and his quartz mill would stamp out silver with no further attention from him. When he telegraphed the legislature's petition to Delegate Cradlebaugh, he asked him to get the position for him "unless something better turns up." What North had in mind was the governorship of Nevada Territory in the event that Nye resigned, or the position of superintendent of the mint all hoped might be established in Nevada.[18] Nye was supposed to return to Nevada in April, but urgent dalliance put off his sailing from week to week until the end of June. By the time he returned to Nevada, Judge North was already a controversial figure.

"My success as a Judge has been much better than I dared to hope," wrote North. "It is generally conceded that at Virginia City they have an abler Bar than at San Francisco . . . that there is no place in the United States where a judge has so difficult and responsible duties as at Virginia." [19] A multitude of mining suits had waited twelve months. "Judges Mott and Jones who preceded me had got the whole community by the ears, and had allowed a large amount of business to accumulate on the calendar. The difficulties they encountered caused them to hesitate and delay until they were overwhelmed." [20] Millions of dollars were involved in every case. Still, North would have preferred to have been appointed superintendent of the mint under his friend S. P. Chase.[21]

When North's term commenced on August 20, 1863, opposition to him was apparent. "When I was appointed some of the most prominent of the attorneys were scared. . . . They thought I must belong to somebody, and I did not belong to them." [22] As lawyers lost suits before North they complained he was too slow to work before oxen and unfit for his position. North "fully concurred" in all criticism. Such modesty was not known on the Comstock within ten miles of William M. (Big Bill) Stewart. When North arrived to open court in Virginia City, the court room was filled with a hundred curious lawyers. "I put on no airs, but took the reins with a firm hand and went to work with a will, and for seven weeks I put those lawyers through [a pace such as they] had never been worked before. Curiosity soon gave place to commendation, and censure was turned to praise." [23] San Francisco and Nevada papers praised North for his expediting of cases. General Charles H. S. Williams, "the most finished lawyer on this [Pacific] coast, except that he is sometimes dissipated," told North that he had done more business as judge in a few weeks than had been done in the previous two terms, and had done it to the entire satisfaction of everybody.

Of course North had not satisfied everybody, not the mineowners who lost millions nor the lawyers who lost cases. His popularity was still great when he turned the court over to Judge Powhattan B. Locke in order to attend the 1863 constitutional convention. North was elected delegate, and the convention elected him president.

O N T H E first ballot, John Wesley North was elected president of the 1863 Nevada constitutional convention, an election that was "almost unanimous." Nevada was seeking statehood under forced draft with Lincoln racing to get Nevada into the Union in time to ratify the amendment to the United States Constitution emancipating the slaves.

North wrote, "We have some delicate questions to settle in our Constitution and as usual I assume my full share of responsibility." As in Minnesota, now in Nevada, there was talk of North's becoming governor of the state, chief justice, or senator. From his experience in the Minnesota convention, he knew that when his views were fully known to the constitutional convention, his chances of state office would be spoiled. "This may turn the scale with me very soon." [1]

He intended to end the states'-rights argument in Nevada, at least, by making Nevada an administrative unit subordinate to a central government. He would write into Nevada's constitution a plain statement never to be misunderstood or misinterpreted, acknowledging federal supremacy over the state.[2] If he had been on the floor of the convention, he would again have championed negro suffrage. His protagonist, William Morris Stewart, who later found it convenient to act in concert with the Radicals in the United States Senate, was no radical in 1863. He was an opportunist who joined the Radicals in the United States Senate only as long as they held power to advance the interests of his masters, the silver kings of Nevada. Then he reverted to type and used his influence to put a southerner on the United States Supreme Court [3] and help defeat the Force Bill which would have maintained

156

Radical reconstruction in the South.[4] To a very great extent, "Big Bill"' Stewart as senator was to blame for the first schism in the Republican party after the war and the postponement of social and educational reforms in the South for a hundred years.

North, on the other hand, began radical reconstruction in Nevada in 1863 by leading the movement to bar the rebels from voting under the new constitution except as they were granted amnesty by Lincoln.[5] As judge, he maintained the many-ledge theory in the interest of small prospectors and miners against the one-ledge theory of the monopolists. Stewart, as agent of the Montgomery street brokers and Nevada mine-owners, tried to put the burden of taxation upon these small mines. North favored taxing the large mines to support a mining school and an educational system, whereas Stewart said that a tax on the mines would discourage prospecting and risk capital. North replied that agriculture and business in Nevada were as much a risk as mining. North and his followers would tax the gross income of the mines; Stewart and his followers would tax only their net income, which, in the fanciful bookkeeping of the times, could be whittled down by installing extensive exploratory shafts, building railroads to the mines, and building quartz mills and elaborate structures at the minehead.

North and his friends won temporarily by writing into the constitution a provision allowing the legislature to tax the gross incomes of the mines — but the provision was permissive only. It became clear to Stewart and the Montgomery street speculators that North could endanger their interests unless the movement to make him governor, senator, or chief justice was stopped. Stewart had three opportunities to stop the North boom: he could defeat the 1863 constitution and delay the formation of a state; if that failed, he could try to control the nominating convention; and he could try to control the new legislature which threatened to elect North senator.

The great mines could defeat the 1863 constitution by the simple expedient of hiring large numbers of "miners" in any area where the vote was doubtful; to prevent this, North and his friends tried to get residence requirements written into the constitution. Stewart could also defeat North's aspirations by misrepresenting the tax issue; with the kept press at his disposal, he could try to convince the prospectors and miners that North wanted to tax every unproductive but hopeful hole in the ground. With an unlimited supply of money he could buy votes, control the press, and attack North as a corrupt judge. Stewart did all these things.

Stewart's influence on Montgomery street, San Francisco's financial district and the birthplace of the martini, was wide. He was just then trying to get all the mine directors to combine to freeze out small companies on the Comstock. The *Enterprise* and the *Union* both got word of the "Stop North" plan to defeat the 1863 constitution at the polls by misrepresentation of the tax provision. Two weeks before the constitutional convention was due to complete its work, the Virginia City press made the "curious discovery" that "Conspirators here are to procure the defeat of the Constitution. . . . Brokers and speculators of Montgomery Street to be the manipulators and distributors of the spoils." [6] Stewart gagged editors with a wad of money. The Washoe correspondent of the San Francisco *Bulletin* reported a few days later, "We do not hear any more of the sensational plot which the *Enterprise* and *Union* of this city announced . . . as maturing in San Francisco to defeat the State organization here." [7] The press attack upon North followed.

"It is enough to make anyone blush to see the intrigues and rascality — the sacrificing of all decency," reported the Washoe correspondent of the *Bulletin*,

A set of vultures after carrion is the only parallel that can be made. In Storey County the fight will be pretty much on the District Judge. I do not know much about the merits of Judge North's decision in the Ophir *versus* Burning Moscow. But I do not belong to the school that because a Judge does not decide in my favor he is therefore to be denounced and put off the bench. If Judge North deserved the censure [for] dishonesty, etc., why do they not produce the documents, and back up their assertions by standing their ground, instead of weakening when he brings them to an account? [8]

Evidence was not needed; assertions were enough to defeat the constitution and, for the moment, North, though the most substantial people on the West Coast came to his defense. Henry Whitney Bellows,

---

HENRY WHITNEY BELLOWS (1814–82) Born in Boston, he entered Harvard at 14, was a private tutor in Louisiana, and returned to Harvard Divinity School in 1837. He preached in Mobile until called to the First Unitarian Church in New York, and he built All Souls Church. One of the founders of the Union League Club, the Century Club, and Antioch College. He edited the *Christian Inquirer* and the *Christian Examiner*. His influence extended to the San Francisco Unitarian society; he named three of their ministers and a president of the University of California. As president of the United

head of the Sanitary Commission and pastor of All Souls Church in New
York, then supplying the pulpit of Starr King's church in San Francisco, had a wide acquaintance among notable men in the city and in
Nevada — such men as William Ralston and A. B. Paul who were in
positions as financiers and mining engineers to know what was going
on. Bellows wired Lincoln, via Seward, "Judge North, assistant [sic]
Judge of the Supreme Court of this Territory is my personal friend. I
will pledge myself for his absolute integrity. His position here is the only
security justice has. For God's sake believe no report to his injury." [9]

To understand the reasons for the attack upon Judge North, we must
examine the clash of mining interests on the Comstock. This lode might
be diagramed as a great silver hand reaching up through the side of Sun
Mountain, holding the peak and Virginia City in its palm. Only the
fingertips showed at the surface. As each finger of ore was discovered,
separated from the adjacent fingers by valueless quartz, each was
thought to be a separate lode or lead, and the discoverer of each lead
claimed the vein of ore with all its dips, angles, and spurs. During
North's time on the bench and for years afterward the mines were relatively shallow; none penetrated the length of a finger of ore, and there
was no strong reason to believe that the fingers would ever join a palm
to form a big bonanza of ore. In theory, the one-ledge argument said this
could happen; but there was no direct evidence that this was so. On the
contrary, all direct evidence supported the view that the fingers were
separate ledges. In settling disputes between holders of the single-ledge
theory and holders of the many-ledge theory, North put on a slicker to
protect himself from the droppings of the candles and descended into
the mines. He saw for himself that the fingers of ore, as far as they had
been mined, were separate and distinct bodies. His decisions were based
upon the only observations possible: he upheld the many-ledge theory.

States Sanitary Commission he visited California and supplied the pulpit left vacant by
Starr King's death. He founded the National Conference of Unitarian Churches in
1866 with the hope of centralizing the work of the liberal churches.

WILLIAM RALSTON (1826–75) Raised at his father's sawmill at Wellsville, Ohio;
clerked on a riverboat until 1850 when he became steamship agent at Panama. In 1856
he established a bank in San Francisco and in 1864 organized, with D. O. Mills, the
Bank of California. He used the resources of the bank to promote manufacturing and
shipping, hotels and theaters, and — unhappily — mines. A close friend was C. N.
Felton who inspired North with Ralston's ideas about irrigated colonies. Newspapers
attacked the "Ralston Ring," especially when the bank failed in the panic of 1873, and
called his death while taking his usual swim in San Francisco Bay suicide.

Time would prove that he was wrong. But at the time geologists disagreed in their expert testimony; one theory was as good as another. All that could be demonstrated then was that the bodies of ore were separated by granite.

Occasionally a mine would cut through the rock separating the fingers of silver ore, and the miners at work in the two fingers thus connected would do battle or build fires to smoke each other out. North could easily detect a drift through the rock to claim illegally the ore of a neighboring mine. Even by candlelight the blue ore could be distinguished from the connecting (or separating) rock. Whom were the mineowners trying to deceive? No judge, no engineer, no miner would be fooled for an instant. The people the mineowners wanted to trick were the investors, far from the mines. If mine A challenged mine B and smoked out its miners, the stock of mine B would fall, and the agents of mine A could buy it while the price was depressed and while litigation lingered in the courts. With stock of the depressed mine in their hands, the owners of mine A needed only an honest judge to state his findings, and the once-depressed stock would again skyrocket. Many mines manipulated their own stocks by reporting they had run into a pocket of worthless rock called a "horse" in the vein of ore. When small owners of stock panicked, the large owners bought up the cheap stock, and the "horse" immediately galloped out of the mine.

Nearly all of the corporations owning claims on the Comstock lode employed as counsel William Morris Stewart,[10] who probably knew more about mining law than any other man, having been head of the resolutions committee which made mining regulations for California, the mining code of the West. The Comstock was defined as all the mining locations along the three hundred feet of the lode, with all dips, spurs, and angles. Within two miles there were a dozen [11] mines, claiming in aggregate about twice as many feet as existed. In addition to the mines on the blowouts (fingertips) of the Comstock lode, there were companies farther down the side of the mountain in a line parallel to the Comstock lode proper (we might think of these as the knuckles of the hand). When the Comstock miners began working the fingertips of the silver hand, they found that the ledge dipped toward the west, while the knuckle locations dipped toward the east, facts that seemed to prove the many-ledge theory. But when the Comstock miners followed the fingers below the surface far enough, they seemed to curve eastward rather than west, giving rise to the theory that the miners on the parallel locations were mining an extension of the Comstock lode.

The fingertip mines on the Comstock lode were the Hale and Norcross, the Savage, and the Gould and Curry. The knuckle mines parallel to them, lower down the mountain, were the Potosi and the North Potosi. The Savage brought suit against the North Potosi, claiming that the latter had entered upon its lode. Chollar likewise challenged Potosi. As soon as the challenge was made, the stock of the knuckle fell. The practice of freeze-out was so common that it is impossible to say which was cause and which effect.

For such dealings, the mineowners did not hire Stewart because he was a great mining lawyer, but because he was just as unprincipled as he represents himself to be in his *Reminiscences*. In this highly inaccurate, ghost-written biography, he is evasive about his controversy with North. Instead of giving his own recollections, he quotes from Eliot Lord's alleged history of the Comstock. Lord is inexact, even calling North "James." With poetic justice, Stewart printed Lord's name wrong. Stewart, quoting Lord, says that North's place on the bench was bought for him, information he had from Stewart. In his *Reminiscences*, Stewart quotes Lord quoting Stewart. In this way Stewart managed to perpetuate a lie disproved by the source cited. Knowing this uncomfortable fact, Stewart says, "Whether the appointment of North was bought with an understanding that he belonged to the litigators who bought him, or whether he had a peculiar mind is immaterial." [12] Stewart, with unbecoming generosity, excuses himself for not going more deeply into this subject by saying, "I do not wish to revive old scandals." We shall discover the reason for his reluctance. He says that North was a very indiscreet man, "He built a quartz mill with money borrowed from litigants." [13] This is a half-truth. The implication is that the loan was a bribe from a mineowner to influence North's decision in a case. Stewart neglects to say that Minnesota Mill arrangements were made before North was drafted to the bench or that two per cent a month usury is a strange way to bribe a judge.

As Stewart said, North was indiscreet; he prepared the way for his own downfall. He avoided the evil of using his judicial position to advance his private interests, but he was too forthright to disguise the appearance of evil. When all Nevada knew that the Minnesota Mill was built to extract choice ores which run-of-the-mill establishments could not handle, it never occurred to North that anyone would for one minute believe that he favored litigants who sent him the richest ores. Once on the bench, North tried to disassociate himself from business. In mid-October, George A. Nourse, the Republican from Minnesota and future attorney general of Nevada, arrived at the North home. He and James F. Lewis, North's law partner and future chief justice of Nevada, took over some of North's private affairs.[14] George Loomis became manager of the Minnesota quartz mill, which went into operation on October 27; a month later, North had drawn $3,500 on the earnings of the mill, and expected it to earn $60,000 a year.[15] Certainly nobody in Nevada would have asked North to divest himself of such a mill for the $1,800, $3,000, $5,000, or even the promised $10,000 salary as judge. At the end of November, he wrote, "A $40,000 Mill is no light load to carry for one who had but $3,000 capital to start with . . . and I am paying a two percent a month interest on about $25,000." [16] The loan was negotiated long before he agreed to serve as judge.

The great fear of Stewart and his clients was that North would attain political power. As governor of Nevada, he might persuade the legislature to tax mines. As chief justice, he might succeed in establishing the many-ledge theory, which would deprive them of their claim upon neighboring mines, or at least prevent the devaluation of the stocks in rival mines. As senator in Washington, North would favorably regard Lincoln's suggestion to tax the mines. His political career must be cut short.

At the opening of the constitutional convention in 1863, he wrote, "I am at present on top of the wave politically; and have been urged by some of the most prominent men in the territory to accept a place in the United States Senate. Many have told me that I could have anything I wanted. I have been urged in the strongest manner to accept a place on the Supreme bench and also to remain District Judge at Virginia. Others have asked me to become the first Governor." [17]

J. Neely Johnson, the former governor of California, and others came to Washoe City to tell North he could have any office, saying, "only let us know what you will take." [18] Minnesota history was repeating itself in Nevada, and Ann North observed, "Such popularity, you know, is sometimes transient." North was actually too busy to look for a state office and he had not the finances to run for the senate against the candidate backed by the unlimited means of the mine owners. He said,

"I have to engineer my own business, at the same time engineer the [Constitutional] Convention; and fill my leisure time with hearing and deciding heavy injunction cases in relation to the mines where from two to four millions of dollars are involved in a single case." [19]

North knew that many of the cases before him were sham battles. Men from rival mines fought in the streets and in the underground and in the courts. A great many of the battles in and out of court were elaborately contrived showpieces staged from Montgomery street to depress stocks. From time to time the San Francisco papers warned against the "bear in the market place." [20] If small stockholders could not be frightened out by depressed stocks, the directors would assess them for "improvements." "Veritas" and others then explained the working of the "freeze-out" in California and Nevada papers. North's sympathy for the small investor made him the champion of the persons so imposed upon. Part of his desire to catch up with the backlog of cases on the docket was to prevent such freeze-outs, to kill the bear in the marketplace before it could damage the small investors, the widows and workingmen who unwisely gambled in "feet."

On all counts, North was a dangerous man to the speculators in Montgomery street who backed William M. Stewart in his plan to force his resignation from the bench.

EJECTION of the constitution of 1863 at the polls was the result of Stewart's propaganda in the paid press of Nevada. Next, Stewart planned to cast suspicion upon North as a corrupt judge. James H. Hardy, a notorious drunk, provided the story of alleged corruption. In one of his less responsible moments, Hardy claimed that when he was attorney for the Burning Moscow in suit against Ophir, Judge North had accepted a bribe in the form of a hundred feet of Burning Moscow. He allegedly told this story to Alexander W. Baldwin; Baldwin told it to Stewart, his law partner, who spread it far and wide just before the nominating convention.

The Carson City (Nevada Territory) *Independent* told of manipulations in the convention, "especially the manner in which Judge North was slaughtered by a certain clique. *He* was the man specially obnoxious to the Storey [county, or Virginia City] delegation, which voted against him as a unit . . . because of his uncompromising integrity, because he cannot be 'buzzed' or used." [1] The Virginia City (Nevada Territory) *Union* pointed to the way in which the county and state conventions were packed against North.

William M. Stewart played a leading part in our [Storey] County Convention, and was successful in the State Convention to a very great degree. He succeeded in defeating Judge North for Governor. . . . It was stated weeks ago, that Mr. Stewart's sole aim was to defeat Judge North and secure a District and County Judge for Storey county, and a Supreme Bench for the new State of Nevada of his own choice. . . . It is a notorious fact that Mr. Stewart had the reputation of dictating the decisions of the District Court, to a very great extent, previous to the time at which Judge North took his seat. . . . Why does he want Judge North removed? Because he cannot be used as a tool.[2]

North called on Hardy and made him repeat the story in the presence of himself, Stewart, and Baldwin. Hardy toned down the bribery story to the satisfaction of North, who then threatened Stewart with a suit for slander on the basis that he had represented Hardy's unfounded suspicion as fact. A suit at that moment would have spoiled Stewart's plans, so he inserted a card in the newspapers acknowledging that the Hardy story as repeated by him was not true. The story had, nevertheless, planted a seed of suspicion in the public mind against North, which was all that Stewart wanted. Once Stewart's card appeared, popular feeling veered round in support of North. But the Hardy story had been useful in stopping North's progress in the nominating convention, and now something had to be done to discredit North before the legislature lest they elect North to the Senate.

At this point, after publishing the card clearing North, Stewart took off for San Francisco to consult the Montgomery street speculators for whom he was a chore boy. He called their attention to the fact that North was the probable author of articles in the Nevada press holding the mining companies up to scorn for not paying taxes to support the Civil War. Obviously, it would not do to send such a man to the United States Senate at a time when Congress was considering Lincoln's proposal to place a federal tax on mining. The mining companies assessed themselves to provide unlimited funds to be used in the election of legislators pledged to more friendly senatorial candidates. Meanwhile, Stewart's friends made light of the retraction of the Hardy story, saying that a man as big as Big Bill, earning millions as a lawyer, could not bother to fight a slander suit and that he had published the card to end a petty annoyance. North's friends were also busy and prevailed upon him to address a public meeting. He spoke brilliantly, clearing himself, which was not hard to do with Stewart's card appearing in the local press. In San Francisco, Stewart's clients were highly dissatisfied with this turn of events; Stewart was sent back to Nevada to brazen out his slander by sending the following letter to North:

Virginia City, January 15, 1864

DEAR SIR:

Herewith inclosed find a notice of a public meeting which will be held at Maguire's Opera House, in this city, to-morrow (Saturday) night, at which time I shall take occasion to defend myself against charges made against me by yourself. If it suits your convenience, I shall be happy to meet you on that occasion.[3]

Stewart was pretty sure that it would not be convenient for North to be present. The excitement and disappointment of the past weeks had again made an invalid of North. The short notice, and the distance from Washoe City to Virginia City, made North's presence unlikely. Stewart hoped to have Maguire's Opera House all to himself for his greatest performance. When the challenge arrived, the adrenalin of anger brought North from his sickbed. He replied in a letter:

Washoe City, January 15, 1864

DEAR SIR:

Yours of this morning is just received, inviting me to meet you at Maguire's Opera House to-morrow evening. In compliance with your invitation, I will be present on that occasion.[4]

The famous opera house, an extension of the San Francisco house of the same name, had been packed before for lesser stars, but never like this. Adah Rehan never drew such a crowd. The *Territorial Enterprise* said it was one of the largest audiences ever congregated in Nevada. Stewart rose with tears in his shifty eyes, an expression preserved in most of his pictures. He drew himself up to that attitude of nobility which may be seen in the picture in which he is the central figure on a landing in the United States Capitol, "Westward the Course of Empire." He had a magnificent act. He was a much-wronged, misunderstood man. He had been branded in the press as a slanderer. Every base motive had been attributed to him — the soul of truth and honor. He had been branded on the stump by men he had thought were friends: Tom Hannah, R. M. Daggett, Tom Fitch, D. Long, Beebe and Corson. He had not a friend in the world to vindicate his precious honor. He must come before them in his own person, cost what it may. What cared he, when honor was at stake, if he offended the great, powerful District Judge North, who would thereafter be prejudiced against him in the earning of his daily bread? It might cost him clients, his livelihood, but he risked all to save his impugned honor.

He had opposed North at the nominating convention because North was an extravagant man. Extravagant — had he not voted for high salaries for state officials? Extravagant — had not North as president of the constitutional convention cast the deciding vote in favor of increasing the salary of the governor even though he himself was notoriously a candidate for that office? Extravagant — yes! But his "greatest objection" was something far more serious. North believed in the EQUALITY OF THE WHITE AND BLACK RACES. He would prove it. He had in his hand the report of the Minnesota Constitutional Convention of 1858 (*sic*). He would read North's very words, a speech in which this radical villain had contended for negro suffrage, saying that the nigger was entitled to vote as much as the good Irish gentlemen here before him. If they would bear with him, he would read exactly what North had said. Now, was there any doubt that North was a radical?

A radical? Why, had not North admitted as much right here in Nevada when he approved taxing the unproductive mines? He was not going to say that North was a *criminal*, but he was a *radical*. But even if he agreed that there was nothing criminal in North's transactions, he still for the life of him wondered how North could undertake such transactions and still retain the confidence of the community. He, for one, would never support such a man for public office. To wit, North had borrowed $15,000 at 1.5 per cent interest a month from Barron while a suit was pending between the Potosi and Grass Valley mines. Barron, as they all knew, was one of the principal owners of the Potosi. Moreover, North owned a quartz mill. He got his quartz from the mines, and these mines were litigants in suits before his court.

He would now call upon A. W. Baldwin to tell his story. Baldwin came forward and repeated the charge that Judge Hardy had made. If Stewart had repeated the charge after having denied it in his published card of retraction, he would have opened himself to serious charges, but by having his law partner do so, he was safe.

The *Territorial Enterprise*, a Stewart supporter, commented, "Strange enough, he (North) attempted no refutation or explanation of the gravest [charge] of them all — that with which Judge Hardy's name was connected, but proceeded to explain at length the circumstances of borrowing the $15,000, and then launched into a vindication of his character on general principles." [5]

The Virginia City paper neglected to note that Stewart himself had retracted the Hardy story in a published card and that North had addressed himself to that accusation at a public meeting a few nights before. The *Enterprise* claimed that the meeting broke up with people still divided in their sentiments between Stewart and North. The Virginia City *Union* was more truthful. After Stewart talked for an hour and a half,

Judge North, in response to loud calls from the audience came forward, and in about fifteen minutes convinced every one in the House with perhaps the exception of Stewart and Baldwin, that a man can have made a speech in Minnesota in favor of all male inhabitants being allowed to vote, occupy the position of Judge of the First Judicial District of Nevada Territory, own a quartz mill, owe $15,000, and still be honest and do justice to the people. He did not reply to Baldwin's remarks in regard to what Hardy had told Stewart and Baldwin. He left that for Hardy to do.[6]

The Virginia City *Union* carried an article on "Judge North and His Slanderers" which said,

We learn that Stewart thinks his meeting on Saturday night was a success; and his purchased organ, the *Enterprise*, publishes in full his weak attack upon Judge North and the English language, and does not publish Judge North's reply. Mr. Stewart said that Judge North had borrowed $15,000 from the banking house of Bolton, Bell and Company. . . . [This loan] was obtained for Judge North by his relative Mr. [C. N.] Felton, who is a large owner in the Grass Valley, [the mine in the suit with Bolton's Potosi]. A mortgage upon a mill worth $60,000 was given as security for this loan. J. W. North was a mill owner before he was a Judge.[7]

North summed up the fracas in a letter to Loomis:

The circumstances were these. William M. Stewart (a son-in-law of Hangman Foote) is the most prominent lawyer in the Territory, and is retained as counsel for all the wealthiest mining companies [at a salary of $200,000 a year] . . . I issued an injunction against the far-famed Ophir Company for which Stewart was counsel; and about the same time decided another important case against him. But a few days passed before I learned that he was openly charging me with the grossest corruption and with having been bribed to decide against the Ophir Company. I went to Virginia City and made him publish a card pronouncing that all those slanders were without foundation . . . I returned home supposing all was right. But he had deliberately determined to destroy me and by free use of money got control of the County Convention, and got a resolution adopted instructing the delegates to the State Convention not to favor my nomination to any State office. That county had sixteen delegates out of the fifty-one in the State Convention. There again he set his slanders in circulation . . . [saying] he wanted to be called out in the Convention to show up my corrupt character. I arranged to have him called out, but he dared not speak them in my presence . . . After the Convention he went to San Francisco and there reiterated the same stale slanders, and I soon heard what he was doing. By this time the people of Virginia City and Storey County had become thoroughly roused with indignation at his conduct, and called on me to expose Stewart. This I did boldly, and successfully. When my antagonist returned home and found the whole tide of popular feeling against him, he became desperate and called a public meeting at the largest theater in the city and sent a note of invitation to me to be present while he "vindicated" himself . . . The audience was *immense*, and I had at least seven-tenths of them to start with and nine-tenths at the close. I never experienced so complete a triumph as I had that night in the meeting that he had called. The meeting wound up with three cheers for me and the groans for him.[8]

The shadow of doubt and Montgomery street money prevented North's nomination, but justice continued to be administered in the first judicial district. The Gold Hill correspondent wrote in the spring,

Judge North has been quite up to the demand of public sentiment in the way of giving just sentences to the convicted. . . . For the future there will be less crime, as law is getting to be a little too strongly administered. Judge North is probably the most staunch, upright Judge we have ever had, and I think will prove as effectual as a whole Vigilante Committee by the time the criminal cases are all disposed of.[9]

North cracked down on what he considered a barbarity of southern origin, the practice of dueling. Mark Twain and Steve Gillis might have been the first victims of the new law providing a two-year sentence, but for a timely warning from North to get out of Virginia City. "Judge North was anxious to have some victims for that law, and he would absolutely keep us in prison the full two years. He wouldn't pardon us out to please anybody," wrote Mark Twain,[10] who followed North's advice and left Nevada before he could be arrested and brought before the court for accepting a challenge to duel.

That term North had on the docket thirty cases involving fifty millions, with no hope of any permanent settlement. "In three cases in five the juries will fail to agree, the remaining two will be reheard if appealed." [11] Nevada was "the most fruitful field for law yet developed in the United States." [12] Men like Stewart made half a million dollars in four years [13]— Belcher gave Stewart a hundred feet as a fee; he sold the stock for $100,000; Yellow Jacket paid him $30,000. By the testimony of his own biography, Stewart bribed and browbeat witnesses, threatened and physically attacked juries and judges, sent toughs to drag them from their homes and force them to sign papers helpful to his case. His power and millions obliterated all sense of shame. The self-assured admissions in his reminiscences make it an outstanding contribution to confessions of criminal irresponsibility. It was only a question of time before North would seek the disbarment of Stewart. Stewart's extralegal threats, his intimidations at the point of a gun, his buying of witnesses and juries — these could not long be tolerated even in lawless Nevada. By the spring of 1864, the issue was not North's conduct, but Stewart's.

"To save myself and my clients from reproach," said Stewart in complete honesty, "I denounced North publicly as a dishonest judge. . . . I also denounced Chief Justice George Turner as corrupt. As for Judge Locke, he was too ignorant for denunciation." [14]

The attack was now upon the whole Nevada judiciary, for only in that way could Stewart prevent his own disbarment. Notice was published that the supreme court would meet on a certain Monday for the purpose of hearing disbarment proceedings against him. As soon as the judges were seated, North presented his resignation. This was no victory for Stewart, for North resigned to enable him to prosecute Stewart for slander; conviction would have led to Stewart's disbarment. Stewart then concentrated upon forcing the other judges to resign. "When I received the notice that I would be disbarred," recalled Stewart, "I told Meyer I wanted an affidavit with exhibits showing that he had paid Chief Justice George Turner for the Hale and Norcross injunction." Abraham Meyer was the local moneylender and president of the Hale and Norcross mine. Turner had by injunction restrained parties from entering upon the Hale and Norcross lode and removing ore. He had also borrowed money from Meyer. That there was any connection between his dealings with Meyer as moneylender and Meyer as president of the mining company was an inference never proved. If Turner needed money, he should have borrowed from somebody with no mining connections; but there was none such in Nevada. Every moneylender had mining connections, every mine was in litigation.

Stewart requested proof from Meyer, who "came back in about three minutes with a receipt signed by Turner for $2,000 and a check drawn in favor of Judge Turner for $3,000, and endorsed by him, making a total of $5,000 paid for the injunction." At least that was the construction Stewart put upon it — as if any corrupt judge would provide for his own destruction by signing for a bribe. Bribes on the Comstock were not receipted, as Stewart must have known from long experience. Moreover, it is impossible to conceive that Abraham Meyer would have paid the judge for doing his duty in a case which Stewart himself characterizes as "so simple, and the injunction so absolutely proper, that no one would have supposed it necessary to bribe a judge."

Stewart said that Turner then sent him word that he would resign if Stewart would "let up on him." When the court reconvened, Turner defended himself against charges made against him, and then he resigned. That left only Powhattan B. Locke. Stewart's account of the way he dealt with Locke is shameless. Stewart invited all his friends downstairs to Pete Hopkins' saloon to celebrate; there they organized themselves into a sort of lynch mob and elected H. O. Beatty president. Champagne flowed, and, at the proper time, two young lawyers "physically strong and endowed with a reasonable amount of courage" were sent by Stewart to fetch Locke. It was obviously a lynching party, for the two heavyweights were instructed to break into Locke's room and drag him out. "If he is locked in his room," said Stewart, "locks can be broken." He could not resist publishing the pun in his biography.[15]

No charges had been made against Locke and he could not conceive that Stewart was his enemy. If he had ever taken a bribe, it was from Stewart, for he had favored Stewart's clients. When the thugs dragged him half-dressed to the saloon, he ran to Stewart for protection. When Locke's resignation was demanded, said Stewart, "Locke turned to me for advice," asking what he should do. "Do?" said Stewart, "Resign, and do it quick!" Stewart called for paper and ink and forced the intimidated man to resign, although he was never charged with being corrupt — Stewart said he was too stupid. Finally, Locke got away from the mob and took refuge in North's home in Washoe City, where he denied the rumors that he had resigned to escape exposure.

Stewart had now succeeded, he thought, in destroying the court which had entertained the motion for his disbarment. His next problem was to prevent Lincoln's appointing a court unfriendly to him. North telegraphed Lincoln that the territory had fallen into the hands of swindlers and urged the appointment of his friend, John T. Swift. Swift was appointed, but did not serve, although he did write a book called *Robert Greathouse* in which he presented Stewart as Mr. Napoleon B. Greathouse. It is a true characterization, of which Stewart said, "I am unable to appreciate his flattery." [16]

Thinking the court gone, Stewart was jubilant. "Nevada," writing from Carson City on August 23, said, "The friends of the Judges regret their resignations, because it will be necessarily, they think, construed to imply a consciousness of guilt of corruption." [17] Stewart could ask no more. But the very next day after "Nevada" had crowed "We are without a Judiciary," and "the wheels of justice no longer revolve," Judge North once more threw the gears into operation against Stewart.

North's resignation in the hands of Lincoln was conditional, to take effect only when an honest judge replaced him and before whom he could prosecute Stewart. "I am compelled by severe and protracted illness to relinquish the office of Associate Justice of the Supreme Court and Judge of the First Judicial District of this Territory," he wired Lincoln, "I hereby tender my resignation to take effect on the appointment and qualification of my successor. I beg leave to assure you that in my opinion the necessity of the people requires an immediate appointment of my successor." [18]

Lincoln had before him the name of North's friend, Swift, the register of the land office in California. In the selection of Swift, North had worked for some time closely with Governor Low of California, Supreme Court Justice Field, and Senator Conness, to stop Stewart's plans. It was only when these friends had guaranteed from Washington that a Stewart tool would not replace him, that North resigned. When Stewart and the mining clique heard this, they cried, "We was robbed!" — or the local equivalent, "We have been sold!" [19]

The *Territorial Enterprise*, widely known for its fiction writers, gave an imaginative account of the events leading up to this new development. "We are called on to record an act of treachery," they began, explaining that on August 22, the judges were "forced to resign." On the twenty-third the Virginia bar selected R. S. Mesick to replace North. A committee consisting of William M. Stewart and two others committed the grave error of addressing the most important political figures on the coast — Governor Low, Justice Field, and Senator Conness — to secure the appointment of Mesick.

"Last evening," said the *Enterprise*, "a despatch was received from Judge Field, stating that a week since, himself, Senator Conness and Governor Low, with the knowledge of Judge North's intended resigna-

tion, and at the request of several gentlemen of this Territory, had recommended the appointment of John F. Swift of San Francisco." [20]

Although Stewart had appealed to them in behalf of Mesick, immediately he sent up the cry that these Californians had no right to
interfere in Nevada matters. It was now clear that Judge North might
continue to sit on the territorial court and have the support of new
judges selected by him and his California friends in dealing with the
disbarment of William M. Stewart.

The only way to prevent this possibility for sure was to end the territorial courts, which could be done by rushing through a constitution
for Nevada and qualifying it for statehood. This would mean state
courts more readily controlled by the mining interests. The *Union* said,
"If we understand the matter, John W. North is still Judge of the First
district, and will remain so until the State Government goes into operation in December — if no appointment is made sooner . . . Judge
Turner, we are also informed, did not resign as was supposed. Somebody has been *sold* more than once in this resignation business." [21]

The final blow came when Governor Low of California intimated that
while he had responded to North's urging and recommended Swift, he
favored North's continuing on the bench. The telegram, dated Sacramento, August 24, to W. M. Stewart, Caleb Burbank, and J. M. Nogues
(the committee of the bar), said, "In my judgment no action should be
taken until the fate of the [Nevada] Constitution is decided. The President has been so advised."

The telegram from Low was truly a low blow to Stewart. The San
Francisco papers read by his clients were attacking *him*, even laughing
at his miscalculation. In the *Bulletin* an editorial, "Hard up For
Judges," said his district was the worst *nisi prius* court in the country
and, speaking of his acts as attorney general of California, that

Mr. Stewart has the reputation of having owned Judges before now,
and wonderful fortune has waited on his efforts as counsellor before the
Nevada Courts. . . . They make it too hot for their Judges and they
resign; but before they go one of them notifies his friends across the
mountains, and gives them an opportunity to ring in a candidate several days before those most deeply interested are even told there is to be
a vacancy.[22]

Even Montgomery street was laughing at Big Bill and his claim that
he had "forced" North to resign. The editor of the *Bulletin* had an ad-

173

vance copy of Swift's letter to Stewart, and predicted it would be a "contribution to literature." The occasion for this letter was the August 25 meeting of the Virginia bar which appointed a committee to inform Swift he was not welcome on the Nevada bench. They threatened to mete out to Swift the "same treatment" that other judges had received. Swift answered:

In my judgment it is not to be presumed that in view of the certainty of the adoption of the State Constitution by the people of Nevada Territory, at the ensuing election, the President will make any appointment whatever. As regards the gentleman you have mentioned in your communication as a fit person for the position [Mesick], I have only to suggest that the recommendation of the members of the Bar whose names are attached to the paper now before me [the committee — Stewart, Burbank, and Nogues], some of whom are identified with much of the litigation, and who have, doubtless, contributed toward the present elevated condition of the Bench and Bar of your highly favored Territory, would be sufficient evidence to the President of the United States, with whom, I believe, lies the *sole* power of appointment, of the fitness of any person they should recommend.[23]

It was clear that North and his friends had got to Lincoln, not only Low, Conness, and Field, but men to whom Lincoln felt particularly close, such as Henry W. Bellows. Less than a fortnight after Bellows arrived on the Eastern Slope to collect funds for the Sanitary Commission of which he was the head, he had an accurate knowledge of Nevada troubles. He wrote,

One of the reasons given for changing the Territory into a State is to get rid of certain U. S. judges. . . . The bench consists of Chief Justice Turner, a young man of thirty-five from Ohio, Judge North from Minnesota, and Judge Locke from Missouri. . . . You can see what enormous interests are hanging in suspense (where $2,000,000 must go with the verdict) and what angry feelings accompany all litigation . . . how liable to suspicion of bribery and corruption judges must be, who have *such* claims and questions to adjudicate; how large and ready the parties [to the suits] must be to fee them, if corruptible, in a new and wild country; how savage the counsel must be, and how personally interested the witnesses — ready to swear — it is said, that white is black, according as one side or the other offers the larger bribe. No decision, therefore, is made that does not create virulent enemies, who use the local press to blacken the character of the judges. Judge Turner is charged very commonly with corruptibility. He is alleged to be worth $75,000 made in three years without business or resources; and it is said only by direct

174

bribery could he have secured such an amount of property. Judge Turner is a vain man of bright manner, and little seeming weight of character. . . . Judge Locke, I have not met. He seems to be thought honest, but *weak* and easily frightened into opinions which are not candid and just. A man [Stewart] told me he *compelled* him to break up court in one place and open it in another for purposes, not discreditable ones, of his own.

Judge North is spoken well of in proportion usually to the intelligence, moral worth, and standing of the speaker. He seems to me a man of inviolable truth, self-respect and dignity of character—a man of settled principles of conduct from which nothing could drive him. I have met no man on the whole coast who has inspired me with greater respect, and such is his personal impression, that a dozen witnesses swearing to his hurt, would not move my conviction of his purity and truth. He, however, does not escape the bitter suspicion and serious charges. Every definite charge he scatters to the winds — but what reply can be made to mischievous rumors? [24]

We may imagine what a good character Bellows gave North when he visited the White House. He had, of course, earlier supported North by telegraph. Bellows was right in his observation that the movement to make Nevada a state was the alternative to continuing the territorial court. Stewart and his clique now fought as hard for the 1864 constitution as they had opposed the 1863 constitution. The differences in the two were immaterial. The permissive tax power was changed to protect the mines, but in all its features this constitution was essentially the document prepared under North's presidency. In fact, there had been no time to make extensive alterations. To liquidate the territorial court, Stewart and the mining interest lavished money on the election at which the constitution was adopted. Almost twice as many votes found their way into the ballot boxes in Storey county as there were voters. The largest vote that Storey had ever polled was 4,348. Since the day of that large vote, lay-offs in mines and emigration to the mines of Idaho, Montana, Colorado, Arizona, and Sonora, had reduced the voters by at least a thousand. An overwhelming vote for the 1864 constitution would have been 3,000, but the vote was 6,000.

"Cosmos," writing from Gold Hill on September 9, said, "Everybody is startled by the fact; but when we have looked around and see that we had notorious ballot-box stuffers in our midst, and they in a position to carry on such work, it is all easily accounted for. . . . At the First Ward, when the companies working in it employed about 500 men, the vote stood at 400, and now, when they have not one-third as many, it is 987." [25]

North did not approve the methods, but he did approve the result. He had come to Nevada to help create a free state. The election cheered him in his serious illness. He received letters signed by nearly forty lawyers of Nevada expressing confidence in him and wishing him speedy recovery. An editor in Nevada wrote, "Let our citizens compare the names of those lawyers who have sustained Judge North, with the names of those who have attacked him, and see which are the best and most substantial citizens."

North sent the editorial to Abraham Lincoln enclosed in a letter carried to Washington by Judge Powhattan B. Locke. North's letter to Lincoln said,

Having been obliged by severe illness to resign my office as Judge, and that after a clique of corrupt men have sought to injure my good name, with no other cause than that I had withstood their corruption; I beg leave to submit to you a brief correspondence between the members of the Bar at Virginia and myself, which will show my position.

The Attorneys who have writhed so restlessly under my administration of Justice for the past six or eight months, are a Mr. Stewart, son-in-law to Senator Foote, now in the Rebel Congress, and his partner [Alexander] Baldwin, a brother of one of the *Chapman* pirates of San Francisco. . . .

All agree that I have done more business in court during the past year than all that was done in the three years preceding. Yet there are about 450 causes now on the calendar; and scores of them are suits on the decision of which millions are turning. Everything is intensified to the highest degree, and corruption has to be met with a firm hand. To hold the helm in these troubled waters is like navigating a whirlpool continually.

While my health lasted I could push business along, and make the rascals toe the mark; but when my health failed they had nothing to do but to abuse the Judge who had held them in check. But I will leave you to learn from others my true position. Professor Silliman and Dr. Bellows have been here and have seen for themselves. Governor Low, Judge Hoffman and others of California, are also fully informed.

I am glad to have had the opportunity of tendering a public service, as I know I have done, and now I am content to resume my place in private life.[26]

North had done the job Lincoln had sent him to do in Nevada. The state would enter the Union in time to supply the needed ratification of the Thirteenth Amendment and support Lincoln's reconstruction. Lincoln told Dana that Nevada was worth many divisions. North had prepared a constitution with "reconstruction" features. Stewart and Nye would go to the Senate. Stewart would have to pay a great price: he would have to go to the Senate supporting North's position and not his own. He would have to become a Radical, though never a sincere one. He would have to violate all his own deep prejudices against the negro, and fight for negro rights and suffrage for which he had castigated North.

North was too ill to wait for disbarment procedure against Stewart in a new court, but he brought action against both Stewart and his paid press before a referee.[27] In this action, he established formally the innocence he had demonstrated in the McGuire's opera house speech. Thus vindicated, North prepared to leave Nevada.

While Nevada was celebrating statehood, he was being carried across the Sierra desperately ill, but going forward in the great fight to reconstruct the Union as carpetbagger in Tennessee.

U RGING her to read the book, North wrote Ann from Washoe and quoted from James Robert Gilmore's *Down in Tennessee*, which he was spending his evenings with:

I long more and more to escape from a life of strife and conflict, and go where I can indulge my tastes in *labors of love*. . . .

I long to go down there, after the war is over, to help build up good society . . . to heal the wounds the war has inflicted.[1]

Ann, living with the children in the home of President Bannister of the University of the Pacific so that they might go to school in Santa Clara, had read the book but not known that "Edmund Kirke" was the famed Gilmore whose peace mission to Richmond was in all the papers.[2] She agreed with her husband that since he could not help fight the war, the least he could do was to "aid in the planting good influences, in many of the desolated places of the south." North was moved by the chapter about the poor whites: not one in a thousand could read, not one in ten thousand could write — yet they constituted two thirds of the white working force.[3] The old temperance reformer was aroused by the story of the preacher who took his text from the "apostle" David: "Try the sperrets" — which spirits the preacher assumed to be liquid; and by the tale of the widow who would not share her barrel of corn liquor lest her children be "nation dry by spring."

North shared Lincoln's view that the poor whites had been led astray by their educated leaders, the chivalry. He expressed enthusiasm to his old abolitionist friends and to the "preacher tribe" in San Francisco for carrying education and a good example to the southern whites. North wanted some encouragement for his "labors of love."

He wrote Gerrit Smith,

I have thought that after the war is over, I might aid a little in restoring the bloom and prosperity as well as the *good society* and *good institutions* to those portions that have been desolated by the war. . . . And then, if I could call around me a score or even a hundred families, which my acquaintance would enable me to do, that would increase the value of property, and give us good society, and enable us to build *Schools,* and *Churches,* and *factories* to bless the people who are already there.[4]

This time, North would not go empty-handed, as he had to St. Anthony, Faribault, Northfield, and Washoe. He would take the proceeds from the sale of mines and mills — his whole capital. As he told Smith, he had no doubt that "large schemes of colonization" would fill up the South. Approaching fifty, he wrote:

In looking forward through the coming years, I always picture to myself scenes of happiness. . . .
Sometimes this little Paradise of hope and promise is located in the bland and genial climate of Southern California. Then, as you know, I have imagined it in Tennessee. . . .[5]

Neither Gerrit Smith nor the "preacher tribe" helped him decide between southern California and east Tennessee. Starr King came to visit him, discussed colonization, and then invited the Norths to inspect his new Unitarian church on Geary street; but then he begged off as having a "rheumatic cold" and sent Charles Low, the brother of the governor, to show them the new church. On Sunday, Thomas Starr King could not preach, and on Friday the Norths heard that he was dead.[6] When Henry Whitney Bellows came out from New York to supply the vacant pulpit, North discussed colonization plans with him as they traveled to Yosemite and New Almaden. Bellows placed all his information about the South, gained as head of the United States Sanitary Commission, before North. Though Bellows had no great hopes for the regeneration of the South, he did not then discourage North. When Bellows returned six months later to his own pulpit at All Souls (Unitarian) in New York, North again visited him and reported: "He thinks well of going South; and does not believe one word about its being unsafe to go."[7] The question of where to build his paradise was resolved for North not by Bellows, nor by Horatio Stebbins (who succeeded Starr

King), nor by North's old friend from St. Anthony, Charles G. Ames, the former Free-Will Baptist who assisted Stebbins in San Francisco, nor by any of the "preacher tribe," but by what the insurance companies called "an act of God."

On Sunday, October 8, 1865, California shook itself like a wet dog and North gave up all thought of then building a colony on such unsteady foundation as the San Andreas fault.

I happened to be in the Unitarian church on Geary street. The choir was singing the last verse of the last hymn, and had commenced the last sentence:

> "The seas shall waste/The skies to smoke decay,
> Rocks fall to dust,/And mountains melt away."

when the building commenced surging in a very indecorous manner. . . . The large pipe in the front center of the organ fell with a crash among the singers. . . .[8]

From Santa Clara, Ann wrote that a sense of danger had grown upon her continually, and she confessed to a great eagerness to leave California.[9] The time had come to go south. The Grass Valley (California) *Union* observed that F.F.V. no longer meant the First Families of Virginia, but Fleet-Footed Virginians. The way was open to northern men. By fall North had sold his mill. Ann wrote that their "pile" was not large, but it would suffice to start some new business if they could find a place where, "this time," they could establish a permanent home.[10] At the close of 1865, North wrote: "I am at last in the Rebel Capital." He had left Washington on December 29 for Aquia Creek aboard the morning steamer, and thought the Potomac much like the Sacramento — muddy.

It was literally the grey of the morning as we looked from the deck of the little steamer through the damp and frosty atmosphere . . . [seeing] acres of canvas and gun-carriages . . . Arlington Heights, General Lee's residence and half a mile each way from it long rows of barracks for the freedmen, which being painted white, gave the whole landscape a picturesque appearance.[11]

He wrote Gerrit Smith that at Richmond he could see how far Providence had carried Lincoln beyond what any of them had dared hope at the time of his nomination.[12] Nearly two thousand freedmen in Richmond celebrated the anniversary of emancipation, but North saw none of the city's white people at the celebration. He learned that a thousand negroes were in school in Richmond, and a hundred thousand in the colored schools of the South. He thought this "a broad flash of light" that could never again be blacked out. He had heard that there was a negro school on the very spot at Appomattox where Colonel Robert E. Lee surrendered to General U. S. Grant.

He also wrote to Salmon P. Chase about the emancipation celebration on the very spot where less than a year before the rebels had met to "fire the southern heart. . . . It was worth a trip from the Pacific Coast, to see that meeting, and to hear their expressions of gratitude to God and Mr. Lincoln."[13] He told his wife that the first speech was by a colored barber, the second by a New Orleans slave who now returned to Richmond to claim his wife and his children, only to find that they had been sold.

When I looked upon the Grand Jubilee in the city of Richmond, I was thankful and proud of my anti-Slavery record. And now, my dear wife, these people need just such friends as we are to guide, counsel, instruct and cheer them on their long struggle upward to intelligence and culture. A finer field of usefulness never opened to mortal man. . . . The F.F.V's will soon be replaced by a sensible and useful class of citizens.[14]

From Richmond, North went south. He told Charles Harris in a letter published for his friends in Washoe that he would not stop short of Knoxville.[15] He reached there on January 13, 1866, and found it "very much a northern city," with many opportunities in business — furniture, implements, lumber, sugar, pottery, glass, wagons, and iron. He thought he could make a fortune in such things as toothpaste and cosmetics, but he aspired to something "substantial and honorable," which would help rebuild the South. The foundry business appealed to him, for the region was rich in iron and coal and deficient in railroads and heavy industry, a situation that must in time create a demand for foundry products.

He went back to New York to transfer his money south to purchase the foundry. Returning to Knoxville just in time to witness a lynching, he wondered if southern prejudices were not a little more virulent than he had supposed.[16] But by the end of February 1866 he was engaged in the foundry business in Knoxville. East Tennessee had few negroes and North regretted that there might be too few of them to afford a field where Ann North could labor as she desired.[17] For his part, he was more concerned with the rehabilitation of the fine white people of the region

181

who were neglected and offended by the attentions the negroes were getting.

It was not long before North discovered in his own household the full nature of the southern negro problem. Superstition, shiftless habits, animal passions, disregard for property rights and truth — the whole dreary inheritance of African slavery — became painfully evident. He dismissed servants for sexual immorality, lying, and irresponsibility. It became more important to find servants than to educate them. On February 26, North described the problem. "Clara and I have got through with our Negro help. . . . We found we had to keep a Negro boarding house; about the same as boarding eight Negroes and three dogs. But we have shut down on it, and yet the dogs bark o' nights just as though they were fed." [18] North could lay no claim to understanding the negro, or even what keeping his own dog meant to a freed negro. He had fought his legal battle, preached abolition, held to the evangelical faith that all men, including the negro, could attain perfectibility; he had tried to enfranchise the negro — and would help do so in Tennessee — but the negro was still a legal entity as impersonal as a corporation. He shared the northern misconception that the negro was just another white man, perhaps as "ignorant as the Irish," but essentially a white man with superficial pigmentation. As such, he loved the negro, or rather what the American negro would become.

North had little to say on the negro problem when he first settled in east Tennessee. Chase had warned him to keep his racial opinions to himself in the South, and in the beginning he did so. But when his family arrived, he could not control their radical enthusiasms. Negro visitors had always been welcome in the North household, Emma had shared her seat in school in Northfield with a negro. The children immediately set out to teach the hired hand, Sam, to read; he progressed faster than Bridget, the Irish cook. They taught in a negro Sunday School and Ann North welcomed to her home the teachers from the Freedmen's Bureau who were ostracized from southern hospitality in Knoxville.

Even the homes of many Tennessee Unionists were closed to the teachers of the negroes. When Ann called upon the Brownlow family,

---

WILLIAM GANNAWAY BROWNLOW (1805–77) His family migrated from Virginia to Tennessee where he was for ten years an itinerant Methodist preacher. Always a strong Unionist, he early predicted that slavery would divide the country and debated she was disconcerted by their racial biases. North visited the Horace Maynards and found the senator's wife "a little tinged with southern notions." [19] Such opinions would change, and, indeed Brownlow changed his, and all that was required, North believed, was the immigration of the right sort of people. He had seen opinions change in Minnesota and in Nevada under the stimulus of northern immigration. He wrote Gerrit Smith that Union men in Tennessee had driven out the rebels, whose places would now be filled by northern men who found, he thought, a cordial welcome in Knoxville.[20] The trouble was that northern people were not yet coming to Tennessee fast enough. He told Chase that northern men who had come south to Richmond and rebuilt the burned city had become discouraged too soon and gone home. Northern men were coming so slowly as to make no stir.[21] Moreover, the right sort were not coming at all. As late as June 1866, Ann North wrote "So *many* white people come here who cannot read, it is lamentable." [22]

One reason North felt confident of the power of immigration was the policy of the state. Tennessee, like Louisiana and Arkansas, had sent an agent to New York to divert the immigrants south.[23] North was doing his part by writing to all his friends, and great numbers were coming from Minnesota and New York. Herman N. Bokum, agent of the Freedmen's Bureau, wrote a handbook about Tennessee for the Board of Immigration established by the Tennessee legislature on December 4, 1867. North organized the East Tennessee Association with Bokum, O. P. Temple, S. I. Lucky, and O. Seymour. By 1869 a sixth of the property in the city of Knoxville would be owned by northerners. In the section where North bought Colonel Ramsay's home, the com-

---

in the interest of slavery in Philadelphia. He organized a newspaper, the *Whig*, in 1838 and published it (with interruptions during secession and his service in the Senate) first in Elizabethton, then in Jonesboro, and then in Knoxville, until his death. It was the largest and the last Union paper in the prewar South. During the war he fled to the North Carolina hills, was arrested for burning bridges, and was sent across Union lines in 1862. His *Parson Brownlow's Book* was a best seller. He was elected governor in 1865, reversed his opinions on negro suffrage, organized state guards to fight the KKK. Stricken with palsy, he was nevertheless elected to the United States Senate in 1869.

HORACE MAYNARD (1814–82) An early carpetbagger, he was born in Massachusetts partly of Narragansett parentage, left Amherst in 1838 to teach mathematics in East Tennessee College. He entered law and politics in 1844 as a Whig, supporting Bell and Everett in 1860, but joining Unionists Andrew Johnson, T. A. R. Nelson, and O. P. Temple in support of the Union, sitting in Congress. He was attorney general under the military government and seated in Congress as a Radical in 1866. When the state fell into the hands of the Conservatives, Grant made him minister to Turkey and Hayes appointed him postmaster general.

munity was almost all northern. He reported, "Knoxville is growing more rapidly than St. Paul ever did." [24]

Tennessee had long been considered part of the undeveloped American West and it was relatively easy to divert the westward migration to a region so long known for its loyalty to the Union. William Darby's *The Emigrant's Guide*, published in 1818, had listed Tennessee as "western," but the pre-war flow of immigration had been discouraged by the planters of middle and west Tennessee. At a time when western governors were encouraging immigration, no governor of Tennessee from 1849 to 1860 mentioned such encouragement in his message to the legislature, whereas every governor of Tennessee did so from 1865 to 1881.[25] Governor William G. Brownlow, who was an ardent supporter of immigration to his state during his association with North, had said at an earlier day, "Leave us in peaceful possession of our slaves, and our Northern neighbors may have all the paupers and convicts that pour in upon us from European prisons." [26]

On immigration, as on all reconstruction policies, Tennessee was divided three ways. The three stars in the flag of the state symbolize its division into mountain, basin, and lowland, or east, middle, and west Tennessee. This division was ethnic and political as well as geographical, with negroes and Democrats increasing toward the west. East Tennessee had comparatively few negroes and many Whigs who had been Union sympathizers during the rebellion. The eight counties surrounding Knoxville had been staunchly Whig.[27] During reconstruction, the Whigs tended to become Radical Republicans and the Democrats Conservative Unionists. This division of the state had acted as a deterrent to establishing any broad policy of immigration. During North's sojourn, east Tennessee became the dominant and controlling part of the state in political matters and was therefore in a position to encourage immigration.

Even before immigration became state policy in Tennessee, North's letters bore fruit. By March 1, 1866, he could report that a dozen families planned to move to Tennessee from Faribault; many who had followed him to Northfield, such as the Jenkins family, were coming to Tennessee.[28] These friends would soon augment North's political influence in East Tennessee. At first he worked behind the scenes in conversations with Brownlow, Maynard, and citizens of Knoxville. He had determined to keep out of politics and devote himself to business.

"I came here with the firm determination to say nothing on political questions, but it is of no use for me to try to hold my tongue." [29]

Certainly he had nothing to lose by being outspoken after the Fourth of July, 1866, when he saved a negro from a lynch mob and became a marked man. The Germans were celebrating the day and called upon Judge North to address them at a picnic. North had been advised by a Knoxville banker "never in this country to interfere in behalf of a nigger!" [30] But before that Fourth was over, all east Tennessee knew where North stood, and so did the banker for whom North later had great need. "The Germans had a 'Pic-nic' about two miles from town," wrote Ann North. "Mr. North and others had just seated themselves to their lunch when they were startled by the cries of a Negro man, who was being pursued by an increasing mob. Finally, the leader, a burly one-armed rebel, got hold of his hair, and was beating his head upon the ground, and the poor man's groans were so loud, Mr. North started."

Heading off the mob, Judge North stopped their pastime, and asked with some vehemence, "Have you no more humanity than to pitch upon one man? The whole dozen of you?"

"They were evidently so amazed that any person should venture to remonstrate against even the murder of a black man, that they stood still, confounded — and the poor victim made his escape. They, after a moment, turned upon Mr. North, and took hold of his arm and coat collar. He continued to talk in his mild, determined way to them."

His plain talk and poise kept the drunken mob from doing him any serious harm until his friends from the picnic gathered in sufficient numbers to save him. "There is no doubt," concluded Ann North, "that the Negro man would have been killed but for his remonstrance. My good husband has kept quiet here; that unforseen opportunity came to show people where he stood." [31]

At the time of the picnic there was a widespread belief that the war would be renewed by desperate rebels. By fall, war threats were heard no more in Knoxville.[32] But passions were so high that Dr. Thomas H. Pearne, North's friend and the presiding elder of the Holston Conference, hesitated to go to the Southern Methodist Conference.

All the Norths began to have doubts about the wisdom of their settling in Tennessee. The children [33] were stopped by strangers and warned not to visit the northern women who had come to Knoxville to teach in Freedmen's Bureau schools. Emma attended the academy with other northern girls who wore, in that year of struggle between Congress and Andrew Johnson, ribbons with the motto "Congress For Ever." When a Johnson parade passed the school, they shouted "Rad! Rad!" at the academy girls. Emma confessed, "It's real fun to tantalize these rebs." [34]

The older North boys worked in the foundry store. On Sundays they all went to the Episcopal Sunday school in the morning and taught negroes in the afternoon. Only Eddie was exempted by his youth from this missionary work. He had caught a "fever" in Nevada which settled in his knee, and one leg was shorter than the other. North read to him in the evenings and Eddie quickly identified himself with Lord Byron. He also accurately placed his father. When Ann told him the story of Job with his boils and afflictions, Eddie suggested that North was just such a man.

Ann North was unhappy in Tennessee. She said she was disgusted with the country and the "shiftless race of people" who brought their produce to market in every sort of odd container, on heads, on arms, across the saddle, on horseback, in wagons drawn by cattle. At ten o'clock when the market house closed, they vended through the streets. The people who had looked so courageous and noble in Gilmore's book did not bear her Yankee inspection well. North's "concern" for the poor whites was not shared by the women of his family, and he was too busy making a bare living to check their ungenerous reports. The rich whites they liked no better than the poor. "Some of the aristocracy have called on us," wrote Ann North, "Some of them are pleasant and I presume very good [but] almost all of them use tobacco in some shape — either smoking, chewing, or dipping [and] get into fights in the Market house." [35] These were not ladies to her liking. "I prefer Northern customs and am longing to see Northern friends."

As the winter holidays approached in 1866, North set out to find a good mechanic for his foundry, one with money to invest. He stopped in Washington to "offer a few suggestions" to Chief Justice Chase, Senator Ramsey of Minnesota, and the Tennessee delegation. Chase told North that he had information that a negro suffrage bill would pass. North predicted that if the franchise bill and school bill both passed in Tennessee that a hundred thousand people would migrate to that state in a year. The franchise bill would keep state affairs in the hands of the Radicals, and the school bill would provide free public education.

In New York, General John Eaton of the Freedmen's Bureau, editor of the Memphis *Post*, prevailed upon North to go with him to the Union League Club where they addressed the members concerning the need for negro franchise and education, but particularly the need for northern emigration. North again met John Jay, with whom he had studied law, and the son of Alexander Hamilton.[36]

Following the Union League meeting, Eaton and North were entertained by the club's founder, Henry W. Bellows, and, using the preacher's connections, they tried to rally financial support for the development of Tennessee. Financiers were frightened off by current reports of guerrilla raids by the Ku-Klux Klan. Men with money would make gifts to schools, but they would not put their risk capital into Tennessee business just then — not *that* risk. North concluded that the Union League clubs sponsored in the South were a mixed blessing. They organized the negroes and provided some schools; they did not, however, set up schools, but *negro* schools. Lincoln had avoided that pitfall in the thirty or forty schools he planned along the Carolina coast; all were open to black and white.[37] The Freedmen's bill passed March 3, 1865, had put the whites first in the title. But in the carrying out of the bill's objectives the emphasis was upon educating the negro for the franchise; hence schools became segregated.

North noticed the poor whites' dislike of the reformers. The reformers had the arrogance of righteousness, the poor whites the arrogance of ignorance. The reformers were conscious of being part of a worldwide moral rearmament from Greenland's icy mountains to India's coral strand. Just as the westward migration was temporarily diverted southward, so the New England schoolmarms were diverted from putting

---

JOHN EATON (1829–1906) Born in New Hampshire, graduated from Dartmouth in 1854, became principal and superintendent of schools in Cleveland and Toledo. Returned to Andover Theological Seminary and was ordained in 1861, becoming chaplain of the 27th Ohio Volunteers. In 1862 Grant put him in charge of contrabands and he became superintendent of freedmen in Tennessee and Arkansas and colonel in a negro regiment. In 1865 he was made brigadier general and head of the Freedmen's Bureau in and about Washington. In 1866 he edited the Memphis Post and the next year was elected superintendent of Tennessee schools. From 1870 to 1886 he was United States Commissioner of Education, later president of Marietta College, and then in 1895 president of Sheldon Jackson College at Salt Lake City. His last service was as head of public schools in Puerto Rico, 1899–1900.

pants on the natives of Pago Pago, or hymnals in the hands of Hawaiians. We know their story only in bits and pieces — how they were among the first missionaries to India and Africa, how they had taught in the South before the war, how they nursed the sick in the wars — but the international character of their work has obscured its significance. Backed by the King James Bible, a dedication to education as the greatest good, a devotion to man's perfectibility and dignity, they descended upon the South as they had upon other benighted parts of the world as avenging angels in hell. That they mistook proprieties for principles, mixed prejudice with high purpose, does not give us grounds for condemning them. The worst that can be said of these sincere and dedicated people is that they were not always wise as we are wise — after the event — nor tolerant of error as we are tolerant of error which we came to share with the South, nor expedient as we were expedient for a century in leaving the negroes to the tender mercies of their former masters, who claimed alone to understand them. The greatest obstacle to their success was their consciousness of being right, a consciousness that engendered the false pride of self-righteousness which clashed with the false pride of southern chivalry.

Little Emma North observed that everybody in the South claimed to be gentry. A definition of a southern gentleman appeared in Forney's *Occasional* column at the time North was a contributor and was probably written by him.

The new Southern definition of the word gentleman is that of a man who betrayed his country he had sworn to support, who hates *niggers*, and endeavors to arouse vulgar prejudices against them; who blows his own trumpet and insists upon his own bravery and authenticity of his celestial origin; who believes that force is better than reason.[38]

Even southern Radicals differed at times from northern, and all Tennessee Unionists did not automatically support the Republican program in the state. For example, a Unionist wrote to Governor Brownlow that immediate legislation was needed to hold down the negro: "It will *never* do to suffer them to roam about at will, go where they please, work or let it alone if they please. A negro must have one to manage him. . . . Those under twenty-one years of age should be bound out to their former masters."[39]

The Tennessee Unionist went on to say that the state jails should be rebuilt, the penitentiary enlarged, and gallows set up in a conspicuous place in every county seat for the ennobling effect this would have upon the negro. This was a far cry from the Radical desire to educate the negro for an immediate franchise. To stay in power, the Unionists had to adopt the northern Radical program. They were eager enough to fight the returning rebels who, as conservatives, were granted amnesty and supported by President Johnson. They would fight them by limiting the white vote, importing foreigners to outvote them, and organizing the negroes to vote against them. Fifteen bills were introduced restricting the white conservative vote, but the legislature balked at extending the vote to the negroes. Finally, the granting of negro suffrage became necessary both to carry out the wishes of Radical supporters in Washington and to maintain control of the state. Negro suffrage was granted not in the interest of the freedmen, but to outnumber the returning rebels. This may be seen in the title of the bill introduced to grant negro suffrage by B. P. Peart, a bill "To aid in the burial of the Southern Confederacy." The bill proposed negro suffrage on the Lincoln model, that is, it was to extend to negroes who had served in the armed forces, negroes of good character who could read and write, and who had been free for five years. Brownlow had originally hoped to augment the voters of Tennessee by carpetbaggers and immigrants from Europe, each of whom brought with him an average of fifty dollars in gold. North had long talks with Brownlow, showing him his correspondence with Salmon P. Chase, who recommended giving the franchise to all negroes. By November 15, 1866, Brownlow could confess to the legislature a change of heart.

The colored race have shown a greater aptitude for learning and intelligence than was expected, . . . While the late rebels, under the encouragement of the President [Andrew Johnson] have shown less disposition to return to true loyalty than hoped for, . . . While I have confessed to those prejudices of caste resulting from education and life-long habits, I am free to say that I desire to act in harmony with the great body of loyal people of the Union [in granting negro suffrage.][40]

The granting of the franchise to the negro had to be followed by the enlistment of a loyal militia to protect him at the ballot box and by the establishment of schools to prepare him for citizenship. Johnson had said that negro suffrage at that time would cause a war of races,[41] but as soon as the negroes received the franchise, the conservatives tried to outbid the Radicals for the negro vote. The negro vote was a Radical illusion of power as long as the negro worked for ten dollars a month and could sell his vote for a dollar to the conservatives. Both negro and poor white had to be educated to their responsibilities.

North devoted a great deal of time to education in Knoxville and the rest of Tennessee. The campaign for free schools in the state got under way with North's recurring observation that it is cheaper to educate one child than to support the aged criminal or pauper that the child might become.[42] A year later, on February 11, 1867, North had written and talked so widely about education that the Knox County Union Convention sent him to the state convention meeting in Nashville on Washington's birthday,[43] a convention that "vociperously" called upon Judge North to address them. This was his hour of triumph and recognition in Tennessee, and what he had to say became of utmost importance to the state.

He was inspired by the setting. The beautiful capitol was the masterpiece of William Strickland of Philadelphia, who was buried a year after its completion in the north wall; a hundred years later it would be discovered that he had even included elevator shafts in the building, though the elevator existed only in models when the building was designed. As North climbed the three-tiered dais to speak, he stood under an American eagle looking to the laurel side of a shield. On either side of him were long galleries filled with a racially mixed audience. Before him were the delegates at their desks and negroes in the side galleries. "When I think of the great things accomplished during Governor Brownlow's administration," he began, "I cannot help feeling that his program wants, to complete its excellence, an efficient system of public schools, open to every child in the State." [44]

The negroes demonstrated their approval, the whites joined in, and North held up his hand to quiet them.

I am reminded of a little incident that occurred some two-hundred years ago. Great Britain had sent her commissioners to her colonies to inquire into their condition. These officials called upon the governor of Connecticut and were informed that a quarter of the entire revenue of the Commonwealth was devoted to education. When they reached Virginia, they were, on the contrary, told by the governor that no schools were fostered in the Dominion. Virginia had no printing presses and the governor hoped there would be none. Both commonwealths have tried their respective policies for two hundred years, and with what result? We had the result stated recently in a newspaper published at Charlottesville, Virginia, to the effect that the South had taken the road to subjugation, while the North had taken the road to empire, and that the South should promptly inaugurate a public school system, laying aside all prejudice against it on account of its Yankee origin.

North's arguments were familiar to many in the Union Convention. He had talked for a year on the subject in private conversations, and had written for the radical press in Tennessee on the need for public schools. His fine orator's voice, the sincerity of his manner, made an old subject new. He continued:

Experience has demonstrated that schools and newspapers are the cheapest money-making machines ever tried by the State. If, during all those years before secession, every family in Tennessee had been taught to read, and had diligently read some good newspaper, no rebellion could have ever lifted its head in this State!

Then, turning to the galleries on both sides, where the negro visitors sat, he said:

But we are progressing. We have now forty thousand newly enfranchised citizens ready to vote in favor of education and loyalty! I am glad to see a portion of them today in the gallery, forming a fitting background for the picture of our noble Lincoln!

Enthusiasm rocked the galleries, and there were cries of approval from the convention.

If these new citizens cannot all read now, they will be able to do so soon. At least, the little bright-eyed sons and daughters will soon learn to read to them, and teach them to maintain their manhood and their loyalty.

When North arrived in Knoxville he had found the white schools paralyzed and waiting for northern help. At Knoxville a northern man from Cincinnati had revived the Female Seminary and enrolled a hundred pupils where sixty had been before the war. The Boys' Academy was doing well under the care of a graduate of Yale. Both institutions suffered for want of proper buildings: they were too poor to repair the damage done by the war. The University of Tennessee at Knoxville was so nearly destroyed that it stood in ruin, with neither the people nor state able to revive it.[45] North saw that the great mistake of northern educators was concentration on the negroes. "In the efforts for the Freedmen (which efforts fall far short of what is needed) there is

191

danger of forgetting the poor whites of the South who need educating quite as much as the Negroes. And, who, if educated, will help educate the Negroes; but, if neglected, will stand in the way of the Negroes' elevation." [46]

At another time North predicted that if the whites of the South were not educated they would resist negro education "for a hundred years." A second error in Radical education North hesitated to point out until he was ready to leave Knoxville: the northern teachers sent south were dedicated to a mission rather than to instruction.

Theological opinions have nothing to do with the fitness of a teacher for his office. . . . And if the teacher is not a good one . . . no "ism" will make him so. Teachers should be selected for their *fitness*, not for their theology. . . . A more profound and monstrous truth is rarely spoken than that uttered by Mr. Motley: "When the schoolmaster, and the school mistress, too, cease to be honored in this land, from that day forth will be dated the decline and fall of our Republic." They dishonor themselves and therefore lose all claim to the respect of others when they pervert their high office by direct or indirect presentment in the school room of their sectarian opinions. . . . The day that Tennessee adopted the Common School System will be, to coming ages, the brightest in her history.[47]

The system North advocated was abandoned when the conservatives gained control of the state; it will be another bright day when Tennessee educators and historians give carpetbagger North full credit for his contribution to the state's school law.

A FOOL'S ERRAND

FACED, by October 1869, with his failure to build his ideal community in Tennessee, North wrote Ann, then in exile from their poverty, that they must strike out west again.[1] He was perplexed about his failure in Knoxville, where he had lavished his capital upon good works, public and private, until his wife had had to return to De Witt or starve. He had gone to Tennessee in the Gilmore spirit — open-handed, open-hearted, wealthy, and ready for labors of love among the poor. Now they delighted in his poverty.

Ten years later, when he had established two flourishing communities in the California deserts, one of them the richest agricultural community in the world, he still wondered how with empty hands he had turned these cactus ranges into garden spots, whereas all his wealth and good will had not been enough to develop the green and glorious valleys of the Holston and French Broad. He found the answer in Albion Winegar Tourgée's novel about Reconstruction, *A Fool's Errand* by One of the Fools.[2] He was comforted at last that he had not been the only fool. He found the book a true representation of the postwar South.[3]

Yet North never brought himself to admit his own peculiar folly of spreading his energies in public benefactions rather than confining them to private business. The foundry, the railroad, the turnpike, and the other business ventures would have been enough for a sick man, without the additional work of promoting free schools nobody wanted, a Unitarian church that only the northern population attended, and a Knoxville chamber of commerce whose chief function was attracting

northern capital as well as immigrants who were, however, soon frightened off by reports of night riders, lawlessness, and pervasive anti-
northern sentiment.

In 1867, after North had exhausted his own resources, he turned to
his father-in-law to keep the foundry going, persuading Loomis to
pledge his fortune as collateral for a loan from the Syracuse Savings
Bank. That North returned with money was sufficient evidence to
Knoxville that they were being exploited. Moreover, he had consorted
with Radicals while he was up north: he and Eaton had addressed the
Union League Club founded by Bellows in New York and he had told
them of the advantages of investing money in Tennessee. In Washington he had taken the Tennessee delegation to dine with the chief
justice and had gone with Chase to Spaulding's church to hear Fred-
erick Douglass. Obviously North was a man intent upon making money
out of Tennessee for himself and for northern capitalists. Unless he
were beaten, he would fill Tennessee with Yankees and foreigners.

Only the Radical Knoxville *Whig* welcomed him home: "A few days
since, Hon. John W. North returned to his home in this city, after several weeks' absence. Judge North is one of the many valuable citizens
of the *North* who have settled in Tennessee since the war terminated.
With the addition to Tennessee of several thousand emigrants of the
enterprise and sterling integrity of Judge N., our State would be renewed, regenerated, and prosperous." [4]

What was needed in Tennessee was an emigrant aid society to do
the Kansas work all over again in the South. In the spring of 1867
North was invited to Boston to address the Unitarians on immigration
to Tennessee (they paid all expenses, or he would not have been able
to make the trip). He wrote, "The old Emigrant Aid Society that did
so much for Kansas has been revived in a small way, and is devoting
its energies to Florida. . . . I hope to call their attention to Tennessee." Lincoln had encouraged the Emigrant Aid Society to start work
in Florida back in 1863, but now there was no Lincoln to encourage
immigration to Tennessee. His place was now filled by *His Accidency*,
President Johnson, whose policy made northerners hesitate to move
south.

In his devotion to public service, North could not stay in Knoxville
to look after his business. His moulders struck for higher wages, and
one of them was "so very humble" that he was rehired. A competitive

foundry was under construction which would pay two and a half a day, or fifty cents more than North could afford.

North had sunk twenty or thirty thousand dollars in the foundry, and had bought an expensive house, befitting his station in life. He had left himself no working capital. A perennial optimist, he hoped to sell the line of improved plows and engines the South needed, but he was soon to find that they were satisfied not to be improved. Only reluctantly did he change his line to the iron pots, kettles, hoes, and old-fashioned plows which the people would buy. In Knoxville, North was surrounded by northern families, and by intelligent Unionists; but he found the rest of the state and the followers of Andrew Johnson, "arrogant and unrepentent." They continued "to curse the government that [was] compelled still to hold them back from crime." [5] North referred, of course, to the kind of activity soon organized as the Ku-Klux Klan.

The only solution North saw was to bring in immigrants and to educate the negroes to take part in governmental affairs. "This work of reconstruction is a long one; and a whole people have got to be reeducated before they can really understand the motives of the men who have saved the Union and abolished slavery." [6]

At fifty-three, he probably had no hope of living to see the day when northerners would be understood in the South. Again he was working well beyond his strength; collapse was imminent. [7]

As usual, North mixed public and private affairs. In the spring of 1867 he was one of seven promoters of the Knoxville and Jacksboro Turnpike Company. Meeting at the courthouse on May 16, they unanimously approved the immediate start of construction. [8] The following month, the governor named North a director of the Knoxville and Kentucky railroad, in which capacity he was to serve without compensation and look out for the interests of Tennessee. "Their compensation," reported the *Whig*, "will be the usual courtesy of a 'free pass' on the road." [9] The directors were to be the watchdogs of state interests and to work in harmony with the stockholders to expedite construction of the railroad which would link Knoxville with the coal fields. By the first week in May of 1867, the Knoxville depot was completed at the rear of the North foundry and the iron was ready to lay as soon as the grading was done. [10]

North's business might have prospered had he taken Chief Justice Chase's advice and kept his ideas to himself. His indiscretion was a letter published in the Syracuse *Journal*, which had advised its readers not to go south. He did some plain speaking in print without stopping to realize that his letter might be published to his disadvantage in Knoxville. Printed under the heading "What They Have Done In Tennessee — The Influence of Northern Men at the South," North's letter was an account of the regeneration of a backward community which could have been the story of any state in the West — indeed, he had said much the same about Minnesota: how the right sort of immigration had taken the territory out of the hands of the vested interests and made it into a Republican state. But the article touched a raw nerve in the South.

John M. Fleming copied the letter in the Knoxville *Free Press* [11] with the suggestion that "all our ignorant, disloyal, immoral, poverty-stricken and imbecile readers study this document and give thanks — aye, let it be read from all the pulpits next Thursday [Thanksgiving]." North did not deserve such sarcasm. He had written,

Mr. Greeley gave wholesale advice to go South, and you [the *Journal*] to stay away. Is it not possible that you are both a little wrong? There are at present in the South hundreds of Northern men, living quietly and pursuing their business as successfully as they could in the North. There are others . . . who are maintaining their ground bravely against local prejudice, and disloyalty . . . doing a noble service to their country. It is an error to suppose that all who go South, and engage in business there, are actuated solely by pecuniary considerations. There are thousands there today who have gone from high moral and patriotic considerations. . . . They believe that the moral warfare now going on there is quite as important as was the contest at arms. . . . The importance of the present war of ideas in the South cannot be overestimated.

He had seen two years of the "redeeming influence" of northern men. But for them, Tennessee would be in the hands of the rebels. Only by their aid was the franchise for the freedmen placed in the state constitution.

You chronicle with satisfaction no doubt, the fact that a free school system has been adopted . . . so that all her children, black as well as white, can receive a free education. Yet could you have seen how that measure was led on and carried through, by the indispensable aid of Northern men, you would have rejoiced with me that so many Northern men have gone South.

He had lived in Tennessee more than a year and a half and had openly advocated the most radical sentiments, but was safe despite the Ku-Klux Klan. No one need fear the "treachery" of Andrew Johnson. There was more to the letter, but nothing particularly offensive. The idea that northern men were "civilizing" the South, however, was enough to anger the *Free Press* and start the boycotting of North's enterprises. The paper would not let the matter drop after publishing the letter of September 23, 1867. The editor began a column called "Northiana" which carried protests such as one from "Illinois," who said she had come to Knoxville for her health. She said North's letter was an insult to every southron and "it is strange that a sufficient number of people can be found to patronize such men." [12] Thus the boycott had begun.

The Knoxville *Whig* came to North's defense, giving a synopsis of his career and adding, "Such Republicans as Judge North, who invest largely of their means to develop our resources, are sneered at by Conservative papers, while scallaways who vote the Democratic and rebel tickets are welcomed with open arms." [13]

If North did not thrive under opposition, he did not give up. He increased his advertising of circular saws, flourmills, canemills, corn shellers, threshing machines, steam engines, and other foundry products. He made the gas equipment to light Knoxville streets.[14] He introduced fireproof iron construction.[15] He organized the Knoxville Industrial Association and became its first president.[16] In the booklet published by the association, North noted that "a free school system has been adopted and put in operation, which opens the doors of knowledge to every child in the State, black or white, rich or poor." [17]

But investors did not come to Knoxville even at excursion rates of two cents a mile.[18] North could not raise enough money to keep his business going. The bankers stared coldly, and even Radical friends were cool. When the Norths called upon the Brownlows at New Year's Mrs. North decided they did not like Yankees. A change in railroad presidents, however, promised some work for the foundry, and a mechanic in Alexandria bought a sixth interest — but sent no money. Creditors were easy on him because North still had "some political influence in a quiet way." [19] Indeed the influence was almost silent. Before taking North's claim to influence seriously, we must recall that he was forever making excuses to his father-in-law for not staying home, and

197

he had just been off on a political junket and had to borrow a hundred and seventy-five dollars to get home.

In this desperate hour, North's only pleasure was riding the railroad he had helped build toward the Kentucky line. Free passes on the Knoxville and Kentucky railroad, thirty-one miles long with fifteen miles more graded without iron, were the only considerations of value received. The Norths made an excursion to the coke center at Coal Creek, where the hotel sheets looked as if generations of miners had slept in them. North also used his pass to explore land for an English colony projected by him and his old friend Elihu Burritt, then in England. Klan pressures limited the passes provided by law: North could not get a pass for John Eaton, now the superintendent of schools in Tennessee.[20]

The impeachment of Johnson still looked "dark" in mid-May when Ann North passed along the gossip that if Senator Joseph Smith Fowler voted "wrong" it was because he wanted to marry Andrew Johnson's daughter; and that John Bell Brownlow, who was paying addresses to Fowler's daughter, had sent home assurances from Washington that Fowler would vote "right"; but that all awaited the result of impeachment with trembling.[21] The failure to convict the conservatives' leader gave Johnson's friends in Tennessee new vigor. If North's creditors had in the past hesitated because of his political influence, that hesitation was now over. Banking capital in Knoxville was in conservative southern hands; the "recent excitement" had frightened off northern money. "Knoxville is the most growing city in the south," he wrote, "One-half our population and business men are from the north. We ought to have a good Northern banking house here." [22]

To raise money North went to New England, but his health was bad, and under this new strain, he ended up in the Massachusetts General Hospital under the knife of Dr. Henry Jacob Bigelow (who had published the first account of the use of ether in a surgical operation). The doctor, like most Bostonians, knew of North's public service and refused a fee, saying, "I will charge it to the country." He took North around Boston and introduced him to men of means, but it soon became clear that nobody would invest in the South until after the election of 1868. Brother Steuben Bacon lent North a hundred dollars to get home.[23]

North sold his foundry to L. H. Rogan, William McAfferty, and William DeGroat, doing business as Rogan and Company.[24] The price was not enough to pay his debts. But now Grant's victory in the election opened the possibility that North could save himself by getting appointed to office. The long wait until after March 4th, 1869; the time he spent electioneering and job-hunting in Washington, and his consequent inattention to business in Tennessee, made North's failure certain.

Ann North took part of the family to De Witt and North was scarcely able to feed the rest. Like many a capitalist in a depression, he looked for a communitarian solution. He had always condemned his grandfather for retreating to a Shaker community under like circumstances, but he now wrote Ann to look into the Oneida experiment. "Whatever errors they may have, as to their social system, their financial policy embodies a living truth. Any system that can secure a whole community from evils of Poverty . . . has elements of truth in it somewhere." [25]

Poverty had overtaken both him and his benefactor. Unable to meet the interest on the notes in Syracuse, North knew his father-in-law would have to ruin himself by taking them up. Belatedly he admitted that he should have looked to his own pecuniary interest rather than devote himself to projects of public good. But even as he wrote he was setting out on the railroad from Cincinnati to Chattanooga to lands where grapes grew abundantly. "If we get ousted from Knoxville, that is a good refuge," said he.[26] He was suddenly aware that his genius had been for real estate. In this he was quite right, for land seldom feels the neglect of an owner turned politician. He recalled that in St. Anthony he had cleared six thousand dollars on an investment of four hundred, and that he had done well at Northfield, except that he had "built too much."

As the summer of 1869 dragged on from one foreclosure to another, North could not raise enough money to bring his wife from New York. He wrote in the fall that he thought the rebels felt a kind of malicious satisfaction in seeing Yankees crushed.[27] Though he wanted Ann with him, he confessed that he could not always get bread for those he was already supporting. "With all my other troubles I am having some boils. It seems that in some things I resemble Job." [28]

In his great distress North paid off his debt to Herman Jenkins, his friend from Northfield, who managed his Knoxville store, and Jenkins went off to Coal Creek to become its postmaster. A few months before,

North's neighbors had serenaded him; now they ransacked his house. He reported, "Our house was entered last night and my pantaloons and shirt were taken from a chair by my bed. My sleeve buttons in my shirt are gone, and the wallet in my pocket which had no money it in . . . We have hard work to get money to live on." [29]

"You ask about money to come home with," he wrote, "I cannot see where it is coming from. You ask about means to live on. I am equally in the dark about [that]." [30] Again, "Clara thinks we can now get along with a dollar per week for provisions." [31]

Brother George provided Ann with money to return to Tennessee. After six months' loneliness, the family was united. North wrote, "If we had given our minds to money we could have been rich, and as mean as people that we know, [but] we have children great men might be proud of. . . . My friends do not reproach me as much as Job's did him, neither do they visit me as his did. They simply content themselves with staying away." [32]

The northerners who constituted half the business population of Knoxville were hurrying home. In October real estate was twenty per cent cheaper than it had been in the spring. Many were departing who had had no such idea three months before.[33] The Radicals could maintain themselves in power as a minority only if they retained the negro vote now intimidated by the Klan, and only if they lost no white Radical voters. Intimidation had its effect. The general assembly was overwhelmingly Radical in the summer of 1868, but it divided sharply on the bill to put down the Ku-Klux Klan. A further break was noted when the governor asked the power to declare martial law against the terrorists in January 1869. The election of August 1869 put the conservatives in power.

Once more North tried to retrieve his lost fortunes by seeking a federal job. In his quest for office under the Grant administration, he was fortunate in his wide acquaintance. He sought a job in Tennessee, but the delegation from the state thought he was "too recently from the North." [34] This was particularly true of Horace Maynard, who had been born in Westboro, Massachusetts, but had removed to Tennessee twenty years before the war. Maynard owed North a favor, for North had used his influence in trying to get Maynard appointed postmaster general, a position he did not receive for another ten years. Regardless

of their coolness toward "recent" arrivals in Tennessee, the state delegation in Washington combined to secure North's appointment as
Grant's Commissioner of Indian Affairs. It was the Minnesota delegation's story all over again.

In support of his application, North had letters from senators and
representatives from Minnesota, Nevada, New York, Tennessee, and
California. He had strong recommendations from Senator Ramsey of
Minnesota, Senators Roscoe Conkling and Reuben E. Fenton of New
York. Carman A. Newcomb, the Methodist minister from St. Anthony,
was now in Congress from Missouri and lent support to the application.
David Heaton of St. Anthony now member of Congress from North
Carolina, and David S. Bennett of New York gave their help. Of
course, Senator James W. Nye was not one to let his old friend down,
and even Stewart was cordial.

North met Senator Stewart in the president's room in the capitol and
Big Bill spoke complimentarily of Minnesota's action in granting suffrage to the negro.

North replied, "Yes, the speech which I made in the Minnesota Constitutional Convention, that you found so much fault with [in Nevada]
has finally triumphed."

"Yes!" Stewart replied, laughing good-naturedly.

North felt a glow of triumph that Stewart had been forced by events
to support Radical principles.[35] Stewart very probably felt some satisfaction in seeing his adversary of Nevada days reduced by the same
principles to seeking his endorsement for a federal office.

North applied directly to Grant. In Philadelphia, Judge William D.
Kelley promised to introduce North to Grant at the Union League
Club. North was kept waiting for hours like the meanest office-seeker.
Later, Kelley called on North at the Continental Hotel, explained that
the slight was not intentional, and took North upstairs to the president's
suite. Grant was friendly but noncommittal. Kelley had visited the
Norths in Knoxville and knew North's prospects. He refused, however,
to lend North the three thousand dollars needed to get clear title to
the North home and put it in Ann North's name. North also tried to
borrow five thousand dollars from his friend, Jay Cooke, with no better
success. All were doubtful about investments in Tennessee.[36]

Fame and fortune did not go together in North's case. He could raise no money, except a Peabody gift for the Tennessee schools, but he was lionized by the Republicans. Kelley and Colonel Forney introduced him to Philadelphia society. He met the political economist Henry C. Carey, the poet George H. Baker, Hart of Carey and Hart, publishers. He met Thackeray's son-in-law Stephen, and a Hungarian who had been sent from Mexico to invite Maxmilian to rule there and who had just published a book in which the Lord's Prayer was translated into a hundred languages. North met or renewed acquaintance with all the greats of the party. He saw Galusha A. Grow knock down one of the chivalry, and altogether had a satisfying time.

He failed only in getting something for himself. Recounting the experience of these weeks, during which Grant had appointed Ely S. Parker to the job North wanted, he wrote: "I went to Washington last spring and had as strong recommendations as any man from this State. They were filed with the Secretary of the Interior, and I suppose they are still. They were to no avail. I should feel humiliated to go there again, and fare as I did then." [37]

Necessity overcame pride, and North appealed to Horace Maynard to use his influence to get him anything at all, but Maynard was "reticent as usual." [38] When North next visited Washington it would be to announce his colony for California.

The last weeks in Tennessee were trying. North and his family were unsafe. Their two older boys were working, but dared not go out at night. Ann North wrote, "The spirit of *Chivalry* still exists here. A few nights ago two young men, friends, went into a saloon . . . one shot the other. The murderer was the son of Andrew Johnson's friend, Hon. T. A. R. Nelson — and was acquitted." [39] Even Congressmen were not safe. The Ku-Klux Klan searched a train with pistols and a rope in hand for North's friend, S. M. Arnell. [40] Such outrages had the support of public opinion. General George H. Thomas reported,

It is mortifying to acknowledge that the State and local laws, and the more powerful force of public opinion, do not protect citizens of the Department from violence. Indeed, crime is committed because public opinion favors it. A criminal who is popular with the mob can set law at defiance, but if a man is only suspected of a crime who is inimical to the community, he is likely to be hanged to the nearest tree or shot down at his own door. [41]

It was clear that the South had never meant the invitation with which they had long challenged the abolitionists — to undertake themselves the responsibility for the negro. The carpetbaggers had done more than that, they had brought great benefits to the poor white population, both in organizing schools and during the famine, feeding 32,612 whites and only 24,238 negroes.[42] But nothing could make the whites like their benefactors, upon whom they blamed all the miseries of a war-torn state and whom they charged with corruption. To say there was no corruption among the carpetbaggers in Tennessee would be to deny a corruption which was rather general in the North as well as in the South, federal as well as local. Yet much of the corruption of the carpetbaggers became legitimate promotion in the hands of returning rebels. Corruption was not an importation, it was homegrown — as common and indigenous as hushpuppies.

Wrote North, "I am not permitted to be of use at the present. The time may come when such counsels as mine may be heeded, in some small degree, by those who lead the party. At present the [Republican] Party is controlled by *rings* and some of them are far from being what they should be." [43]

Rumors reached northern Republicans and Horace Greeley wrote that Governor Senter of Tennessee "was regarded as having been too much mixed up with the discreditable Railroad jobbing of the last few years. It is believed that a few men have made considerable money while the Union has lost nearly as much and the State far more." [44]

Trying to rally honest Republicans, Eaton wrote North several times asking him to attend Republican state conventions, but North and other honest Republicans were in financial distress because of the boycott of Klan and kin. In answer to one appeal, North wrote, "And besides that I am not a Delegate. And besides that, I do not belong to any of the *rings*, and therefore would have little influence in shaping things." [45]

Reluctantly, North left political life for good: "Nothing would suit me better than to take hold and help to build up a true Republican Party in Tennessee, so far as I am able. But traitors have been so conspicuously in favor in our State and reliable men of so little account, that I have about concluded to give up all thoughts of ever trying to do any things again in this State." [46]

Letters and telegrams from Eaton could not move him from his resolution. He could sacrifice no more for the good of Tennessee. He had sacrificed his fortune, his father-in-law's fortune, the welfare and education of his children, the respect of his friends, the trust of many who had invested in Tennessee — and even sacrificed the patient trust of his wife.

Nevertheless, he made one last effort.

A COLONY FOR TENNESSEE

IVEN his experience of the preceding months, North should have been convinced by the spring of 1869 that Tennessee could not at that time be reconstructed by northern men and northern investments. He blamed Andrew Johnson, hoping that with the new administration of General Grant northern men would have more security in the South. A great immigration of northern men to east Tennessee might well outweigh the resurgent rebels in middle and west Tennessee. "There is no doubt now," he wrote his Unitarian friends in Boston, "that this tide of immigration is turning to the South, and before the close of General Grant's administration there will be a change in the condition of all these States that is little dreamed of at present." [1]

Men were even then in Knoxville from Iowa, Kansas, Maine, and other northern states, and letters of inquiry were pouring in from all quarters. Though many had bought small farms, no one had yet taken advantage of the large tracts with mineral wealth and water power which, it is true, required capital, but offered the real opportunity for making money. The people of east Tennessee had begun to think of home associations and business associations for the promotion of immigration — they had begun because North had, addressing them in the city hall in Knoxville, described the homestead association venture he had noted in California. [2]

The Industrial Association of East Tennessee held weekly, well-attended meetings in the Knoxville city hall. "All parties unite in this association with the best feeling and with great enthusiasm," North wrote, "All agree that this move is in the right direction and must produce excellent results." [3] County associations were also being formed in other parts of east Tennessee on the model of North's Knoxville Association. He had failed, however, to induce the legislature to adopt these associations as a statewide plan. "Thus far the Legislature has done very little in aid of this." He outlined the objectives of the east Tennessee promoters:

We have at Knoxville an organization known as "The Industrial Association of East Tennessee," which has for its object: — 1. To obtain and disseminate information in regard to all industrial pursuits. 2. To increase the number and variety of our manufactures. 3. To improve our agriculture. 4. To promote the development of our mines and quarries. 5. To enlist our business men and capitalists in promotion of home industry.[4]

For North, there was nothing new in this program: it was what he had urged in Minnesota and in Nevada with great success. Now as then, he was urging the northern capitalists to bring their skills and money to the new land's opportunity, but what he always had in mind was the increase of northern *ideas*.

A month later, in another in a series of letters to the *Christian Register*, he declared that though the fear of what Andrew Johnson might do had held back northern emigrants, during the month Grant had been in office immigration had reached a magnitude hitherto unknown. Some of the large estates he had previously mentioned had now been sold to northern capitalists. He pointed out that if one were to draw an "air-line" map from Boston to Knoxville, it would pass through New York, Philadelphia, Washington, and Lynchburg. Railroads ran the entire distance (seven hundred miles from New York), and it seemed reasonable that the kind of immigrant he wanted would come in numbers, particularly since he had arranged for railroad excursion fares of two cents a mile.

He had used his time with Forney, while waiting for an introduction to Grant at the Union League Club in Philadelphia, to good advantage. Besides publishing the articles on Tennessee North wrote for Forney's Philadelphia *Press* and Washington *Chronicle*, Forney had agreed to establish a land agency for Tennessee in the *Chronicle* office, and to see that all applicants got information and excursion-rate passes on the railroad south. As soon as Congress adjourned, Forney was going to bring a very large party of investors and settlers to Tennessee.[5]

If all the editors in Boston and New York were to take the same interest in the development of east Tennessee that Forney did, North believed they would be doing the country a great service. "Hundreds of thousands in the North are only waiting for information and for opportunity to cast their lots with us in the South." [6]

North called upon all editors to follow Forney's example, gather around them gentlemen with intelligence and capital, and come south. "If other editors would do the same thing, they can hardly imagine the good they would accomplish. Emigration from the North carries with it loyalty, safety, capital, schools, churches, enterprise, and all that the South needs to make it the most beautiful and prosperous portion of our country." [7] North did not merely call upon editors in general, but he addressed them personally. To S. W. Bush of the Unitarian paper he wrote:

The one thing needful is for suitable persons to step forward and organize the enterprise. Who will begin the work? Will not you, Mr. Editor, lead off as agent in organization of the first colony? After one has been carried through successfully, multitudes will follow the example. [Multitudes did follow — but in California.] If help is needed at this end of the line, I will do all in my power to secure success. What say you? Shall this work be done at once? and will you do it? — Yours, very truly, J. W. North. [8]

North was still using the Methodist technique of calling people to be saved, though to a different purpose now, according to his views. But he was still the evangelist and the sincere call to righteousness still worked. It had worked with Forney; it had worked with Greeley — although Greeley would not, after due consideration, plant his colony in the South; it worked with Bush. On April 3, the editor of the *Christian Register* announced that he had been converted and that

As soon as arrangements can be made we should be able to give more information respecting the price of land, where situated, and the like. A colony, such as suggested by Judge North, will be formed if there is sufficient encouragement to warrant the attempt. Anyone who desires to engage in this, or wishes further information on the general subject, will please communicate with S. W. Bush, No. 26 Chauncy Street, Boston. [9]

Henry Whitney Bellows also supported North's colony in his *Christian Examiner* and *Liberal Christian*. "I shall not fail to bring forward your views," he wrote North. "*Any* emigration . . . would be a blessing! What you want is people who have the school-house and the Church in their blood. It is this . . . that has saved the northwest, and must save the south." [10]

In two letters, North enlarged upon his plan for a colony in east Tennessee. Having failed so often, he hesitated to put forth the plan as his own idea. In fact, he was then so dejected that he probably had little confidence in his plan. In its social aspects, the plan was North's, but in its business arrangements it was Californian. Greeley, like North, had observed the development of the homestead associations in California, and had begun to present in the *Tribune* his plan for the colony that later became Greeley, Colorado. Perhaps to give the plan more prestige, North attributed the whole of it to Greeley.

Some of the Northern people, now here, are earnestly thinking and talking of organizing colonies for settlement in this State, as recommended in the New York *Tribune*. The plan proposed by that paper, is that a number of persons unite and subscribe, and pay in, a sufficient sum to purchase a large tract of land, say 30,000 or 50,000 acres, which in some instances may be purchased for one dollar an acre. These [subscribers] appoint some person or persons of their number as trustees to make selection of property and obtain title. After this the property can be divided into small tracts suitable for farms, mill sites, town sites, etc. etc.

It takes little imagination to see that the "etc. etc." was the point at which J. W. North intended to step in to develop the coalfields and quarries, build sawmills, and do whatever else he had in mind for the Cumberland mountains. He could not resist mentioning that if iron, coal, or marble were found (he had already found them!) they might be surveyed and set apart for "appropriate use."

After this digression, North went on to give the particulars of the homestead association; one might suspect that he had before him an editorial from the San Francisco *Bulletin* of 1861, describing the workings of the new California homestead association law.

After the property is thus divided, it may be sold in parcels at public auction; and those who have subscribed can bid for a choice; and their certificates of payment on the original subscription will be taken with ten percent added in payment for their individual purchases. Let a New England colony make such a purchase, then subdivide and take possession of the property; and the moment they enter into possession the property will be more than quadrupled in value.

208

North did not say that such had been the experience in California, but it was a shrewd note to strike when appealing to Yankees. He did not mention the California homesteading, which by 1869 in many cases had degenerated into little more than unsavory real-estate promotions. The settlers in *his* colony were to be men of quite different character and ideals.

Such purchases, if made with judgment [North's], must be not only safe, but profitable. In this way, those who engage in the enterprise can have their Northern friends for neighbors. [There was to be no more rubbing shoulders with brawling fishwives at the Knoxville market!] A New England village may be built in the center of the settlement, with church and schoolhouse, lyceum, library, manufactories and mechanic shops, such as are seen at home.

On April 3, the day that North's first description of his proposed colony was being read by New England Unitarians, he wrote another letter to the *Christian Register*, saying that Andrew Johnson was in Knoxville to set himself right with the former rebels, and that two trains of colored troops had passed through Knoxville to the deep South to take charge of the "chivalry" — to teach them how to behave like orderly, law-abiding citizens. "As to colonizing," he added, "can you obtain names of persons who would unite in a $50,000 purchase, and send two or three of their number to select a location? Or, are there not some persons who wish to come South, who would join in such an effort to select a place, and then unite in getting up the colony?"

North was now unemployed and entirely without money; he could not stand further delay. He knew that if these persons came South the selection was easy. He had already made it. "I have several localities in my mind," he admitted, "and I have no doubt that suitable places can be had where very many advantages would be combined." Then he put his heart on paper:

I have often thought how pleasant it would be to live in a society wholly made up of educated, enterprising, progressive people; where every neighbor is a companion and friend; where each will vie with the other in building the schoolhouse, the church, the lyceum, the library, and the reading-room; and where the views of all would harmonize in an onward march toward all that is pure, and beautiful, and good. We may never realize our highest hopes, even after doing the best we can; but good, united effort will put us a long way in advance of where we are.[11]

Events in east Tennessee demonstrated that such a colony as North proposed would not be tolerated there. North failed to understand that the South had not been socially integrated in the nation for generations, but was an enclave. The movement of our own nationals or foreigners to any part of the great West was normal, natural, and encouraged; but any migration into the South was invasion. Month after month he continued in Knoxville without sensing this truth, because east Tennessee was in turn an enclave of free people within Tennessee. Only when the true South, middle and west Tennessee, gained control of the whole state, did North admit reluctantly the impossibility of establishing a New England community at the mercy of the chivalry. The proprietors of the colony saw no reason to handicap their investment by establishing the colony in east Tennessee, where it would be deprived of federal protection, when the whole wide West lay before them.

At sixty-five, J. W. North took a last look at the Holston, French Broad, and the Tennessee, wandered for the last time through the Market House where the echoes of his orator's voice still rang in a hundred stirring speeches, went down to the railroad for the last time, and bought his ticket north and west. Ho for California! He would begin again, at sixty-five. He would go forth a prophet of a new age, a new life. Knoxville believed him a false prophet, and as he left the city, he shook its dust from his feet.

A COLONY FOR CALIFORNIA

Holding a meeting in the city of Chicago on the tenth anniversary of the nomination of Abraham Lincoln were those hopeful people who had expressed immediate interest in the founding of a colony somewhere in California. Some were disillusioned carpetbaggers from the South, all were old friends or admirers of J. W. North. Most of them came from the southern tier of counties in Michigan or from the Cedar Valley in Iowa.

In 1869 North had interested Dr. James Porter Greves in his plan for a colony in Tennessee. Greves, a New Yorker who had gone west to Michigan to be one of the original proprietors of Marshall and had then pioneered in Milwaukee, had been sent by Lincoln at the outbreak of the Civil War to minister to the sick prisoners when federal arms captured the Carolina coast. He had later taken part in the resettlement of negroes upon lands confiscated from the rebel planters. Still later, he went to Nevada by way of Nicaragua and opened an assay office at Reese River. One of the mines he had an interest in was named the J. W. North. After the war, he joined North in Tennessee, and it was there that they matured, in the fall of 1869, the plan for a colony. When it became clear that such a colony would not succeed in Tennessee, North issued a broadside from Knoxville, published March 17, 1870 and mailed to all who had expressed an interest in the colony plan, "A Colony for California." [1] The first public announcement was made by North in Washington, D.C.[2]

Greves spent the months before the excursion to California in Marshall, Michigan, where he gained some support among the old friends

211

with whom he had founded that city. At the same time, Ebenezer Griffin Brown [3] of Belle Plaine, Iowa, passed out circulars among his friends in the Cedar Valley. Those interested, whether in Michigan or Iowa, were mostly New Yorkers, and they were joined by other New Yorkers from Buffalo and Syracuse. All knew North personally or by reputation and sympathized completely with his ideals. The California colony excursionists were impressed by irrigated agriculture they saw at Salt Lake City and voted to establish the new colony in the desert, whereas North preferred a colony at Los Angeles, then a disreputable cow town.[4]

More important than any colonist was the principal financial backer of the colony, Charles N. Felton of San Francisco. In Nevada he had supplied the money for George Loomis's sawmill and had put up the money for Loomis's purchase of a half interest in the Minnesota Mill. He had had long and complicated financial relations with North, whom he had known in New York, and with whom he was connected by marriage (Felton and young Loomis had married sisters).

Felton had left Syracuse and joined the Forty-Niners at about the same time North went from Syracuse to Minnesota. When Felton ran for sheriff of Yuba county the worst his opponent could say about him was that he wore six-dollar imported white shirts. In a day when some San Franciscans were sending their shirts to China to be laundered, this would not seem a very serious charge, but the implication was that such a dandy could not be man enough to hold the job of sheriff in lawless Yuba. Felton was equal to the challenge, and said, "I imported these shirts and my studs are genuine. California laws do not forbid my wearing them if I choose. I will continue to wear what I please, and if you do not like it, you can go to hell." [5] He was elected, and more than once presented his starched white bosom as a target for the lawless, unafraid. He became a financier in San Francisco while North was in Nevada, and had an interest in Ralston's Spring Valley Water Company, which supplied San Francisco. He was a member of the Ralston Ring, and was present when Ralston was fished out of the San Francisco Bay dead and carried to his palatial home in a dramatic climax to the crash of his fortunes. Felton's fortune did not end with the crash. He had speculated widely in land in Oakland, and for six years was assistant treasurer and treasurer of the San Francisco mint. He was sent by California to the forty-ninth and fiftieth Congresses, and was elected

senator in 1891 to succeed George Hearst (Leland Stanford is supposed
to have bribed the California legislature with Southern Pacific money
to elect him). A large part of the Felton fortune was made with North
in Nevada. He at least owed North another chance to make his fortune
by establishing a colony in California.

When the excursionists met in Chicago, they had no idea where the
new colony would be. It would be in California and perhaps southern
California, but that could mean any place south of San Francisco — in
the Santa Clara valley, the San Joaquin valley, on in the neighborhood
of Los Angeles. Wherever it might be, the nature of the colony was
quite clear: "We expect to have schools, churches, lyceum, public library, reading room, etc., at a very early date, and we invite such people to join our colony as will esteem it a privilege to build them." [6]

In short, the colony was to be a better St. Anthony, an improved
Northfield, and another Washoe City free from saloons. It was to be a
temperance colony, communitarian in design. The socialistic features
of the original plan did not long survive the association with one of San
Francisco's leading capitalists. North had planned that the irrigation
facilities needed would be constructed and owned by the community,
and this he might have achieved at Los Angeles where he desired to
settle the colony; but when the directors decided upon buying in the
desert at the future Riverside, the irrigating works had to be so extensive that capitalization was necessary on a large scale. Felton went into
the project to make money, not to back a communistic venture. Nevertheless, plans about the location were still vague when the excursion
started. North rushed ahead to see Felton in San Francisco.

The Union Pacific and Central Pacific had just been completed.
Everybody wanted to take the transcontinental ride in the spring of
1870. The Boston Board of Trade ran an excursion from Boston to San
Francisco, consisting largely of millionaires and their families. "The
best blood of Boston" rode in "eight of the most elegant cars ever put
on rails," consisting of refrigerator car, two hotel cars, two magnificent
saloons, two "elegant" commissaries, with a fine library, two organs,
and a mobile printing press from which issued a newspaper called the
Trans-Continental. These cars were hurriedly created in forty days by
Pullman in several shops. [7] The North colonists for California did not
roll down Market street in San Francisco to be greeted by all the wor-
thies of California as did the "bon ton" of Boston, but they did ride in

"celebrated Pullman Palace Drawing Room and Sleeping Cars," [8] and were in California in time to welcome the millionaires. Excursion parties over the Pacific railroad were even then almost daily occurrences.[9] This was also the year that Nathan Cook Meeker and Horace Greeley were settling the Union colony at the future Greeley, Colorado. Greeley, often quoted as advising young men to go west, had really directed them to all points of the compass and had even advised them to stay home. He had little faith in settlement of the West by individual farmers taking up land, but believed in cooperative colonies — his own Union colony, North's California colony, and similar establishments based upon such common interests as temperance. The Union colony at Greeley, Colorado, had the advantage of being only half as far from Chicago; Los Angeles was remote both in distance and travel time.

When the North excursion assembled in Chicago, they numbered about a hundred. Tickets for the excursion were good for sixty days, ample time to see Salt Lake City, Greeley's colony, Yosemite, the Mariposa trees, and San Francisco. "The grand excursion party, of which so much has been heard lately," reported the Chicago *Tribune,* "will leave Chicago May 18 for California, over the Chicago, Burlington and Missouri River." [10] The Marshall *Statesman* reported that they would take the "fast express," and that the party had left Marshall, in most excellent spirits.

The California excursionists raced to depot lunchrooms hoping to be served before the train's departure was announced. "Meals en route are 'six bits,'" wrote the *Statesman*'s reporter, consciously falling into a westernism which he translated for Marshall readers as six shillings or a dollar in greenbacks. "I don't know what so large a country was made for. The land, with now and then a solitary exception, is worthless for farming purposes. . . . Since entering the Territory, the Indians have appeared in considerable numbers — bands of them being at nearly every station. So far, they have been harmless, although in some places we learn they have been troublesome." [11]

It is quite possible that the excursion party expected the Indians to attack the train. While they were in Chicago, the newspapers reported that Indians had made a raid on the Kansas Pacific Railway.[12] The Indians were a nuisance on the Union Pacific: a large party of them — a hundred mounted Indians on each side, with the rope wrapped around their bodies — stretched a rope across the tracks in an attempt to stop the iron horse. The train approached, the rope was taut across the tracks, the result was discouraging to the survivors.

All that spring trouble with the Indians in the West and in Canada had been headlined in the press. North's excursionists were ready for the worst. A few hours before they entered South Pass, the Indians had run off all the horses in the neighborhood and wounded one man. The leading chiefs were even then preparing to go east with demands upon Washington in general, and upon one general in particular.[13] An Indian, General Ely S. Parker, was Grant's commissioner of Indian affairs, the job that North had tried to get. Providence had saved him for other things, he believed. With negotiations in prospect, the Indians along the excursion route were quiet but sullen. "They seemed to be about as good looking as our Michigan Indians," said reporter Seth Lewis, "and quite as attractive in point of cleanliness."

That ungenerous implication set the newspaperman apart from the company of humanitarians who were, even as he wrote, filing into another car for a Methodist meeting and a sermon Lewis called (the qualities were obviously related) "short and very good."

Lewis wrote about the California desert as evidence of drought. The colony proprietors were spared his description of southern California, for he and other excursionists were content to linger in San Francisco at the Grand Hotel, "the best in the city," and renew old friendships with Michigan and Iowa strays. He wrote, "I suppose Mr. Schuyler and Dr. [Sanford] Eastman will start on Monday, for Los Angeles. I think hardly any of us will go that trip. California sight-seeing seems to disgust most of our party, owing to the enormous expensiveness."[14]

It is little wonder that many of the investors in the colony for California preferred to stay in the more civilized parts of California in 1870 and examine the possibilities of colonizing the more accessible irrigated parts of the state as well as Salt Lake City and Greeley. The difficult travel to southern California was more than they could reasonably undertake for pleasure. Special rates were offered by Phineas Banning's steamship company for the trimonthly passage from San Francisco to San Pedro, the port of Los Angeles. The voyage was long and often rough. There was nothing to see in the City of the Angels but a few adobe huts built for Mexicans who had come to tend cattle on a thousand barren hills during the gold-rush demand for meat, a disreputable Nigger Alley, dusty streets full of desperadoes and drunken Indians, ditches adapted as much to sewage as irrigation, a pueblo church in decrepitude unrelieved as yet by any romantic Ramona tradition. The rancho life of Mexican days, with colorful horsemen racing through the streets, had been in decline for ten years as the Americans bought up the hillsides for orange "groves" that were still scattered scrub. The Pueblo of Our Lady Queen of the Angels was a filthy setting for heinous crime which, indeed, broke forth in a bloody pogrom of the Chinese a few months later. There was every reason for substantial tourists to stay away.

Yet for the undiscouraged few who journeyed southward to plant a colony, there were signs of progress. As many people then lived in Los Angeles as there were whites in all of California on the eve of the gold rush — eight thousand. A fine hotel, the Pico House, was ready to open in a few days (on June 19), and the adjacent Merced theater and Masonic temple would soon lend an Anglo-Saxon architectural respectability to the Plaza. Cockfights, horseracing, and an occasional bullfight recalled "better" days, and on feast days the pueblo became almost handsome with decorated houses and decorative costumes.

The Los Angeles and San Pedro Railroad, completed a few months before by Phineas Banning, had only nineteen miles of track, stretching from the port at San Pedro to Los Angeles. No connection with the other six hundred and ten miles of railroad in California was even contemplated, but the state expected to construct an additional hundred and fifty miles of track that year [15] and, sooner or later, a railroad would cross the mountain barrier into southern California. The site of the colony had no connection with Los Angeles except an unimproved wagon road improvised by the "Spanish" padres and captains a hundred years before.

North's son recalled that "there was no railroad within four-hundred miles of San Bernardino [the county seat] except a short road leading from Los Angeles to San Pedro, and practically all the travel to San Bernardino County [in which Riverside would have an uneasy being until Riverside County was formed] was by steamer from San Francisco to San Pedro, and by team from Los Angeles to San Bernardino." [16]

The desert which is now the flourishing groves of Riverside county was then a forbidding place. It was, like Nevada when North first went there in 1861, a wasteland, crossed only by a trail to Yuma, Tucson, and El Paso, and seldom braved by lone travelers except prospectors of the tin mines and the goldfields, where gold had been discovered many years before the more important discovery at Sutter's mill. The only habitation near the future Riverside was a scattering of adobe huts at Spanishtown, which flash floods, cloudbursts, and constant desert winds had all but worn and crumbled to the desert pavement. These flat earthen houses scarcely rose above the level of the dunes; the only indication of life in them was the group of lounging Mexican herdsmen who rolled about the doorways in laughter at the Americans who proposed to pay good money for this worthless land — two or three dollars an acre for land valued formerly at seventy-five cents. Later, when the Riverside settlers set out their plants, the herdsmen would delight in stampeding their herds through the gardens.

The old settlers of San Bernardino were equally amused at this attempt to make something of the desert. They were suspicious of the young men of the colony who tried to interest the old settlers of San Bernardino in new ways. The Southern California Colony Association was not the first to amuse the herdsmen of Spanishtown and disturb the old settlers of San Bernardino. In November 1869, the Silk Center Association had purchased the desert area to grow mulberry trees and collect the state subsidy on silkworm production. The leading spirit of that movement was Louis Prevost, whom North had known in Santa Clara during his vacations from Nevada when his children were at the University of the Pacific. Prevost had then been regarded by silk producers as the man who would make silk production in California equal to the French enterprise, so that California could vie with France in silks as well as wines. He was about the only member of the Silk Center Association who knew anything about cocoon processing, though, and unfortunately he died. The Silk Center Association lands were up for sale when North and his party reached Los Angeles.

At the Pico House, North and his friends held many conferences with the investors of the Silk Center Association, but North remained determined to plant his colony in Los Angeles. He predicted that Los Angeles would become one of the great cities of California; all it needed was people from New York, Iowa, and Michigan. The rest of the excursion party disliked the pueblo and were shocked by its politics and brawls. They had come to found a temperance colony, and Los Angeles reeked of stale beer and hot wines. Patiently North explained that im-

migration could change all that — perhaps he saw the Methodist building rising opposite the Pico House on the Plaza. The Mexicans and
Indians could be induced to improve; in the meantime they would be a
labor force for all sorts of enterprises which he had discussed with Los
Angeles men. The colonists, lacking his experience at St. Anthony and
Washoe City, were skeptical. The Southern California Colony Association directors were deadlocked.

On August 25, 1870, Dr. Kelita Davis Shugart, who had grown impatient in Belle Plaine, Iowa, arrived in Los Angeles and visited the
Jurupa rancho with Dr. Greves and the chief investors of the colony
and the remnant of the Silk Center Association men. He cast the deciding vote in favor of locating the new colony at the future site of Riverside. Bitterly disappointed, North went to San Francisco to talk with
the colony's backer, Charles N. Felton.

Felton saw in the possible silk culture at Riverside a quick return
upon his money. The state subsidy was important, for it meant money
to be had simply in return for planting mulberry trees. With the Silk
Center Association men to assist and advise, the new colony could get
off to a good start. Furthermore, Felton's friend William Ralston had
built a silk factory which could use the product of the colony. North
returned to Los Angeles reconciled to the site. The new owners of the
Jurupa and Rubidoux ranchos wandered across their waterless acres
hopefully.

North stood at the present site of the Mission Inn, soon to be the
retreat of poets, writers, and musicians of distinction, while his com-
panions walked through the cacti and the sword-leaved agaves to
climb the bare desert mountains where in a few years would be held
the first Easter sunrise service. Here and there flowering yucca suggested the unrealized fertility of the ground upon which the new community was platted, signaling from the mountain to the men on the
plain who paced off the first streets. Less dedicated men would have
stopped to laugh in despair. The work was hot in the shadeless desert,
as these men of rare vision and purpose marked out their future houses,
schools, churches, library, and lyceum — lot by lot, block by block, for
a city a mile square.

The first building to be erected was Judge North's office, built on land
afterward occupied by the railroad depot of the Riverside and Santa
Ana and Los Angeles Railway Company. Nearby was his house, where

in later years his children would dedicate the Ann Loomis North rose garden. Religious services were first held in his office by the Methodist Higbie, the Congregationalist Bates, and the Anglican C. F. Loop. The first public building was a school built in 1871 at a cost of twelve hundred dollars.[17]

A few stakes in the wide desert were the beginning of the city of palm-shaded streets and flowering gardens that inspired Carrie Jacobs Bond to write her *Perfect Day* — the curfew that now carols across the City of Bells at the close of every rich day.

Colonial experiments were in the air in this decade before the disappearance of the American frontier, when the only land available in large tracts required cooperative effort in large-scale irrigation. Most of the land west of the hundredth meridian needed irrigation and hence capitalization. Cooperative colonies alone could do the job, for the money required to finance irrigation was beyond the resources of the individual farmer. Many of the excursionists purchased land even if they did not settle in the new colony: they saw how the Mormons had made Deseret a place of beauty in a single generation, how Greeley colonists had prospered in weeks.[18]

A printed pass issued to prospective colonists, signed by J. W. North as president of the Southern California Colony Association, was honored by railroads and steamers.[19] Once more North was gathering about him people of high principles and ideals, as he had at St. Anthony and Northfield, as he had at Washoe and Knoxville, and as he would again do at Fresno and Oleander. His enthusiasm and high purpose radiated like lines of force from a magnet, and, once magnetized, his followers were even more quickly attracted the second or third time. Fewer of his old friends followed him to Riverside because they had succeeded in Nevada or Knoxville, but a host of new friends joined him during the first year. At least fifty families invested in 1870, and thirty or forty moved at once to the colony.

North had released a pent-up flood of people from the northern tier of communities from New England, New York, Ohio, Ontario, Michigan, Wisconsin, Iowa, and Minnesota. They were, by his standards, the "right sort" of people to make southern California the garden spot of the West.

$\mathbf{V}$ARIOUS facts conspired to arouse interest in colonial settlements in the 1870's, among them the failure of Reconstruction, disillusionment with eastern politics, and the rise of corporate business. North was ready to give up all thought of private gain if he could but realize his ideals in a model community based upon cooperative or communitarian ideas. Riverside (the name was changed from Jurupa in December 1870) was originally planned as a temperance community like Greeley, Colorado Springs, and many other western colonies. Greeley was his chief competitor in 1870, and North said very frankly, "We do not expect to buy as much land for the same amount of money in Southern California as we could obtain in the remote parts of Colorado or Wyoming; but we expect it will be worth more in proportion to cost than any other land we can purchase in the United States."[1]

This emphasis upon material gain suggests that his desire for a cooperative colony did not last long once he recovered hope and ambition after his great disappointment in Knoxville. Still, the emphasis was upon the non-material ideals of education, cultural organization, and controlled social environment which were part of the New England tradition. In reading North's letters on the subject one is reminded of the Puritan Colonel Rainborough who said, "I think that the poorest he that is in England hath a life to live as the richest he."

A hundred or more colonies would spring up in the West during the early Riverside experiment, many of them close neighbors to North. The small farmer had been disappointed by the Homestead Act which was of little use in the dry lands beyond the hundredth meridian, land that subsequent acts would turn over in large sections to grazing. The cost of early irrigation at Riverside was more than $225,000.[2]

To water the mulberry trees they hoped to plant, the Silk Center Association in 1869 had begun a survey for a canal leading to the Jurupa rancho, posting a notice for the appropriation of water from the mountain streams. Don Juan Bandini had received the eleven-league Rancho Jurupa from Governor Alvarado on May 22, 1840, and had, as one American put it, quartered quadrupeds on the tract. Bandini sold the ranch to B. D. Wilson, affectionately called Don Benito. The "quartered quadrupeds" were stolen by Indians making forays from the Piute country to the east, and Mexican settlers were brought in, by establishing the town called Agua Mansa, to protect the horses and cattle. The Mexicans soon became as troublesome as the Indians, and to make the rancho pay, the owner had to live on it with enough settlers and workers to guard the animals. B. D. Wilson sold Jurupa rancho to Louis Rubidoux, a son of the St. Louis fur-trading merchant. Rubidoux had settled in New Mexico and was on good terms with the Mexican authorities — so good, in fact, that he was jailed in Los Angeles during the Mexican War. But when the war was over, the United States recognized the Rubidoux patent to Jurupa rancho.

His brother Joseph had founded St. Joseph, Missouri, and his brother Antone was a scout with Kearny's Army of the West. Louis Rubidoux would have become a colonizer like Joseph and a leader like Antone, for he proposed a Missouri colony in the Southwest. His addresses to meetings in Butte county, Missouri, pledged five hundred settlers to make the westward passage to a new settlement. All were to meet at Sapling Grove, Kansas, in May 1841, but when the time came, the Missouri merchants, who objected to the emigration of their customers, had convinced all five hundred to stay home. Louis Rubidoux went west alone, probably with some idea of establishing a settlement in California, since he purchased Jurupa rancho; but the Mexican War and the gold rush intervened. He died on September 23, 1868, and a year later his heirs sold the Jurupa rancho to the California Silk Center Association.

At the first meeting of the Silk Center Association held in the Los Angeles office of George Clark the superintendent, T. W. Cover, was instructed to buy the Rubidoux lands.[3] He bought six sevenths of the three thousand acres of Jurupa rancho for mulberry trees. A good co-

coonery was as profitable as a quartz lode: ten million mulberry trees had been planted in California since 1864, silkworm eggs were selling at from $3 to $10 an ounce, and the state paid a bounty on trees planted — $250 for planting over five thousand trees, and $300 for every hundred million cocoons. But all the association's hope of fortune died in April 1870 with Louis Prevost. Their immediate problem was disposing of Jurupa rancho. Those who had invested heavily or explored possibilities for irrigation still wanted to set out mulberry trees in the desert; per- haps, they thought, they could combine with the settlers of the Southern California Colony Association; on September 12, 1870, they joined forces.

The Reverend I. W. Atherton, first resident minister at Riverside, left an account of an early visit to the desert mesa in Robert Hornbeck's book, *Roubidoux's Ranch* (pp. 146–148). He says,

It was by invitation of and in company with Judge North that we went on a tour of inquiry and inspection. The trip was made from Los An- geles via San Bernardino. On leaving San Bernardino we made for the extreme northern point of the mesa, intending to traverse it for some miles to the south. There was no trail where we attempted to cross the [Santa Ana] river. Very soon there were signs of quicksand. Happily, by a lively concert of action on our part, both horse and buggy were soon gotten out of the threatening trouble . . . and gained the plateau. What a place and scene met our view! A bare, dry, sun-kissed, and wind-swept mesa, stretching for miles toward the south, having not a tree or a shrub in sight, and only the scantiest possible remains of what we assumed to have been, at one time, a growth of grass. Up and down this mesa, the length, breadth . . . we rode. Every now and then, with a tool in hand, we would dig up and sample the soil. . . . And then and there, I think, the decision was formed [to plant the colony], if water and plenty of it could be secured. . . . That was Riverside in the seed and germ — its first actual conception.

And with the idea shaping itself in his brain, the judge and his com- panions returned to Los Angeles, via the Chino ranch.

The founders of the Southern California Colony Association held all the offices and all the money, but the Silk Center Association was in practical control in the sense that they had begun the irrigation project and everyone else was depending upon them to complete their plans. The first winter, Higby (Higbie) and Goldsworthy of Los Angeles com- pleted the canal survey, and the work of construction began in October 1870. The canal was twelve feet wide — narrowing to eight feet at the bottom — and three feet deep. The ditch was crooked and badly planned. To avoid long flumes over arroyos, the canal zigzagged to the narrowest part of each gulch, and low places on the mesa were by-passed. The longest of the flumes, five-hundred and twenty-eight feet long, was at Spanishtown. It was so poorly constructed that while seven or eight hundred miner's inches were delivered to it, only five or six hundred miner's inches of water got beyond that point. By July 1871 the canal was a mile and a quarter below Riverside, and it had cost fifty or sixty thousand dollars. Disappointment was two-fold: of the fifteen hundred miner's inches of water entering the headworks, only two or three hundred inches reached the lands at Riverside; worse, it reached them too late for planting that year.

North offered the settlers free water during the first year if they would plant their lands, but only fifteen acres were planted. The thirty or forty families living at Riverside were glad enough to have the water for domestic use, however. Though the canal was makeshift and disappointing, it had many notable features. It diverted the Santa Ana river by means of a brush dam consisting of layers of brush with the feathered ends upstream, pinned down by willow stakes pounded into the sandy bottom. The current itself built the dam by depositing silt in the brush. As the fine sand built up against the brush dam, it became watertight, withstanding floods until 1883–84. Water entered the canal through a headgate cut in the rock of a hillside, and the canal was carried around the western face of the hill before beginning its descent of an inch a mile to Riverside and the overflow beyond. A regulator, escape-way, and sandbox, for the elimination of sediment and surplus water, were all constructed of wood. The flumes, over eleven hundred feet of them, were also of wood — a very scarce commodity in the desert.

In 1871 the canal delivered four hundred and fifty miner's inches of water, which nearly doubled the next year, and tripled by 1874. The acres irrigated increased from fifteen in 1871 to one hundred in 1872, five hundred in 1873, and one thousand fifty in 1874. This reflected improvements in the flumes and canals to prevent loss of water, and use of more water by the Riverside farmers. The sub-canals carried water to blocks of twenty acres; the water was flooded over the land, with dry seasons between the floodings. Irrigation lasted thirty days in summer and sixty in winter. Water was let into the sub-canals three, four, or sometimes five times a year. Before each irrigation, furrows were plowed across the fields between the fruit trees, and the furrows connected to allow gravity to spread the water evenly over the plat. To keep the adobe soil from hardening, the furrows were harrowed during the dry periods. The water company sold the colonists water for twenty-five dollars an acre with a small annual charge of one dollar an acre.[4]

Only a skilled promoter and optimist, surveying the dry desert and little ditch of the Santa Ana, could have come up with a name such as Riverside. The motion to change the name of the community was put to the board of directors on December 14, 1870, by T. M. Luther. It had been known until then as Jurupa, but there was some thought of calling it Joppa. North thereafter made the most of the name in his letters of promotion, always suggesting that the name described the city of the future rather than the present colony in the desert. North was not long in realizing his announced aim of securing "at least 100 good families," to invest a thousand each, in the purchase of land. At the same time he invited to join him all good, industrious people who could, by investing a smaller amount, make any contribution to the general prosperity. "We wish to form a colony of intelligent, industrious and enterprising people, so that each one's industry will help to promote his neighbor's interests, as well as his own." [5]

With $52,000 provided by C. N. Felton, North not only built the original forty-thousand-dollar canal, but also tried to stop the seepage, repair the leaks, fight the gophers, and build an office. The office of the Southern California Colony Association was a neat wood-framed building lathed and plastered, measuring eighteen by twenty-four feet and divided into an office for the president and one for his son, John Greenleaf North, who made twenty dollars a month as telegrapher. The office was on Market Street, a half block south of the now famous Mission Inn, which was then but a vacant lot. The first thought was a school for twenty-five students, of which North supplied three. Plans were made for a library, but meantime North shared his extensive library with all readers. In planning the mile-square town, he laid it out in a typical Yankee checkerboard pattern, leaving a public square, but calling it, as a concession to the southwest, a plaza.

From his meager earnings as president of the colony he soon bought a gristmill on the Santa Ana at the point where the main tributary, Warm Creek, joins the river. On the first-use principle, the mill car-

ried with it the water rights of the Warm Creek water. By 1874 when
North bought the mill it was already clear that the Santa Ana irrigation
ditch would not be adequate to the needs of the settlers and he planned
carrying Warm Creek across the wide arroyo of the Santa Ana on a
flume. As gophers undermined the Santa Ana ditch, the seepage cut the
promised water in half, but North was never able to raise the money
to build his flume. It was, however, later completed by his son John
when he was superintendent of the water company.

Some cooperation actually developed in the colony. When a ship-
load of Tahiti oranges was found to be rotting in port at San Francisco,
they were bought for the colony and all hands began separating the
seeds from the pulp for planting.[6] This cooperation carried out the spirit
of the community, even though it demonstrated that the wheat and
corn farmers had no knowledge of citrus fruit culture: budding, not seed
planting, was needed. In San Francisco, North let his imagination wander, sustained by what he had seen grown in Santa Clara and Los Angeles, and what he had read in the Bible of fruits appropriate to paradise. He spoke of oranges, lemons, figs, English walnuts, olives, almonds,
raisin grapes, wine grapes, peanuts, sweet potatoes, sorghum and sugar
beets, "more than double the yield in the East." He estimated a thousand dollars' profit a year per acre from silk culture and tropical fruits.
The pepper tree, pomegranate, and oleander would provide shade or
beauty. Income was soon three thousand dollars an acre in Riverside.

To perpetuate the colony as an intimate community, North urged
newcomers to buy only small plots of land, which they might work intensively. This would keep the people together to "enjoy the society of
near neighbors." Ten acres might yield ten thousand dollars; who would
want more? There were other reasons for this desire to concentrate the
colonists in a town: it was hard to get water to more scattered holdings.
And almost equally important was the fencing of lands.

The farms of the settlers at Riverside were in range lands, and the
established ranchers were not likely to respect unfenced farms. The
cattle of the several ranches followed the grass and the water courses
across the unfenced range, and invariably ended up trampling down
the seedlings in the irrigated lands at Riverside. The ranches were unfenced and even unmarked, except in the rudest way — by trees, stones,
and brush piles. Boundaries were customarily run by two men on horseback; one would place a pole with its point in the ground while the

second rode the length of a rope and placed a second pole in the ground; the first horseman would pull up his stake and ride again the length of the rope and place his stake again, and so on. Casual surveying of open range naturally brought the rancheros into conflict with the farmers. An act of 1850 protected the ranches: it allowed farmers to fence lands, but they could not drive the cattle and horses off unfenced farms without being liable for damages. In northern California fencing was easy, for there was wood at hand to build fences of. But in the desert of southern California wood was expensive. Though Joseph Glidden at De Kalb, Illinois, was already stretching a wire from his barn to a tree and twisting barbs into it, it would be some time before barbed wire would be available in southern California. The settlers at Riverside planted all sorts of hedges, but even when they grew high enough, the cattle and horses stampeded through them. Australian eucalyptus trees were planted as fences, but the seed cost five dollars an ounce.

Dr. George S. Loomis, whose wife had died during the days of the Norths' deepest distress in Tennessee, came west to live with his daughter at Riverside. He wrote, "Bands of horses are being driven past here or are met on these vast, arid plains in wild strife. Handsome bands of sixty to eighty horses passed here Sunday, Monday and Tuesday, and yesterday — There is a much larger Spanish population in this country than I had supposed." Just a few miles from Riverside, there was a "dusty village of adobe huts called Spanish Town." [7]

North saw the struggle between the rancheros and the farmers as "a contest between advancing civilization and obsolete barbarism." [8] "A poor neighbor has put in ten acres of Wheat," reported North, "He must now expend near three hundred dollars to fence it; to guard against other peoples stock." If the ranchers were forced to fence their own stock, the poor wheat farmer could put in another fifty acres of wheat instead of having to spend the money to fence his land. The fencing problem was one of three that made North wish his friends had listened to him and settled at Los Angeles; the other two were lack of transportation and disputes over water rights.

In North's circular about Riverside, he had pointed out that it was on the proposed line of the Southern Pacific Railroad. It seemed reasonable that the line being built through the San Joaquin Valley would cross the mountains to Los Angeles, but railroad builders were not always reasonable men. They announced that they would not build into Los Angeles, but would cross from Mohave to San Bernardino. Los Angeles then provided a $600,000 subsidy, a right-of-way, and a sixty-acre depot site to induce the Southern Pacific to tunnel through the San Fernando mountains and build over Tehachapi Pass, but by the time the railroad reached Los Angeles, North had moved away. He was never quite certain that Riverside could produce the inducements necessary to get the railroad to the colony as promised. When San Bernardino would not subsidize the Southern Pacific, the route was changed to pass through the Slover Mountain colony (Colton, California) near Riverside. The cost of shipment from Los Angeles to Riverside was equivalent to the cost from Los Angeles to Chicago. A second high-cost utility was water, which was in the hands of the capitalists who had invested large amounts of money in the development of the colony; they looked to its sale as a permanent revenue-yielding investment. As long as North was in a position to control the water arrangements, he could do so in the interest of the colonists; very shortly, however, it became clear that his backer, Charles N. Felton, would combine with other water companies in charging all the traffic would bear.

Water was measured in flume boxes with a regulated outlet. Many of the small farmers working heavy soils on small tracts could not use the water as fast as it was delivered, while others with large tracts and several workmen complained that they needed a larger head of water than could be delivered. By the summer of 1874, most of the irrigation problems had been solved at Riverside, but just then two new colonies began to compete with Riverside for water. S. C. Evans of Indiana and W. T. Sayward bought the B. Hartshorn ranch for a colonization venture and began to build a canal; the result was the New England colony. At the same time, San Francisco capitalists, including L. L. Robinson, General Carpenter, and General Hutchinson, owners of a tin company known as the San Jacinto Sobrante ranch, planned a Santa Ana colony using the canal of the New England company.

The new canal, constructed at great expense (North was not alone in underestimating costs), was built on the principle that water moving fast enough at the source would run uphill in an open ditch. The two new colonies found that their canal would have to pass through Spanishtown and Riverside; the proprietors of both — the Mexicans and the Southern California Colony Association — refused right-of-way. To protect its water rights, the North company purchased the Matthews

Mills property on Warm Creek, and prepared to contend in court that first use gave them rights to the water. Rather than burden the aging North with litigation, Felton in May 1875 sold his interest to his rivals.[9] On June 1, W. T. Sayward replaced North as president of the Southern California Colony Association.

Though officially J. W. North's connection with Riverside was ended, he had succeeded in peopling the desert community: immigrants were coming to California in 1874 at the rate of three thousand a month,[10] from the northern states and from Europe. The Pacific Railroad made passage easy, agents of the railroads meeting immigrants at the docks and giving them bargain passage west. The newcomers went only as far as the railroad terminus. North's efforts had been directed toward getting them by steamship and stage to Los Angeles, where he could sell them upon the advantages of Riverside. A minor gold rush brought miners to Riverside and from there they went on to their placer discoveries. Each steamer landed a "considerable party" of farmers at Wilmington in search of land. They had dreamed of great thousand-acre wheat farms and it took some selling by North to persuade them that they could make more with less effort on a "little farm well tilled." [11] Dr. Greves reported that Riverside was "buoyed with hope."

Unfortunately, North's hopes were inversely related to the hopes of the colony. He had been foremost in urging a railroad connection, but when the railroad surveys were made, it was found that most of his own farm was — because of the faulty surveying methods — land the government had given to the railroad. The government land he claimed now advanced in value because of the improvements made in the colony. The success of his enterprise had put his own farm beyond his means of buying it from the railroad. The future of Riverside was secure, but its founder was insecure — and restless.

North was the center of all complaints both from colonists and from the capitalists C. N. Felton, J. H. Stewart of San Bernardino, and Henry Hamilton, editor of the Los Angeles *Star* — none of whom lived in Riverside. Lush weeds grew in the canal and Indians were hired to wade in the three-foot canal to cut them with scythes. Hosts of naked Indians of all ages in the drinking water was too much for the colonists.

When Don Benito Wilson sold Jurupa, he had taken the grantee to one of the bare peaks and pointed out the eastern boundary — or "corners" — the mountains of Spanishtown and the Pachappa. This line was run by the surveyors Goldsworthy and Higbie (the latter a minister and trusted by North.) But when William T. Sayward bought out Felton's interest in the colony, he claimed to have discovered a pile of rocks marking the true boundary, which he "floated" to his own advantage and the elimination of many marginal claims on government land, including North's own. The squatters met and appointed North their attorney and he proved Sayward's claim fraudulent or mistaken, saving his own eighty acres and the twelve hundred more acres of his friends. The pleading of this case took North to San Francisco and he began to wonder if his calling was not, after all, the law. When some of his closest friends, in their experimentation with desert crops, began to grow the opium poppy for sale to the Chinese community in Los Angeles, he was even more sure of it.

Those who had restrained his enthusiasm for new projects were dead. Dr. George S. Loomis was dead; so was Clarissa North. This remarkable woman had matured with her brother intellectually, had read Huxley, Spencer, Tyndall, and Ingersoll with him. When she died in Riverside, her request that only her brother read a few words over her grave was complied with. Ann North suffered from the heat of Riverside, and spent the summers in San Francisco and the East. Their youngest boy, Eddie, had decided to make a career of music, and had published a song. North took the same view as Bellows took with his son Russell — that music was all very well as an avocation, but in this world of serious problems, a preoccupation with the decorative arts kept young men from helping to solve more important, practical problems. Serious attention to the fine arts was a waste of brains. With great sorrow and some embarrassment, North saw Eddie's poor little song published. He had raised his children for better things — to help change an evil world, and that not by writing the songs the nation sang. It was disheartening to North to see his own impracticality mirrored in his son in this exaggerated form. Another son had left the family circle, inheriting uncontrolled the wanderlust controlled in the father. He was lost from his family's sight. North was beginning to fear that he had not been a very good parent.

He was in no mood to seriously enter the business of law, even with such good partners as Deal and Lewis. W. E. F. Deal had also been known to Judge North in Nevada, where he had been a clerk in the law office of Perley and De Long. Deal's father was Dr. W. Grove Deal, a Methodist preacher, who had bought Sutter's fort in 1849 and at his own expense used it as a hospital in the cholera epidemic of that year. Judge James F. Lewis of the Nevada and California bar now entered into partnership with North for the second time. They had been partners in Washoe beginning in the summer of 1862, and Lewis later climbed to success in Nevada. He had boarded with the Norths for ten dollars a week, a high rate justified only by the high cost of food in Washoe, where milk at the time sold for a dollar a gallon. Exceedingly shy, melancholy, and home-loving, he slept in the law offices and was so timid that he shut himself in for two days rather than let the Norths know he was sick. When they learned of it they moved him to their crowded home. He was once threatened by a secessionist bully named De Witt, who had knifed several others and was whetting his blade for Lewis. Seeming scarcely the sort of man to succeed in Nevada, he nevertheless did; when North left Nevada, Lewis was the new editor of the Washoe newspaper.

After North's desultory practice of law in Riverside and San Bernardino, it was gratifying to be a member of such a well-known firm as North, Lewis, and Deal in San Francisco, where promoters and entrepreneurs talked of grand schemes. The Norths had many friends in the city, felt at home in the Geary Street church, and could find interest and companionship in the lyceums and associations of the Bay cities. Nevertheless, North's dream of an ideal community remained unfulfilled, and San Francisco was not a city to suit his ambitions and prejudices. His many friends there, plus all the enthusiasms of the stockholders, proprietors, and developers of mines, forests, and agricultural lands, did not counterbalance the forty-two breweries and endless saloons. This was a period when "a copper-lined man can take an observation through the bottom of his drained glass once a day for *ten years*, and not visit the same place twice." [12]

North was distressed with the failure of the raisin-grape vines at Riverside. They had grown luxuriantly, giving promise of an abundant harvest, only to wither on the vine one year in the face of the hot blasts that blew down from the mountains, or the next year to be filled with grit and sand by the Santa Ana. Somewhere in California, there must be an ideal climate for this profitable crop. Thus preoccupied, he could not linger long in the city, and at times he perhaps regretted having left Riverside.

He had left just as the colony was about to become world-famous as a health resort. E. G. Brown's little twelve-by-sixteen-foot cabin had become a fashionable dwelling called "The Anchorage," where wintering visitors could amuse themselves at tennis, croquet, tenpins, and similar innocent amusements. Adoniram Judson Twogood of Onondaga and Iowa now had an annual ten-thousand-dollar citrus crop at Riverside. North left Riverside, as he had all his other pioneer ventures, too soon to enjoy the fruit of his labors. Soon after his death, *Bradstreet's* listed Riverside as the richest city per capita in the United States.[13] And earlier, shortly after North's departure, English capitalists flooded it with money as productive of prosperity as mountain water.

Prosperity brought some relaxation of code. The original intention had been to write into every sale of land the explicit provision that liquor could never be sold or consumed on the land. Nevertheless, two saloons had opened in Riverside. The town still remained a "temperance place," for the charter and one hundred and twenty ordinances had established that character: Ordinance Number Eight provided that anyone found drunk would be fined an amount up to twenty dollars, which could be worked off at labor at a dollar a day. The Board of Trustees ordained this penalty on December 13, 1883, but they were closing the barn door after their temperance horse had been stolen. Beside the temperance views of North and his friends was the hard fact that a Mexican town was nearby, that Mexicans were needed to work the fields, and that one way or another they would circumvent the restrictions on wine. Many of the settlers were willing to open Riverside to liquor to retain a work force, and perhaps saw some inconsistency in barring intoxicants while growing wine-grapes. Still, by 1892, when an Englishman wrote his reflections on Riverside, the town was still temperance, and the two public houses were threatened with extinction.[14]

The sober character of the industrious settlers had raised the price of unimproved lands with water rights to $250 to $500 an acre, which might show an annual profit when worked of $1,000 to $3,000 an acre.[15] By 1875, Riverside had become an ideal community for capitalists and persons with small investments. To this extent, North had succeeded. His plans were fulfilled with respect to schools, churches, library, and lyceum, to say nothing of cricket, tennis, and gun clubs, a Cotillion club and whist club.

What had North gained in Riverside? For himself, very little. A decade after his death his portrait would appear in the "Workers for the West." The editor could say, "Judge North, founder of Riverside, California, occupies an enviable place in Western history. The results that flowed from his labors are much wider than the limits of the beautiful community he founded, yet in Riverside alone he and his associates have a monument more beautiful and lasting than any that could be made of stone or bronze." [16]

George Wharton James, who knew North, made this appraisal:

Judge North was too busy helping others and directing municipal affairs to become a money-maker. . . . He had learned years ago, in the old Methodist homestead, . . . that "Ye cannot serve God and mammon." . . . Hence in none of his ventures did he reap a large pecuniary reward. When he left Riverside in 1880 [sic] to go to Fresno County, he took very little money with him, though his wisdom and foresight had enabled many other people to accumulate competencies.

In the later years of his life, I knew him well. He had seen that vast areas of land in the San Joaquin Valley, owing to its longer period of summer heat, were better adapted for the growth and curing of raisins than was Riverside. . . . Just as he had seen Riverside spring into prosperity that no necromancy ever surpassed, so he saw Oleander and its surrounding colonies become one of the greatest raisin-producing centers of the world.[17]

At seventy-five, J. W. North would again attempt to plant his ideal cooperative colony, and become the father of the raisin industry in California. The pattern for Oleander was established — with schools, churches, lyceum, library, reading room — and that major asset, John Wesley North.

REVOLUTION
IN THE CENTRAL VALLEY

Q̲U̲I̲T̲E̲ unable to content himself in the San Francisco law office
with a great agricultural revolution going on in the Central Valley of
California, North saw that baronial holdings dating back to the Spanish land grants were being broken up into family-size farms. His success
at Riverside and the success of the Anaheim colony near present-day
Disneyland were the models upon which proprietors were turning great
estates into small agricultural holdings.[1]

Foremost in these colonial ventures was the Washington Irrigated
colony at Fresno, organized by North's friends, J. P. Whitney, Wendell
Easton, and A. T. Covell. Easton was proprietor and general manager,
and Covell was resident agent and superintendent. The colony covered
five sections, later eleven, south of the Central California colony at
Fresno. To understand what a revolution these colonies wrought in California, we must recall what California farming was like when North
arrived in 1870.

North had seen California change during the Civil War, passing from
the doldrums following the decline of the gold rush to new activity as
the income from Nevada mines poured into San Francisco and was
invested widely in California. Railroads had radiated from Sacramento
and a few of the old gold-mining towns changed to centers of ranching
and prospered despite drought, flood, and earthquake. The Central Valley of California is divided into a northern and a southern half: grain
ranches of vast acres developed in the Sacramento Valley and cattle

and sheep ranges spread out in the San Joaquin Valley where tule swamps were drained and irrigation reached the dry plains.

While North developed the Riverside area, the Central Valley also prospered. Great fleets of grain ships carried supplies to England, for with the successful draining of the swamps and irrigation of the plains in the San Joaquin Valley, the cattle and sheep ranges gave way to grain farming. To the north of the state capital, the California and Oregon Railroad (later the Southern Pacific) reached Chico and crossed the Sacramento River at Los Molinos to serve Red Bluff and Redding. The Central Pacific, which had connected with the Union Pacific in 1869, now moved south into the San Joaquin Valley to serve the grain centers, making or breaking the towns of the valley. Towns like Empire and San Joaquin City refused to grant a subsidy to the Central Pacific (now the Southern Pacific) and were passed by; near Empire the railroad built a town they wanted to name for William Ralston, but when he modestly refused the honor, they called it Modesto. Likewise, the railroad ignored San Joaquin City in favor of Fresno — a matter of considerable importance to North when he decided to pioneer in that area where the first vineyard was planted east of Fresno in 1873. He watched with enthusiasm the advance of the railroad to the south, creating cities along its course and leaving ghost towns in its wake. Of the towns passed by, only Visalia, which had been rejected by the railroad in favor of Tulare, managed to survive the lack of railroad connection.

The railroads would have been content to serve the large ranchos and baronial estates. But North's example at Riverside, and his later work at the Washington colony at Fresno and at Oleander, helped dictate the revolution from large holdings extensively worked to small holdings intensively farmed. His work in the San Joaquin Valley was a continuation of the work he had begun in Nevada, where he had tried to break up the Mormon land grants and Spanish-title land grants in favor of the small farmer who might wish to pre-empt a few acres of the river valleys. He had tried to bring in small farmers to replace the great planters in Tennessee. He had succeeded at Riverside in converting the Jurupa and Rubidoux ranchos into small holdings. He was even more successful in the San Joaquin.

The Central Pacific had created Fresno and had given impetus to the vineyards. By the time North settled there in the 1880's, the great gang plows such as had stimulated his imagination toward industrialized farming, when he saw the steam plow at Chicago before the Civil War, were coming into use. Ten-horse teams drew great plows across the immense ranches. For all North's enthusiasm for industrialized farming, the numberless acres in the hands of one man, one family, or one corporation, seemed now to be defeating his communitarian ideal. At one place in the Sacramento and San Joaquin valleys a man of modest means could hope to compete with the large ranches; this was at Fresno, where the raising of grapes would not lend itself to industrialized farming. Here the large tracts of land were being subdivided for colonization, and here he decided to end his days.

North had a choice of engaging in the great industrialized wheat farming or the small intensive grape vineyards. Fifty men held half the irrigable land in California [2] and with his ability to raise money for corporate enterprise North might well have become manager of one of the great tracts. He knew that as settlers continued to come the great tracts would be broken up into family farms. Everything pointed toward this intensive agriculture on small holdings; with such soil and climate a small, well-tended farm could produce two or three crops a year. The great industrial kind of farming did not get the most out of the land; it was better suited to the one-crop regions of the plains of the American and Canadian West. An inspection of the great Central Valley of California today shows the influence of men like North. In the Sacramento Valley (the northern half of the Central Valley), where grain farming on extensive acres was carried on longest, there are palatial mansions widely spaced, where the ranch kings held court like feudal barons. In the San Joaquin Valley (the southern half of the Central Valley), where the colonizing ventures broke up the large tracts first around Fresno and later over the whole valley, simple cottages show that farmers of modest means and small acres grow their grapes, figs, olives, walnuts, almonds, and citrus and other deciduous fruits on irrigated ranches. This cottage agriculture which North encouraged, when the whole Central Valley was mostly in the hands of the land barons, now extends throughout the valley. Irrigation required capital which could be achieved by capitalists taking up the land, as they are now doing again for the raising of cotton, or by cooperative communities and colonies. The industrial cotton farms today import Mexican labor, but the industrial farmers of North's day did not have the labor in California for a more intensive farming, whereas the colonizing ventures had the many hands of their members.

By example at Riverside and by direct superintendence at Fresno, North helped produce "A thriving settlement of intelligent and enterprising people located upon the colony. Neat homes, orchards, and vineyards became numerous. Fields of alfalfa supplied abundant food for teams and animals." [3] Wendell Easton at the Washington colony set up a cheese factory. Bear organized a brass band, George Rowell established a dramatic club — all in keeping with the theory of North that colonial cooperation should be economic and *cultural*. In June 1880, North undertook the general agency of the colony and moved to Fresno. Immediately, between 1880 and 1882, the Washington colony grew vigorously with people "from Eastern States, some English and Scotchmen of means and culture, and some from the Islands, some from San Francisco, and some from Sweden and Denmark — there not being a loafer or grog-shop on the colony." The very success of the land sales deprived North of a job, for G. G. Briggs purchased all the unsold land of the colony and became its sole proprietor.

There were six colonies planted within six miles of Fresno. The Central California colony was within three miles of the city. Its proprietor, W. S. Chapman, and its manager, Marks, had included the price of water rights in the price of the land. The twenty-acre lots were sold with a one-fifth down payment, but the network of ditches was so costly that water paid for was not immediately delivered. The complaint was that "by misrepresentations without number, [settlers] were cajoled into purchasing desert lands at $50 per acre that would have been dear at five . . . The water which they were promised in abundance has only been dribbled out." [4] The promised vines, shade trees, bridges, fruit dryers, and factories existed only in the projectors' promises. Two miles away was the Scandinavian Irrigated colony founded by Charles A. Henry of San Francisco on the Riverside model in November 1878. Six miles from Fresno were the Church colony and Eisen Vineyard.

The Washington colony was five miles from Fresno, and, while North was there, the colonists built a central town a half-mile square — and a school [5] built on a tract of land originally owned by North's friend from New York, A. T. Covell. [6] When North moved into it in June 1880, it had been organized for only two years. During that time the land was surveyed and canals built, but when the other water companies would not cooperate, ten miles of main and branch canals had to be built to the Kings River. Lots were sold in summer, 1878, houses, some substantial, had been quickly built the year before North arrived. North lived in the worst sort of makeshift shack, "batching" it with only his visions of a great community to overcome his loneliness for his wife.

"A Colonist," who could be none other than J. W. North, writing to the local paper, said,

The larger portion of the buildings erected are cheaper structures, a few having built more substantial and tasty homes . . . Up to this time there has been planted as follows: Fruit trees, 7,500; Grape vines, mostly raisin varieties, 275,000; including cuttings, nearly all of which are making a fine start; Alfalfa, 120 acres, which after the first season, produces five and six good crops of hay each year. The above is distributed amongst over forty different Colonists, on their 10, 20, and 40-acre farm, and will result in much greater benefit to the country than three times the amount of improvements put up and owned by one, two, or three individuals on the same land. A better class of buildings, fine orchards and vineyards, with numerous pleasant and happy homes will soon be found in large numbers hereabouts.[7]

It was typical North promotion copy, and as usual it came true. North made the point that forty colonists were already occupying land formerly held by one man, and he had no time in his first promotion piece for the exotics — the eight-thousand-dollars' worth of Japanese persimmons and camellias. The less said about them the better, but the five or six crops of hay a year would bring eastern farmers by the hundreds when the clip sheets from the *Republican* were mailed to a myriad friends, acquaintances, correspondents, and newspaper editors.

The railroad made it easy for the immigrants to come to the San Joaquin Valley. In 1860 there had been only three or four towns in the valley, and a few stock-raisers, such as Lux and Miller, Jeff Davis, and John Sutherland, had made fortunes in a few years. But after the railroad was built through in 1870–71, the county changed completely, with immigrants coming every year.[8] In the winter of 1872, through the efforts of North and others, the fence law passed the legislature, compelling cattlemen either to fence in their stock or drive the herds to open ranges.

By the time North arrived in Fresno, it was a city of two thousand people, counting frequent visitors, and had a "handsome three-story Court House." A. T. Covell used North's system of excursions to bring investors and settlers from San Francisco, offering a flat rate of twelve dollars covering transportation, meals, hotel, and teams to carry the excursionists to the surrounding lands.[9] North carried on these excursions, bought a handsome team, and opened a substantial law office with his son in the best building, the Donahoo block. By spring of 1882, the colony had 229 residents.[10]

When North undertook the job of general agent for the Washington colony at Fresno, Ann believed that they had at last escaped the debilitating desert heat and would live out their lives in the bright, brisk city where North would sell colony lands from a comfortable office on Montgomery street. While she was sewing the wedding garments for Emma to go east to marry Edmund Clarence Messer, she received in Riverside a letter full of optimism and mentioning that North would have to spend part of his time on the spot in Fresno. Indeed, if he were to sell lands in the colony, he would have to show enough confidence in the colony to take up land himself.

Lacking money after North's investment in land to go east with her daughter for the wedding, she could escape the desert summer only by a prolonged visit to the Andersons, friends of Minnesota and Nevada days, in Santa Cruz. Taking Mary with her, she sent Eddie to his father so that he could tend the office in Fresno while North built his house at Oleander, leveled thirty acres for irrigation, rooted nine thousand vines, set out six hundred and seventy-five fruit trees and five hundred and sixty ornamentals, planted several acres of alfalfa, and put additional acres into peach pits — all on money borrowed from his son George. With men coming on from Scotland, England, and New Zealand, North said he had to demonstrate what could be done in this seemingly worthless desert.

When Ann left the Andersons, she moved to a boarding house at 700 Post street in San Francisco and refused to pioneer again. Apparently she called going to the Oleander community a wild goose chase, for North replied that it was no such thing. Land was hard to sell in the desert in the summertime, but he was occupied all day with possible buyers. In the evening he did not mind the loneliness, for he could wander across the wastes, fellow of coyotes, rabbits, and antelope ("my nearest neighbors"), and see an ideal community maturing all about Fresno.

Not yet plastered, his house was overrun by red ants from whom he

238

managed to save himself by standing the legs of the bed in cans of turpentine. Ann North was not equal to this kind of pioneering again, but she finally consented to spend a month with him in December 1880, afterward returning to San Francisco. On January 11, 1881, he wrote, "This is not nearly so dark a time as it was three months ago. Keep up courage, Dearest, things will yet come right."

Though North could not write after dark because the flies and bugs put out his candle, he managed to write a few thousand letters to clients and to old friends who might be persuaded to "come on." Governor William Rainey Marshall recalled years later in a letter to Ann North that his old friend had seriously urged him to come to California and "take hold" at Fresno. Marshall did not want to pioneer, but North's description of California may have had some effect: Marshall died in Pasadena. The governor was not the only friend North wrote to: he wrote to the Rice County *Journal,* and when his column-long letters stopped, Wheaton, now the editor in Northfield, called upon him to begin again. He also wrote letters about current topics — the assassination of Garfield and the wisdom of Robert G. Ingersoll — as well as penning judicious praise of the Oleander colony for the Belle Plaine (Iowa) *Union,* the Fresno *Republican,* and other papers. As for himself, he put every dollar into land and a future "bright with promise."

As we might expect, the month that North took over the agency of the Washington colony, "A Colonist" attacked the local Democrats in the Fresno *Republican.*[11] James A. Garfield had just been nominated in Chicago, and the Democrats were shouting for reform. Let the reform start, said the article, at the local level, in Fresno county, where graft had prevented the building of roads satisfactory to the colonies. In September, after his arrival, North did some campaigning for Garfield. There was a "Rousing Meeting" in the Grange hall in the Central colony, with many outside looking in at the windows after the hall was full, to hear Judge J. W. North. "The Judge said he was not a politician, nor engaged in political matters, but he felt he knew the value of Republican principles. In a speech of thirty minutes, he ably reviewed the relative positions of the two parties, gave his personal experience as a resident of the 'Solid South,' and earnestly exhorted all good citizens to support the Republican party in the coming election."[12] His son John Greenleaf North was a delegate to the Republican National Convention.

REVOLUTION IN THE CENTRAL VALLEY

Judge North was on hand for the pre-election meeting in the plaza before the Wigwam in Fresno, to tell of his personal experience as a resident of the South and to call on all patriots to vote for Garfield. North was conducted down Mariposa Street to the Wigwam on Front Street by a band and four-horse-wagon load of people from Washington colony, displaying a handsome flag. On election day, the Fresno county Democrats won, but by a hundred and ten fewer votes than usual. Given time, North could repair that. After the inauguration of President Garfield, he wrote, "I notice one thing in which this inauguration differed from the first one of Mr. Lincoln. He was sworn into office before he went out upon the platform to deliver his Inaugural. General Garfield (not being in danger of assassination) delivered his Inaugural first." [13] This letter to his daughter Emma, now married to Messer of the Corcoran art school in Washington, D.C., bore the address, Oleander, California. North had embarked upon a colony project of his own, but he still had connections with the Washington colony as agent for Thomas E. Hughes and Sons of Fresno. A correspondent of the *Farming World* (Cincinnati, Ohio) noted that only a good class of people was wanted at Fresno, and that "J. W. North and Son, at Fresno, California, are carrying on a general land agency business, representing some ten thousand acres, varying in price from $3 to $50 per acre. These gentlemen are safe and reliable, guarantee clear titles, and will in every way aid the homeseeker to secure the right location. They solicit correspondence. . . ." [14]

North's experience at Fresno was very much like all that had gone before at Riverside, Knoxville, Washoe, Northfield, and St. Anthony — enthusiasm to be maintained, letters to be written and answered, articles for the newspapers to be toiled over, and persons to be shown about. He took a party of eastern lumbermen up Kings Canyon to see the great trees, and pointed out the sawmill possibilities of the river. Yet this time there was a difference. He was the famed founder whom younger generations wanted to honor. In March 1882, Riverside called him back to speak at the citrus fair. In 1884, he was invited to read a paper on irrigation at the State Irrigation Convention. Minneapolis also invited him to return to the scene of his labors, in the fall of 1883, when he was so poor that he had to borrow money to buy a new suit so he could meet the millionaires of the Twin Cities with whom he had founded the St. Anthony section of Minneapolis. He visited the great

240

university he had begun almost singlehandedly, and President Folwell "insisted that I should tell all I remembered about the origin of the University which he had his Phonographer write down." [15]

North visited the towns he had founded and rode upon the railroad he had built. He was entertained by the citizens of Northfield, and went on to New York for a reunion of abolitionists. The first anti-slavery association in New York had been set up October 2, 1833, and the sesquicentennial was celebrated in the Broadway Tabernacle with the sole survivor of the founders, Elizur Wright, in the chair.[16] North wrote, "The Anti-Slavery gathering closed its sessions last evening at a late hour and I made the closing speech." [17]

Ann North had avoided the heat of the San Joaquin Valley summer by visiting her daughter Emma in Washington. She was greatly concerned about the state of their finances. North, then at home in his modest cottage in Oleander, spent the Fourth of July reading his latest hero, Robert G. Ingersoll. He wrote his wife, "As Ingersoll says 'if you have but one dollar to spend, spend it like a Lord.' Extreme carefulness, economy, and anxiety can make but a few dollars difference. . . ." [18]

In the spring of 1881, North wrote, "The Minnesota [Railroad] Bonds seem now to promise me some relief. The bill has passed to [pay] fifty-cents on the dollar on them. This will bring me five or six thousand dollars nearly, all of which will have to go to pay borrowed money. I hope to save a thousand or fifteen-hundred dollars with which to get a suitable home for your Mother and Edward and Mary, and to get a horse and buggy." [19]

When G. G. Briggs of Yolo county bought the lands at the Washington colony, North had enough money to buy eleven lots for $6,300.[20] His lands were called Oleander, and centered at Cedar and Adams streets.[21] Diagonally from the North estate was the schoolhouse on section 299, which North, in his poverty, had given away. Oleander was described as seven miles southeast of Fresno and three miles from the railroad at Fowler, with which the community had telephone connections. Twenty-five hundred acres were in raisin-grapes. The hamlet had several places of business, two raisin and fruit-packing houses, and the public school.[22] North deeded the section to the Oleander School District trustees on December 15, 1886,[23] for one dollar.

He deeded as much of his property as he could manage unencumbered to his children. His youngest daughter, Mary Ann North, received half a lot for a dollar, and similar arrangements were made for other children. John G. North had been the most successful. He was the first telegrapher in Riverside, and went to work at the United States mint in San Francisco in 1874, returning to Riverside in 1881. He lived on the twenty acres at Cypress Avenue and North Street and was incorporator of the Citizens' Water Company and of the Riverside Water Company. He followed in his father's footsteps, becoming land agent for Richard Gird's Chino ranch at Pomona, and became general manager of the Bear Valley Land and Water Company at Redlands. He was delegate to Republican conventions, and was successful in business until the panic of 1893 left him with one dollar. Then in his fortieth year, he studied law and was admitted to the California bar on April 10, 1894.

Neither John G. North nor the other children were in need of their father's generosity in dividing his holdings among them, and perhaps this was fortunate, for North seldom had clear title to his lands. He was deeply in debt to George A. Newhall, the San Francisco capitalist and president of its chamber of commerce. From August 1887, to December 1889, North gave three promissory notes to Newhall for $4,500, $1,500, and $2,061.70.[24] Newhall was too good a businessman to consider these loans adequately secured; they were given well beyond the value of the property, and upon North's expectations rather than upon the assessed value of the lands that supposedly secured them.

Years before, soon after arriving in Minnesota, when North thought his poor health would send him into an early grave, he had expressed his intention of providing for Ann if he should die. He had made numerous wills, and from time to time had tried to put property in her name, but necessity always prevented his securing to her any private fortune or income. Forty years later, his death left her with all his worldly goods, but that was a far less than adequate provision for her welfare. Two lots in the Washington Irrigated colony were heavily mortgaged to Newhall. Besides his watch and a library of seven hundred volumes, there were only the household furniture, farming tools, raisin trays, sweat boxes, two wagons and a buggy, three horses with harness, two cows, and a yearling calf,[25] an estate any small farmer of indifferent talents might have accumulated in one good season.

The modesty of the home in which North ended his days may be judged from the value placed upon the furniture — twenty-five dollars.

At the end of his life he was surrounded by books worth twice as much as his furniture, and could look out of his window upon a fine school he had donated to the community. The small grey horse Sam and the spring buggy he drove to town were together valued at twenty dollars. The large grey horse and the bay with a white star on its forehead formed the work team of Dick and Nick, valued at twenty dollars; they were worked with a spring wagon and a one and three quarter axle wagon worth twenty-five dollars. The sets of harnesses were valued at seven and a half. Thus, the animals and equipage North used to impress his callers and show newcomers the wonders of California were worth four times as much as the furnishings of his house. The property left by North to his widow came to $5,302.50, including his watch, library, tools, furniture, wagons, and animals. Even this was mortgaged to George A. Newhall for $8,061.70; Ann inherited a three thousand dollar debt.[26]

In the light of this appraisement, the good intentions expressed in his will show North a supreme optimist to the end:

"I, John W. North, of Oleander in the County of Fresno and State of California . . . give and devise to my beloved wife, Ann L. North, all my real estate . . . together with all personal property, notes, mortgages, books, and property of every kind and nature . . . it being my desire that my said wife shall be my only legatee." [27]

He left "nothing to either of our six children, whom I love with equal and devoted affection . . . I desire to give the highest evidence of love for and confidence in my said wife, who, through all our married life has been to me far more than I can express."

It was an old will, witnessed on March 5, 1882, by Charles L. North and George F. Stamford. It could have been written at any time in his life, and the sentiments and the results would have been much the same. Ann could inherit hopes and dreams worth millions of dollars — but millions that were made by others caught up in the tide of his vision, in the founding of Minneapolis, Faribault, Northfield, the Cedar Valley Road, the University of Minnesota, the states of Minnesota and Nevada, the finest quartz mill in Nevada; in the surveying of the Nevada Territory; in the founding of iron works and foundry in Knoxville, a free public school system in Tennessee, Riverside and Oleander, a section of the Republican party upon abolitionist principles, and, in some part, founding the United States itself upon the principles that have made it one great nation.

By the direction of John Wesley North, his body should have been cremated without ceremony, and his ashes and dust spread as a blessing upon the Los Angeles plain between the mountains and the sea. Los Angeles had been his choice for the ideal community he had sought to found, and in his death he would become a part of it, a testimonial of his faith in the future greatness of the City of the Angels. Even in death his expectations were frustrated; he was buried in the family plot at Riverside. But even in this last wish, history will justify North; the Los Angeles community of homes, schools, churches, libraries, and lyceums is expanding as he predicted to people the desert with homes far beyond Riverside and take his remains to its bosom.

NOTES AND INDEX

NOTES

Evangelical Humanism

[1] John Wesley North, manuscript, "Random Sketches of a Crude Life," *North Papers* 1414, Huntington Library, San Marino, California (*North Papers* cited hereafter as *NO*).

[2] *NO* 1414.

[3] *Ibid.*

[4] William Reddy, *First Fifty Years of Cazenovia Seminary*, Cazenovia, New York, 1877, p. 97.

[5] *Ibid.*, p. 98.

[6] *Ibid.*

[7] *NO* 1414.

[8] George Wharton James, *Heroes of California*, Boston: Little, Brown, 1910, p. 298.

[9] North also studied in the offices of Benedict and Boardman in 1843, and later in Syracuse in the office of Forbes and Sheldon.

Free Soil and Liberty

[1] North to Emma Bacon North Messer, July 23, 1871, *NO* 891.

[2] Emma North Messer, "Memoirs of a Frontier Childhood," *Overland Monthly Magazine*, August, September, and October, 1924, pp. 339–340, 395–397, 437–440.

[3] Gerrit Smith, *Address*, October 1, 1857, *Smith Papers*, New York Public Library.

[4] Amos Kendall to Lewis Tappan, March 4, 1843, *Lewis Tappan Papers*, Library of Congress.

[5] North to Ann Loomis, June 30, 1848, *NO* 1400.

[6] North to Ann Loomis, July 3, 1848, *NO* 1402.

[7] North to Ann Loomis, July 8, 1848, *NO* 1403.

[8] *Ibid.*

[9] Syracuse (New York) *Journal*, August 30, 1848, p. 2, c. 6, and family records of Miss Anne Shepard, Palmdale, California.

[10] North to Gerrit Smith, August 27, 1867, *Smith Papers*, Syracuse University Library, Syracuse, New York; photostat in *NO*.

[11] North to Gerrit Smith, January 6, 1849, *Smith Papers*, Syracuse University Library, Syracuse, New York; photostat in *NO*.

[12] Syracuse (New York) *Standard*, March 12, 1885, clipping, Onondaga Historical Society, Syracuse, New York.

[13] Syracuse (New York) *Standard*, November 20, 1854, clipping, Onondaga Historical Society, Syracuse, New York.

[14] John T. Roberts, "Business Men of the Village," Onondaga Historical Society, *Publications*, New Series, Vol. I, No. 1, January 1910, pp. 35–36.

[15] Ellen Birdseye Wheaton to Carlotte Amelia Birdseye, December 24, 1849, in *The Diary of Ellen Birdseye Wheaton*, Donald Gordon, ed., Boston, 1923, p. 11.

Island Home

[1] St. Paul (Minnesota Territory) *Chronicle and Register*, Vol. I, No. 2, September 1, 1849.

[2] William R. Marshall at St. Anthony

Falls to Henry H. Sibley at Mendota, June 22, 1849, *Sibley Papers*, Minnesota Historical Society, St. Paul, Minnesota.

[3] Franklin Steele at Fort Snelling to Henry H. Sibley at Mendota, November 27, 1848, *Sibley Papers*.

[4] Franklin Steele at Fort Snelling to Henry H. Sibley in Washington, December 18, 1848, *Sibley Papers*.

[5] Return I. Holcombe, *Minnesota in Three Centuries*, New York: Publishing Society of Minnesota, 1908, printed by Mankato *Free Press* Printing Company, Vol. II, p. 97.

[6] Franklin Steele at Fort Snelling to Henry H. Sibley in Washington, November 27, 1848, *Sibley Papers*.

[7] Henry M. Rice in New York to Henry H. Sibley in Washington, April 8, 1848, *Sibley Papers*.

Pioneers at the Falls

[1] Washington (D.C.) *National Era*, January 24, 1850, p. 1, c. 6–7.

[2] Isaac Atwater, *History of the City of Minneapolis, Minnesota*, New York: Munsell, 1863, Vol. I, p. 423.

Minnesota, 1850

[1] John Francis McDermott, *The Lost Panoramas of the Mississippi*, Chicago: University of Chicago Press, 1958, p. vii.

[2] Ann North to Loomises, March 14, 1850, *NO* 104.

[3] Ann North to Loomises, May 3, 1850, *NO* 111.

[4] St. Paul (Minnesota Territory) *Chronicle and Register*, May 27, 1850, p. 2, c. 6.

[5] *Ibid.*, editorial, p. 2.

[6] Ann Hendrix Lewis to Mary Ann Lewis Loomis, July 16, 1850, *NO* 20.

[7] Fredrika Bremer, *The Homes of the New World; Impressions of America*, Mary Howitt, tr., New York: Harper & Bros., 1854, Vol. II, p. 27.

[8] *Ibid.*, p. 32.

[9] *Ibid.*, p. 55.

[10] *Ibid.*, p. 57.

[11] *Ibid.*, p. 56.

[12] Ann North to Loomises, September 1, 1850, *NO* 515.

[13] *Ibid.*

[14] North to Loomis, September 3, 1850, *NO* 515.

[15] *Ibid.*

[16] North to Loomis, October 13, 1850, *NO* 769.

Minnesota, 1851

[1] North to Loomis, January 19, 1851, *NO* 142. Charges against Ramsey are in 32nd Congress, 2nd Session, Executive Document 29; his justification, in *Globe*, United States Senate, February 24, 1854.

[2] North to Loomis, March 9, 1851, *NO* 775.

[3] Edward Duffield Neill, *The History of Minnesota from the Earliest French Exploration to the Present Time*, Minneapolis: Minnesota Historical Company, 1882. The Reverend Mr. Neill said, "By the efforts of J. W. North, Esq., a bill creating the University of Minnesota at or near the Falls of St. Anthony was passed and signed by the governor," p. 547.

[4] Atwater, *op. cit.*, Vol. I, p. 40.

[5] North to Loomis, March 9, 1851, *NO* 775.

[6] North to Loomis, March 5, 1851, *NO* 777.

[7] North to Loomis, August 19, 1851, *NO* 778.

[8] University of Minnesota *Directory*, Vol. XIII, No. 8, November 10, 1913: "To Colonel North, more than to any one man, belongs the credit of starting the movement which resulted in the establishment of the University of Minnesota."

[9] Atwater, *op. cit.*, Vol. I, p. 33.

[10] North to Loomis, December 26, 1851, *NO* 164.

[11] North to Loomis, August 19, 1851, *NO* 778.

[12] North to Loomis, December 26, 1851, *NO* 164.

Prohibition Year, 1852

[1] North to Loomis, September 12, 1852, *NO* 174.

[2] North to Loomis, February 22, 1852, *NO* 168; Ann North to Ann Hendrix Lewis, February 20, 1852, *NO* 168.

[3] North to Loomis, January 2, 1852, *NO* 780.

[4] North to Loomis, February 22, 1852, *NO* 168.

[5] *Ibid.*

[6] Ann North to Ann Hendrix Lewis, October 3, 1852, *NO* 551.

A Highway for Our God, 1853–54

[1] North to Loomis, May 1, 1853, *NO* 188.
[2] *Ibid.*
[3] North to Loomis, November 6, 1853, *NO* 793.
[4] North to Loomis, November 20, 1853, *NO* 794.
[5] *Ibid.*
[6] Ann to Loomises, May 23, 1853, *NO* 190.
[7] Ann to Loomises, November 12, 1853, *NO* 201.
[8] North to Loomis, May 15, 1853, *NO* 788.
[9] North to Loomis, January 1, 1854, *NO* 795.
[10] North to Loomis, February 5, 1854, *NO* 796.
[11] H. M. Rice in Washington to David Olmsted, August 3, 1854, quoted in Neill, *op. cit.*, p. 610n.
[12] H. M. Rice in Washington to Alexander Ramsey in St. Paul, June 20, 1854, *Ramsey Papers*, Box 4, Minnesota Historical Society.
[13] Neill, *op. cit.*, pp. 595–597. In source Farnam is spelled Farnham.
[14] Ann North to (brother) George Loomis, June 11, 1854, *NO* 535.
[15] North to Gerrit Smith, June 23, 1854, *Smith Papers*, Syracuse University Library; photostat in *NO*.
[16] North to Loomis, February 5, 1854, *NO* 796.

Republican Party

[1] Holcombe, *op. cit.*, Vol. II, p. 484.
[2] North to Loomis, February 5, 1854, *NO* 796.
[3] North to Loomis, January 4, 1855, *NO* 802.
[4] T. H. Williams, "Account of a Trip to Faribault," ms dated January 21 [23], 1855, Minnesota Historical Society.

Northfield

[1] North to Loomis, March 16, 1856, *NO* 806.
[2] *Constitution of the Northfield Lyceum*, microfilm, Minnesota Historical Society.
[3] Ann North to Loomises, May 3, 1857, *NO* 269.
[4] Warrantee Deed, Northfield Public Library, Northfield, Minnesota, copy in Minnesota Historical Society.
[5] Ann North to Loomises, October 5, 1856, *NO* 260.

[6] North to Loomis, January 11, 1857, *NO* 808.

Two Constitutions for Minnesota

[1] T. F. Andrews, *Debates and Proceedings of the Constitutional Convention for the Territory of Minnesota to Form a State Constitution Preparatory to Its Admission into the Union as a State*, St. Paul, Minnesota: George W. Moore, printer, 1858, p. 21.
[2] *Ibid.*, p. 22.
[3] *Ibid.*, p. 33.
[4] *Ibid.*, pp. 58, 61.
[5] William Anderson, *A History of the Constitution of Minnesota*, Minneapolis: University of Minnesota, 1921, p. 98.
[6] St. Paul (Minnesota Territory) *Pioneer and Democrat*, August 25, 1857.
[7] North to Silas Hawley, published in the St. Paul *Press* and copied in the Virginia City (Nevada) *Daily Union*, September 2, 1865.
[8] Ann North to Loomises, November 25, 1868, *NO* 499. Marshall's letter is quoted.

M. & C. V. Railroad

[1] *Report of the Commissioners, Minnesota and Cedar Valley Railroad*, 1857–58, Minnesota Historical Society.
[2] *Ibid.*
[3] Shields to Charles P. Daly, May 6, 1857, *Charles P. Daly Papers*, New York Public Library.
[4] *Report of the Commissioners.*
[5] Shields from Baltimore to Sibley, January 12, 1857. *Sibley Papers*, Minnesota Historical Society.
[6] *Report of the Commissioners*, June 8, 1858.
[7] North to Sibley, May 24, 1858, *Sibley Papers.*
[8] *Report of the Commissioners*, June 8, 1858.
[9] North to Loomis, March 7, 1858, *NO* 274.
[10] Ann North to Loomises, April 11, 1858, *NO* 277.
[11] North to Sibley, October 27, 1858, *Sibley Papers.*
[12] North to Loomis, November 13, 1858, *NO* 810.
[13] Ramsay Crooks to Sibley, November 22, 1858, *Sibley Papers.*
[14] North to Sibley, December 2, 1858, *Sibley Papers.*

[15] *Ibid.*

[16] North to Loomis, December 17, 1858, *NO* 812.

[17] Shields to Daly, November 19, 1858, *Daly Papers.*

[18] Ezra Abbott to Sibley, December 5, 1858, *Sibley Papers.*

[19] R. M. S. Pease to Sibley, January 29, 1859, *Sibley Papers.*

[20] Ann North to Ann Hendrix Lewis, March 13, 1859, *NO* 608.

[21] North to Sibley, April 6, 1859, *Sibley Papers.*

[22] North to Loomis, April 10, 1859, *NO* 815.

[23] *Stock Ledger of the M. & C. V. Railroad Company*, Vol. II, Minnesota Historical Society.

[24] Ann North to Ann Hendrix Lewis, June 5, 1859, *NO* 611.

[25] F. M. Crosby to Philander Parmalee, June 19, 1859, *Philander Parmalee Papers*, Minnesota Historical Society.

[26] Ann North to Loomises, June 19, 1859, *NO* 296.

[27] North to Loomis, June 19, 1859, *NO* 816.

[28] Ann North to Loomises, July 5, 1859, *NO* 612.

[29] Petit to Sibley, September 12, 1859, *Sibley Papers.*

[30] Ann North to Loomises, September 26, 1858, *NO* 280.

[31] Interstate Commerce Commission, *Corporate History of the C. M. St. P. and P. Railroad Company in Minnesota.* I.C.C. Val. Docket #1072, pp. 636ff.

[32] Interstate Commerce Commission, *Final Report*, pp. 550–558, on file with Engineering Department, Railroad and Warehouse Commission, State Office Building, St. Paul, Minnesota.

Short Corner

[1] North to Loomis, January 30, 1859, *NO* 631.

[2] F. M. Crosby to Philander Parmalee, June 19, 1859, *Parmalee Papers*, Minnesota Historical Society.

[3] Crosby to Parmalee, August 9, 1859, *Parmalee Papers.*

[4] Ann North to Ann Hendrix Lewis, April 17, 1859, *NO* 610.

[5] Ann North to Loomises, May 29, 1859, *NO* 294.

[6] Atwater to John T. Stevens, October 31, 1857, John T. Stevens, *Personal Recollec-*

tions of Minnesota and Its People, Minneapolis, 1890, p. 419.

[7] Hermann Trott to Charles P. Daly, November 21, 1857, *Daly Papers*, New York Public Library.

[8] Ann North to Ann Hendrix Lewis, March 30, 1859, *NO* 609.

[9] Z. Chandler to E. D. Morgan, April 30, 1859, *Morgan Papers*, Box 19, Folder 1, State Library, Albany, New York.

[10] L. C. Clepham to Ramsey, August 15, 1859, *Ramsey Papers*, Minnesota Historical Society.

[11] Ann North to Loomises, November 20, 1859, *NO* 301.

[12] North to Loomis, December 19, 1859, *NO* 822.

[13] Judd to Morgan, March 9, 1860, *Morgan Papers.*

[14] Ramsey to Morgan, March 13, 1860, *Morgan Papers.*

[15] Syracuse (New York) *Journal*, April 3, 1860.

[16] North to Loomis, May 15, 1860, *NO* 826.

[17] Correspondent "S" from Chicago, May 15, 1860, to Indianapolis (Indiana) *Daily Journal*, May 17, 1860.

[18] North to Loomis, May 15, 1860, *NO* 826.

[19] Addison G. Proctor, *Lincoln and the Convention of 1860*, Chicago: Chicago Historical Society, 1918, pp. 6–7.

[20] North to Loomis, May 15, 1860, *NO* 826.

[21] Leonard Swett to Josiah H. Drummond, May 27, 1860, *Herndon-Weik Papers*, Chicago Historical Society.

[22] Fond du Lac (Wisconsin) *Commonwealth*, May 23, 1860, J. A. Smith, editorial correspondence.

[23] *Ibid.*

[24] North to Loomis, June 3, 1860, *NO* 827.

[25] North to Loomis, November 21, 1860, *NO* 831.

[26] North to Ramsey, November 23, 1860, *Ramsey Papers.*

[27] North to Loomis, November 21, 1860, *NO* 831.

[28] North reported the talk with Lincoln in the letters cited in notes 26 and 27 above.

[29] North to Ramsey, November 23, 1860, *Ramsey Papers*; North to Loomis, December 2, 1860, *NO* 832.

[30] North to Ramsey, November 23, 1860, *Ramsey Papers.*

[31] North to Loomis, December 2, 1860, *NO* 832.

[32] North to Loomis, February 25, 1861, *NO* 838.

[33] North to Loomis, March 7, 1861, *NO* 839.

[34] North to Loomis, March 8, 1861, *NO* 840.

[35] North to Loomis, March 23, 1861, *NO* 843.

[36] Roy P. Basler, ed., *The Collected Works of Abraham Lincoln*, New Brunswick, N.J.: Rutgers University Press, 1953, Vol. VI, pp. 296–297.

[37] North to Loomis, March 23, 1861, *NO* 843.

[38] Basler, *op. cit.*, Vol. IV, pp. 294–295.

General North

[1] Basler, *op. cit.*, Vol. IV, p. 250.

[2] See Mark Twain's account in *Roughing It*.

[3] James M. Edmunds to North, April 13, 1861, National Archives, General Land Office (hereafter cited as N.A., G.L.O.), Letters to the Surveyor General, Nevada.

[4] J. C. Birdseye to Edmunds, March 29, 1861, N.A., G.L.O., Miscellaneous Letters Received, Surveyor General, Nevada.

[5] Edmunds to North, April 13, 1861, N.A., G.L.O., Miscellaneous Letters Received, Surveyor General, Nevada.

[6] North to Edmunds, May 17, 1861, N.A., G.L.O., Miscellaneous Letters Received, Surveyor General, Nevada.

[7] North to Ann North, May 20, 1861, *NO* 919.

[8] *Ibid.*

[9] Edwin Hubbell Chapin, *Select Sermons*, New York, N.Y.: H. Lyon, 1859.

[10] San Francisco (California) *Evening Bulletin*, June 14, 1861, p. 1, c. 1, p. 3, c. 4.

[11] North to Ann North, June 23, 1861, *NO* 925.

[12] James Shields to Mrs. Maria Lydig Daly, June 10, 1861, *Daly Papers*, New York Public Library.

[13] North to Ann North, June 16, 1861, *NO* 924.

[14] North to Loomis, July 6, 1861, *NO* 928.

[15] *Ibid.*

[16] On Sam Brown, see George S. Lyman's *Saga of the Comstock Lode*, Ch. 26 and *passim*.

[17] North to family, July 13, 1861, *NO* 903.

[18] North to Ann North, July 18, 1861, *NO* 931.

[19] North to family, August 13, 1861, *NO* 937.

[20] National Archives, Department of State, Territorial Correspondence, Nevada, Vol. I.

[21] Edmunds to Nye, N.A., G.L.O., Letterbook, 1862.

[22] Edmunds to North, December 26, 1861, N.A., G.L.O., Letterbook, 1861.

[23] North to Edmunds, February 17, 1861, N.A., G.L.O.

[24] Memorandum, November 27, 1861, N.A., G.L.O., Letters Received, Surveyor General, Nevada.

[25] North to Edmunds, August 14, 1861, N.A., G.L.O.

[26] North to Edmunds, September 30, 1861, N.A., G.L.O.

[27] Letters to the Surveyor General, Nevada, 1861–63, p. 43, N.A., G.L.O.

[28] North to Edmunds, December 27, 1861, N.A., G.L.O.

[29] Edmunds to North, August 16, 1861, N.A., G.L.O.

[30] Edmunds to J. P. Usher, September 29, 1863, *Report of the Commissioner of the General Land Office*, Washington, D.C., 1863, p. 42.

[31] San Francisco (California) *Evening Bulletin*, July 1, 1861, p. 3, c. 4.

[32] Edmunds to North, October 28, 1861, N.A., G.L.O.

[33] North to Edmunds, July 17, 1861, N.A., G.L.O.

[34] Syracuse (New York) *Courier*, November 21, 1877.

[35] Edmunds to Caleb B. Smith, in *Report of the Commissioner of the General Land Office*, accompanying *The Annual Report of the Secretary of the Interior*, Washington, D.C., 1862.

[36] North to Chase, December 25, 1862, *Chase Papers*, Library of Congress.

[37] North to Loomis, November 2, 1862, *NO* 849.

Judge North

[1] San Francisco (California) *Evening Bulletin*, November 14, 1862, p. 2, c. 2–3.

[2] North to Loomis, November 2, 1862, *NO* 849.

[3] Gold Hill (Nevada Territory) *News*, April 29, 1864, p. 3, c. 1.

[4] Nevers, "Nevada Pioneers," Pac. MS G 10, Bancroft Library, Berkeley, California.

[5] Dr. Charles L. Anderson to Merial H.

Anderson, December 21, 1862, PG 266, Bancroft Library.

[6] *Ibid.*

[7] *Ibid.*

[8] Ann North to Loomises, July 5, 1863, *NO* 366.

[9] Ann North to Loomises, September 6, 1863, *NO* 360.

[10] National Archives, Attorney General's Papers, Letters Received, Nevada, Group 60.

[11] *Ibid.*

[12] Latham to Lincoln, April 18, 1863, National Archives, Attorney General's Papers, Letters Received, Nevada.

[13] Syracuse (New York) *Journal,* January 14, 1863.

[14] Syracuse (New York) *Journal,* June 20, 1863.

[15] Syracuse (New York) *Journal,* May 1, 1863.

[16] Corson to North, June 2, 1862, National Archives, Attorney General's Papers, Letters Received, Nevada.

[17] *Ibid.*

[18] North to Chase, December 25, 1862, *Chase Papers,* Library of Congress.

[19] North to Loomis, November 29, 1863, *NO* 853.

[20] *Ibid.*

[21] North to Chase, December 25, 1862, *Chase Papers,* Library of Congress.

[22] North to Loomis, November 29, 1863, *NO* 853.

[23] *Ibid.*

President North

[1] North to Loomis, November 29, 1863, *NO* 853.

[2] San Francisco (California) *Evening Bulletin,* September 15, 1863, p. 1, c. 1.

[3] *Congressional Record,* 50th Congress, 1st Session, p. 475.

[4] *Congressional Record,* 51st Congress, 2nd Session, p. 1667.

[5] San Francisco (California) *Chronicle,* January 10, 1888; Carson (Nevada) *Daily News,* January 9, 1888.

[6] San Francisco (California) *Evening Bulletin,* November 28, 1863, p. 3, c. 5.

[7] San Francisco (California) *Evening Bulletin,* December 1, 1863, p. 5, c. 6.

[8] San Francisco (California) *Evening Bulletin,* January 8, 1864, p. 3, c. 7.

[9] Bellows to Seward, July 23, 1864, *Robert T. Lincoln Collection,* 34802, Library of Congress.

[10] William Morris Stewart, *Reminiscences of Senator William M. Stewart of Nevada,* George Rothwell Brown, ed., New York and Washington: Neale Publishing Company, 1908, p. 129.

[11] They were Sierra Nevada, Ophir, Mexican, Middle Lead, Gould and Curry, Savage, Chollar, Gold Hill (several claims), Yellow Jacket, Crown Point, Belcher, and Overman.

[12] Stewart, *op. cit.,* p. 153.

[13] *Ibid.,* p. 159.

[14] Ann North to Loomises, October 26, 1863, *NO* 374.

[15] Ann North's postscript to North to Loomis, November 29, 1863, *NO* 853.

[16] North to Loomis, November 29, 1863, *NO* 853.

[17] *Ibid.*

[18] Ann North to Loomises, November 25, 1863, *NO* 376.

[19] North to Loomis, November 29, 1863, *NO* 853.

[20] San Francisco (California) *Evening Bulletin,* August 3, 1863, p. 3, c. 4; May 21, 1862, p. 3, c. 5–6; August 21, 1862, p. 2, c. 1.

"Corrupt" Judge

[1] Virginia City (Nevada Territory) *Daily Union,* January 5, 1864, p. 1, c. 7; copying the Carson City (Nevada Territory) *Independent.*

[2] *Ibid.*

[3] San Francisco (California) *Evening Bulletin,* January 21, 1864, p. 3, c. 6.

[4] *Ibid.*

[5] *Ibid.*

[6] *Ibid.*

[7] Virginia City (Nevada Territory) *Union,* January 19, 1864, p. 2, c. 1.

[8] North to Loomis, February 7, 1864, *NO* 855.

[9] San Francisco (California) *Evening Bulletin,* April 4, 1864, p. 2, c. 1; article by Gold Hill correspondent, March 28.

[10] Charles Neider, *The Autobiography of Mark Twain,* New York, N.Y.: Harper, 1959, p. 118.

[11] Virginia City (Nevada Territory) *Territorial Enterprise,* May 15, 1863, quoted in San Francisco (California) *Evening Bulletin,* May 21, 1863, p. 2, c. 1.

[12] San Francisco (California) *Evening Bulletin*, April 30, 1863, p. 3, c. 4.

[13] Stewart, *op. cit.*, p. 151.

[14] *Ibid.*, p. 160.

[15] *Ibid.*, p. 162.

[16] *Ibid.*, p. 163.

[17] San Francisco (California) *Evening Bulletin*, August 27, 1864, p. 2, c. 1.

[18] North to Lincoln, August 22, 1864, *Robert T. Lincoln Collection*, microfilm, 35720, Library of Congress; Virginia City (Nevada Territory) *Territorial Enterprise*, August 24, 1864; San Francisco (California) *Evening Bulletin*, August 26, 1864, p. 2, c. 1.

[19] *Ibid.*

[20] *Ibid.* See also *Robert T. Lincoln Collection*, microfilm, 35706, Library of Congress.

[21] Virginia City (Nevada Territory) *Union*, August 26, 1864, quoted in San Francisco (California) *Evening Bulletin*, August 29, p. 3, c. 6.

[22] San Francisco (California) *Evening Bulletin*, August 27, 1864, p. 2, c. 1.

[23] Virginia City (Nevada Territory) *Union*, August 31, 1864; San Francisco (California) *Evening Bulletin*, September 3, 1864, p. 1, c. 4.

[24] Bellows' description of Nevada, July 25, 1864, *Bellows Papers*, Massachusetts Historical Society, Boston, Massachusetts.

[25] San Francisco (California) *Evening Bulletin*, September 13, 1864, p. 2, c. 2.

[26] National Archives, Attorney General's Papers, Presidential, Group 60.

[27] *NO* 1386. Mary North Shepard's attempt to correct the Nevada histories castigating her father as a corrupt judge received no eager assistance from Nevada officials. After her frustrating correspondence with E. H. Beemer, Washoe County clerk, he finally wrote that the number of the case of J. W. North *vs.* W. M. Stewart was 211, and the case of J. W. North *vs.* J. T. Goodman and D. E. McCarthy was 212. After still further correspondence, on August 1, 1938, Clerk Beemer by M. Dowd, Deputy, provided the following transcript: "according to the findings of the Arbitrators which the parties agreed to the following is taken from the findings: 'We must therefore pronounce the conduct and motions of Defendant Wm. M. Stewart, after that date (Dec. 22, 1863) as wrong and unjustifiable. . . .' As a corollary from the foregoing decision, it follows that defendants Wm. M. Stewart, I. [Joseph] T. Goodman and D. E. McCarthy pay the costs of these proceedings in accordance with the terms and stipulation."

Labors of Love

[1] North to Ann North, December 11, 1864, *NO* 975.

[2] San Francisco (California) *Evening Bulletin*, September 19, 1864, p. 1.

[3] James Robert Gilmore, *Down in Tennessee, and Back by Way of Richmond* (Edmund Kirke, pseud.), Carleton, N.Y., 1864.

[4] North to Gerrit Smith, December 17, 1864, *Smith Papers*, Syracuse University Library; photostat in *NO*.

[5] North to Ann North, January 1, 1865, *NO* 984.

[6] Ann North to Loomises, March 7, 1864, *NO* 381.

[7] North to Ann North, December 21, 1865, *NO* 1063.

[8] Washoe (Nevada) *Times*, October 14, 1865, p. 2, c. 3–4.

[9] Ann North to Loomises, October 15, 16, 1865, *NO* 431.

[10] *Ibid.*

[11] North to Ann North, December 30, 1865, *NO* 1069.

[12] North to Smith, February 3, 1866, *Smith Papers*, Syracuse University; photostat in *NO*.

[13] North to Chase, January 1, 1865 [1866], *Chase Papers*, Library of Congress.

[14] North to Ann North, January 1, 1866, *NO* 1070.

[15] Washoe (Nevada) *Eastern Slope*, February 3, 1866.

[16] North to Ann North, February 20, 1866, *NO* 1085.

[17] North to Ann North, January 14, 1866, *NO* 1078.

[18] North to Ann North, February 26, 1866, *NO* 1088.

[19] North to Ann North, January 18, 1866, *NO* 1080.

[20] North to Smith, February 3, 1866, *Smith Papers*, Syracuse University Library; photostat in *NO*.

[21] North to Chase, January 1, 1865 [1866], *Chase Papers*, Library of Congress.

[22] Ann North to Loomises, June 4, 1866, *NO* 438.

[23] William B. Hesseltine, "Tennessee's In-

vitation to Carpetbaggers," *East Tennessee Historical Society Publications*, Vol. IV, 1932, p. 105.

[24] North to Loomis, January 11, 1868, *NO* 871.

[25] C. G. Belissary, "Tennessee and Immigration, 1865–1880," *Tennessee Historical Quarterly*, Vol. VII, No. 3, September 1949, p. 230.

[26] Hesseltine, *op. cit.*, p. 103.

[27] New York *Tribune Almanac*, 1868.

[28] North to Ann North, March 1, 1866, *NO* 1089.

[29] North to Ann North, March 1866, *NO* 1094.

[30] Ann North to Loomises, July 8, 1866, *NO* 442.

[31] *Ibid.*

[32] Ann North to Loomises, October 14, 1866, *NO* 452.

[33] Emma Bacon North (Messer), George Loomis North, John Greenleaf North, Charles Loomis North, Edward North, and Mary Ann Lewis North (Shepard).

[34] Emma North to Mary Ann Loomis, September 23, 1866, *NO* 54.

[35] Ann North to Loomises, August 26, 1866, *NO* 447.

[36] North to Emma North, January 5, 1867, *NO* 888.

[37] Washington (D.C.) *Chronicle*, November 19, 1867, p. 2, c. 2–3. North was a regular contributor to Forney's papers in Washington and Philadelphia, and many of his articles on Tennessee appeared under Forney's own column signed "Occasional."

[38] James A. Rogers from Brownsville, Tennessee, to Governor W. G. Brownlow, May 15, 1865, *Brownlow Papers*, Tennessee State Archives, Nashville, Tennessee.

[39] State of Tennessee, General Assembly, Senate *Journal*, 1866–67, Nashville, 1867, pp. 11–12.

[40] Nashville (Tennessee) *Union*, January 13, 1866, p. 3, c. 2.

[41] "A Friend to Education," Nashville (Tennessee) *Union*, January 10, 1866, p. 1, c. 6–7.

[42] Knoxville (Tennessee) *Whig*, February 13, 1867, p. 2, c. 2.

[43] Knoxville (Tennessee) *Whig*, March 6, 1867, p. 1, c. 1–5.

[44] North to Gerrit Smith, February 3, 1866, *Smith Papers*, Syracuse University Library; photostat in *NO*.

[45] *Ibid.*

[46] "The Destruction of Free Schools," Knoxville (Tennessee) *Whig*, January 6, 1869, p. 3, c. 3.

A Fool's Errand

[1] North to Ann North, October 6, 1869, *NO* 1239.

[2] Albion Winegar Tourgée, *A Fool's Errand*, by One of the Fools, New York: Fords, Howard, and Hulbert, 1880.

[3] North to Ann North, Fresno, California, August 28, 1880, *NO* 1314.

[4] Knoxville (Tennessee) *Whig*, January 16, 1867, p. 3, c. 2.

[5] North to Smith, June 30, 1867, *Smith Papers*, University of Syracuse Library; photostat in *NO*.

[6] *Ibid.*

[7] Ann North to Loomises, January 5, 1868, *NO* 472.

[8] Knoxville (Tennessee) *Whig*, March 20, 1867, p. 3, c. 1.

[9] Knoxville (Tennessee) *Whig*, April 12, 1867, p. 3, c. 2.

[10] Knoxville (Tennessee) *Whig*, May 8, 1867, p. 3, c. 1.

[11] Knoxville (Tennessee) *Free Press*, November 24, 1867, p. 2, c. 1–2.

[12] Knoxville (Tennessee) *Free Press*, November 28, 1867, p. 2, c. 2.

[13] Knoxville (Tennessee) *Whig*, December 4, 1867, p. 3, c. 2. In the margin of the copy in the Library of Congress, J. B. Brownlow noted, "The Democratic Organ of Knoxville warred upon all the Northern men coming there from the North who were Republicans but had more *respect* for them than for the few who abandoned the principles they professed during the war."

[14] Helms' *Directory of Knoxville, 1869*, Knoxville: T. Haws and Co., 1869, p. 47.

[15] *Ibid.*, p. 11.

[16] Knoxville Industrial Association, *Facts and Figures Concerning the Climate, Manufacturing Advantages, and Mineral Resources of East Tennessee*, Knoxville: T. Haws and Co., 1869.

[17] *Ibid.*, p. 11.

[18] *Ibid.*, p. 21.

[19] North to Loomis, January 14, 1868, *NO* 872.

[20] North to John Eaton, January 11, 1868, *Eaton Papers*, University of Tennessee Library, Knoxville, Tennessee.

[21] Ann North to Loomises, May 17, 1868, *NO* 482.

[22] North to Smith, June 10, 1868, *Smith Papers*, University of Syracuse Library; photostat in *NO*.

[23] North to Ann North, December 4, 1868, *NO* 1173.

[24] *History of Tennessee from the Earliest Time to the Present; Together with an Historical and a Biographical Sketch of from Twenty-five to Thirty Counties of East Tennessee* (East Tennessee ed., Knox County), Chicago and Nashville: Goodspeed Publishing Company, 1887, p. 858.

[25] North to Ann North, July 3, 1869, *NO* 1199.

[26] North to Ann North, July 16, 1869, *NO* 1204.

[27] North to Ann North, October 3, 1869, *NO* 1238.

[28] North to Ann North, July 3, 1869, *NO* 1199.

[29] North to Ann North, September 17, 1869, *NO* 1229.

[30] North to Ann North, September 8, 1869, *NO* 1224.

[31] North to Ann North, August 25, 1869, *NO* 1220.

[32] North to Ann North, July 18, 1869, *NO* 1205.

[33] North to Ann North, October 6, 1869, *NO* 1239.

[34] North to John Eaton, November 26, 1869, *Eaton Papers*, University of Tennessee Library, Knoxville, Tennessee.

[35] North to Ann North, March 12, 1869, *NO* 1182.

[36] North to Ann North, November 20, 1868, *NO* 1166.

[37] North to John Eaton, May 13, 1868, *Eaton Papers*, University of Tennessee Library, Knoxville, Tennessee. North later picked up his recommendations on his way to California. Nothing remains in the Archives but an empty envelope.

[38] North to John Eaton, October 11, 1869, *Eaton Papers*.

[39] Ann North to Loomises, September 27, 1868, *NO* 494.

[40] State of Tennessee, General Assembly, Extra Session, 1868, Senate *Journal*, p. 5; House *Journal*, p. 9.

[41] Thomas to Grant, November 19, 1868, reported in Philadelphia (Pennsylvania) *Press*.

[42] North to Eaton, May 20, 1869, *Eaton Papers*, University of Tennessee Library.

[43] Greeley to Eaton, July 9, 1869, *Eaton Papers*, University of Tennessee Library.

[44] North to Eaton, May 20, 1869, *Eaton Papers*, University of Tennessee Library.

[45] North to Eaton, October 11, 1869, *Eaton Papers*, University of Tennessee Library.

[46] *Ibid.*

A Colony for Tennessee

[1] "Letter from Judge North," *Christian Register*, Boston, March 6, 1869, p. 3, c. 3.

[2] When North landed in San Francisco in 1861, the *Evening Bulletin* was commending the associations formed under the California Homestead Act, and associations advertised for investors. North's colonies adopted the same plan of company investment and colonial land purchases.

[3] "Letter from Judge North," *Christian Register*, Boston, March 6, 1869, p. 3, c. 3.

[4] *Ibid.*

[5] "Letter from Judge North," *Christian Register*, Boston, April 3, 1869, p. 3, c. 2.

[6] *Ibid.*

[7] *Ibid.*

[8] *Ibid.*

[9] Editorial, *Christian Register*, Boston, April 3, 1869, p. 2, c. 1.

[10] Bellows to North, October 24, 1868, *NO* 9.

[11] "Letter from Judge North," *Christian Register*, Boston, April 17, 1869, p. 3, c. 2.

A Colony for California

[1] Copies of the broadside are in the collection of the Huntington Library, San Marino, California, Numbers 258580 and 258581. Reference is made to the circular in John Greenleaf North's *Riverside, The Fulfillment of a Prophecy*, reproduced with the compliments of the Riverside Land Company, from *The Land of Sunshine, the Magazine of California and the West*, Vol. XIII, December 1900, pp. 467–480.

[2] Emma North Messer to Fred B. Snyder, July 5, 1932, Minnesota Historical Society.

[3] *The History of Benton County, Iowa*, Chicago: Western Historical Company, 1878, pp. 443–446; *An Illustrated History of Southern California*, Chicago: Lewis Publishing Company, 1890.

[4] *Ibid.*, pp. 497–499.

NOTES

[5] Syracuse (New York) *Standard*, December 15, 1891, clipping, Onondaga Historical Association.

[6] "A Colony for California," broadside, Huntington Library, San Marino, California.

[7] Detroit (Michigan) *Daily Post*, May 25, 1870, p. 4, c. 4.

[8] Chicago (Illinois) *Tribune*, May 17, 1870, p. 4, c. 2.

[9] Chicago (Illinois) *Tribune*, May 25, 1870, p. 4, c. 3.

[10] Chicago (Illinois) *Tribune*, May 17, 1870, p. 4, c. 2.

[11] Marshall (Michigan) *Statesman*, June 1, 1870, p. 2, c. 5.

[12] Chicago (Illinois) *Tribune*, May 17, 1870, p. 1, c. 4.

[13] Detroit (Michigan) *Post*, May 31, 1870, p. 1, c. 4; June 2, 1870, p. 1, c. 3.

[14] Marshall (Michigan) *Statesman*, June 8, 1870, p. 2, c. 4.

[15] San Francisco (California) *Alta*, May 15, 1870.

[16] John Greenleaf North, *op. cit.*, p. 480.

[17] *An Illustrated History of Southern California*, p. 463.

[18] Merlin Stonehouse, "The Michigan Excursion for the Founding of Riverside, California," *Michigan History*, Vol. VL, No. 3, September 1961, pp. 193–209.

[19] In *NO* 1261, enclosure, is a pass worded as follows:

This certifies that [Mrs. Emma Phelps] of [Marshall, Michigan] is a member of the Southern California Colony, and that [she] is entitled to reduced fare on the Rail Road lines, and on Steamers as per arrangements with [J. W. North].

The bracketed words are handwritten in the printed form.

Riverside Colony

[1] Circular, 1870, Huntington Library.

[2] William H. Hall, *Irrigation in California* [Southern], Sacramento: California State Department, 1888, p. 204.

[3] Wallace W. Elliott, *History of San Bernardino County, California*, San Francisco: W. W. Elliott and Company, 1882. The directors of the two colony groups combining forces were J. W. North, president; James P. Greves, secretary; H. Hamilton, Dudley Pine, W. B. Brink, John H. Stewart, Barbara

Childs, George J. Clark, W. J. Linville, K. D. Shugart, and T. W. Cover.

[4] George Wharton James, *Heroes of California*, Boston: Little, Brown, 1910, pp. 306–307.

[5] Circular, 1870, Huntington Library.

[6] Pryor Russell, a Forty-Niner, secured the Tahiti oranges.

[7] Dr. George S. Loomis to Margaret Hasty, July 10, 1872, *NO* 42.

[8] North to B. D. Wilson, January 29, 1872, *Wilson Papers*, Huntington Library.

[9] Elliott, *op. cit.*, p. 131. Felton began drilling for oil in the San Fernando Mountains. See Fresno (California) *Daily Evening Expositor*, May 31, 1882.

[10] Los Angeles (California) *Herald*, April 15, 1874.

[11] Los Angeles (California) *Herald*, April 11, 1874.

[12] Benjamin F. Taylor, *Between the Gates*, Chicago: S. C. Griggs, 1878, p. 81.

[13] *Out West*, Vol. XXV, October 1905, pp. 515–519.

[14] *Californian Illustrated Magazine*, Vol. II, November 1892, pp. 790–807.

[15] *Ibid.*, p. 793.

[16] Charles F. Lummis, *The Land of Sunshine, the Magazine of California and the West*, Vol. XV, June 1901–December 1901, p. 187.

[17] James, *op. cit.*, p. 307.

Revolution in the Central Valley

[1] Elliott, *op. cit.*, pp. 114–115.

[2] "In 1870, 1/500 of the population of California owned one-half or more of the available agricultural lands of the State," Carey McWilliams, *Factories in the Field*, Boston: Little, Brown, 1940, p. 23.

[3] Elliott, *op. cit.*, p. 115.

[4] Fresno (California) *Republican*, July 24, 1880.

[5] *California As It Is*, San Francisco: San Francisco Call Company, 1888, p. 50.

[6] Fresno (California) *Republican*, July 12, 1879.

[7] Fresno (California) *Republican*, June 5, 1880.

[8] Fresno (California) *Republican*, March 23, 1878.

[9] Fresno (California) *Republican*, August 17, 1878.

[10] Fresno (California) *Daily Evening Expositor*, April 21, 1882, p. 3, c. 1. Since J. W. North assumed control, 1,080 acres had been sold. North moved to Donahoo's Block in April 1882. See *Expositor*, May 3, 1882. Before that his office was next door to the Ogle House, where he did business as "Fresno Real Estate Office, also, Office of Washington Irrigated Colony." See *Expositor*, April 3, 1882, p. 3, c. 5. All farmers with spring wagons or buggies were called on April 11 to show excursionists around for two days.

[11] Fresno (California) *Republican*, June 19, July 31, 1880.

[12] Fresno (California) *Republican*, September 11, 1880.

[13] North to Emma Messer, March 20, 1881, *NO* 898.

[14] Copied in the Fresno (California) *Daily Evening Expositor*, June 9, 1882.

[15] North from Northfield to Ann North in Washington, D.C., September 13, 1883, *NO* 1370. The phonographer's copy is in the Minnesota Historical Society: "University [of] Minneapolis, September 11, [1883], Mr. John W. North of Oleander, California, being duly examined testifies as follows. . . . I was residing here in St. Anthony in 1850–51. I was a member of the legislature in the winter of '50 and '51 and introduced the bill to charter this institution. I got the charter passed in the legislature and succeeded in getting it located here at St. Anthony. After the passing of the bill I was one of the regents of the University and treasurer of the board. I started a subscription and raised $3,000 . . . procured a teacher and started the institution. . . ."

[16] New York *Tribune*, October 3, 1883, p. 2, c. 1.

[17] North in New York to Ann North, October 4, 1882, *NO* 1371.

[18] North in Oleander to Ann North in Washington, July 4, 1883, *NO* 1350.

[19] North in Oleander to Emma Messer in Washington, March 20, 1881, *NO* 898.

[20] Fresno County Deed Book, Vol. XXX, p. 579; Vol. XXXII, p. 77.

[21] Thomas H. Thompson, *Official Historical Atlas Map of Fresno County*, Tulare, California, 1891.

[22] Fresno County Deed Book, Vol. LII, p. 20.

[23] *Ibid.*, p. 420.

[24] Superior Court Records, Fresno County, p. 488.

[25] Superior Court Records, Fresno County, A. A. Holmes, judge. "Decree of Distribution of Estate, Ann L. North, executrix of Last Will and Testament of John W. North . . . filed 7 February 1891, heard 14 February 1891."

[26] Superior Court, Department No. 2, Records, Fresno County, p. 488. Estate of John W. North, Inventory and Appraisement, April 15, 1890.

[27] Superior Court Records, Fresno County, p. 488. Certificate of Proof of Will, filed 22 March 1890 and recorded in Vol. II of Wills, p. 358.

INDEX

INDEX

INDEX

Marshall (Michigan) *Statesman*, 214–216
Mason, Roswell B., 113
Massachusetts Anti-Slavery Society, 13n
Matthews Mills on Warm Creek, 227–228
May, Samuel J., 11, 13n, 13–14
Maynard, Horace, 183, 183n, 200, 202
Mazeppa, 151
Medary, Samuel, 92, 95
Meeker, Nathan Cook, 214
Memphis (Tennessee) *Post*, 187, 187n
Mendota, Minnesota, 23, 24
Menken, Adah Isaacs, 151
Merrill, Elijah Washington, 56, 58
Mesick, R. S., 172
Messer, Benjamin Edmund, 16, 70, 82
Messer, Edmund Clarence, 238
Methodists: 185, 207; influence of preachers, 4; camp meetings, 4–5; reluctant to oppose slavery, 6; assist North in Connecticut, 10; church history published, 10n; try to withdraw North's preaching license, 10; divided on slavery, 10, 81; family devotions, 17; plain talk of, 19; conscience of, 40; congregation moves to Minnesota, 83; in Northfield, 89, 182n
Meyer, Abraham, 170–171
Middletown, Connecticut, 7–8
Military reserve, 65
Miller, Stephen, 121
Millpond at St. Anthony, 44
Mills, D. O., 159n
Mills: site, 79; at Northfield, 86, 88, 90, 93; at Washoe, 152; at Riverside, 224; *see also* Minnesota Mill and Northfield
Milwaukee (Wisconsin) *Sentinel*, 131n
Mining: Emma mine, 127n; square-sets, 146; laws in Nevada, 151, 160; in politics, 157; control by Montgomery street, 157–158; ledges, 157, 159–160; "horse" in mine, 160; Comstock, 161; *see also* Montgomery street
Minneapolis and Cedar Valley Railroad: 103–114; North treasurer of, 76; chartered, 90; surveyed, 93; North director of, 93, 103; Mendota meeting, 103; Shields elected president, 103–104, 111; connections planned, 104; route of, 104; construction, 105; grant for depot, 105; Sibley director of, 105–106, 108, 109, 112; grading, 105, 107; shops at Northfield, 105, 110; bonds sold, 107; mandamus secured, 108; payment withheld, 108–109; Northfield meeting, 110; failure of road, 110–111; Wheaton joins, 110–111; Chamberlain con-

trols, 112; deal proposed to North, 112; rechartered, 112–113; cost of, 113
Minnesota: an idea without borders, 22; description (*1849*), 22–23; first mansion in, 23n; Sioux war, 23n; leading men in (*1849*), 23–25; Historical Society, 23n, 24n, 35, 74; Marshall governor of, 25; generosity of settlers, 27–28; superior to East, 27–28; immigration to, 27, 36, 37, 39; ideal community planned, 28; routes to (*1849*), 29; cost of removing to, 30; economy of (*1849–50*), 31; winter in, 32; few cats in, 34; no cows in, 34; lonely frontier, 35; historians of, 35, 42; North's description of, 38–39; building costs in, 40, 51–52, (*1850*) 43–53, (*1851*) 54–63; competing with California, 43; roads in, 44; river traffic, 44–45; medicine in, 48; Fredrika Bremer visits, 49–51; Scandinavian immigrants to, 50–51; politics (*1851*), 52–53, 56, (*1853*) 75, 77; second territorial legislature of, 52–53, 59, 62; federal lands for University of, 56; changes orientation from South to North, 64–65; railroad fever in, 72, 74; railroad lands in, 75, 76–77; Republican party in, 75, 80; excursion to, 77; prairie flowers in, 77; politics (*1855*), 82–83, (*1857*) 95–96, (*1859*) 114, 115–116; Cannon River valley described, 83; constitutional convention called, 95; becomes state, 95–102; state borders, 99–100; failures in *1857*, 109–117; ginseng in, 117; Republican delegation to *1860* Convention, 121
Minnesota Mill, Washoe, Nevada Territory, 141, 152, 161, 162
Minnesotian, 25n
Mission Inn, Riverside, 218
Mississippi River: dividing line, 22, 64; head of navigation on, 26, 44–45; panorama of, 29, 43; description of falls, 32; navigation closed, 34; opening of navigation, 39; effect of opening, 41; ice jams, 44; islands destroyed by, 44; influence on Minnesota, 64–65; excursion on, 77; Lake Pepin, 77; bridge, 78; ferry, 78; waterpower, 79; downriver trade fails, 118
Missouri colony proposed, 221
Moccasin Democrats, 75, 83
Model Worker, 20
Modesto, California, 234
Montgomery street: financial district of San Francisco, 157–158, 163, 165, 169, 173, 238
Morgan, Edwin D., 116

INDEX

INDEX